HISTORIC DISTRICTS OF AMERICA

The South

Alabama - Florida - Georgia - Kentucky
Louisiana - Mississippi - North Carolina
South Carolina - Tennessee - Virginia

By Ralph W. Richardson

HERITAGE BOOKS, INC.

Published 1987 By

HERITAGE BOOKS, INC.
1540E Pointer Ridge Pl., Bowie, Maryland 20716
(301)-390-7709

ISBN 1-55613-088-0

NOTE

This guidebook is the first in a series of regional guides covering the continental United States. Other regions under preparation are:

MID-ATLANTIC
MID-WEST
NEW ENGLAND
WEST

I have had to rely, of necessity, on information compiled by countless individuals over many years of the Historic District program.

It is quite possible, therefore, that errors have crept into some of my information (or errors occurred in my handling the original information). I hope users of this Guide will contact me at the address below, in cases of major error or changed circumstances regarding a given District.

In addition, if you want to insure my adding a particular district in any updating of this volume, please have your local Historical Society or Chamber of Commerce get in touch with me.

Ralph W. Richardson
Historic Districts of America
POB 9202
Naples, FL 33941

TABLE OF CONTENTS

ACKNOWLEDGMENTS

My compilation of this Guidebook has been possible primarily because of the program of Federal-State-local cooperation which is the basis for the National Register of Historic Places. Descriptions for the majority of the National Register districts have been based either on selected volumes of the Register, or (for districts placed on the Register since 1978) on nomination documents provided to me by the various State Historic Preservation Offices.

In addition, my research has been possible because of the invaluable cooperation I received from hundreds of sources; they include Chambers of Commerce, Local Historical and Preservation Societies, city offices, and numerous individuals. These sources answered my questionnaires, provided tour brochures, and patiently responded to my queries. Their cooperation has been of special importance in identifying "Local" districts and in providing details on annual homes tours and other special events. I only wish space allowed me to acknowledge each and every case of such help.

Specifically, however, I wish to express my sincere appreciation to the following institutions and individuals:

Alabama Historical Commission, Mr. F. Lawrence Oaks, Executive Director; Staff, National Register.

Florida Department of State, Division of Archives, History and Records Management; Mr. William N. Thurston, Historic Preservation Supervisor.

Georgia Department of Natural Resources, Historic Preservation Section, Elizabeth A. Lyon, Chief; Charlotte Ramsay, Information Specialist.

Kentucky Heritage Council, State Historic Preservation Office; Mr. Robert M. Polsgrove, Historic Sites Program Manager.

Louisiana Department of Culture, Recreation, and Tourism, Office of Cultural Development; Mr. Robert B. DeBlieux, Assistant Secretary (State Historic Preservation Officer).

Mississippi Department of Archives and History, Division of Historic Preservation; Mr. Brian Berggren, Architectural Historian.

Nashville (Tennessee) Metropolitan Historical Commission; Elissa Tuleen.

National Register of Historic Places, National Park Service; Carol D. Shull, Chief of Registration.

New Orleans Preservation Resource Center.

North Carolina Department of Cultural Resources, Division of Archives and History; E. Virginia Oswald, Survey and Planning Branch.

South Carolina Department of Archives and History, Reference and Research Unit.

Tennessee Historical Commission; Mr. Herbert L. Harper, Executive Director and Deputy State Historic Preservation Officer.

Virginia Department of Conservation and Historic Resources, Division of Historic Landmarks; Margaret T. Peters, Public Information Officer and Editor.

SOURCES

My research has been based on formal publications such as the National Register, internal state reports, historic district-nomination forms, responses to two special questionnaires, local tour brochures and related materials, correspondence, and personal visits.

Major Sources

National Register of Historic Places (U.S. Department of the Interior, National Park Service:GPO); 1972 edition, 1976 edition, Volumes I and II.

National Register of Historic Places Inventory-Nomination Forms (from various State Historic Preservation Offices).

National Register in Alabama (Alabama Historical Commission, 1978).

Preservation is Progress, Planning Office report, City of New Orleans, 1980.

National Register Accession Book, Mississippi Department of Archives and History, Division of Historic Preservation (excerpts).

Notes on Virginia, semi-annual publication of Virginia Department of Conservation and Historic Resources, Division of Historic Landmarks; excerpts from 1976–1986 issues.

Miscellaneous Sources

Historic Districts: Identification, Social Aspects, and Preservation, Preservation Press, National Trust for Historic Preservation, Washington, DC 1975.

Illustrations

All illustrations are from the Historic American Buildings Survey (HABS), Library of Congress, Washington D.C.

INTRODUCTION

I have compiled this Guide as a means of sharing the infinite charms and pleasures of our nation's Historic Districts with other travellers. My particular interest is in those Districts where a cluster or more of older buildings offers us a "sense of time and place," a glimpse of how life might have been in another time, another place. This Guide, therefore, excludes archaeological and certain other special-category Districts, plus a limited number of Districts considered as not being of general interest.

Even with such exclusions, there are over 4,000 Historic Districts throughout the U.S. which either are listed in the National Register of Historic Places, or designated solely by a local government. In the South alone, there are over 1,000. Although the majority of these Districts are residential, other major categories include commercial, military, academic, and industrial. In terms of history, they range from early colonial days to the era of commuter suburbs. As for architecture, they contain examples of just about every facet of the art, from humble cottages to stately Georgian mansions, from Victorian eclectics to modest bungalows. Commercial, military, and industrial style-changes also are well represented.

The first formal designation of a Historic District in the U.S. came in 1931, when Charleston's Battery District was placed under the protection of a local ordinance to help protect the area's early architecture. New Orlean's "Vieux Carre" (French Quarter) was the second local Historic District, and dates from 1937. Federal legislation first provided for the designation of Historic Districts through the "Historic Preservation Act of 1966." That same Act authorized creation of the National Register of Historic Places, administered by the National Park Service.

That Register, an inventory of our national heritage, has grown steadily through the years and now contains over 40,000 entries; it is estimated that Districts constitute about one tenth of the total. New entries for the Register, including Districts, are first evaluated and then nominated by the various State Historic Preservation Offices annually; approved additions to the Register normally are published by the Federal Government each February or March. In addition, there are hundreds of Districts not included in the National Register, but designated solely by local government authority.

Any District listed in this Guide has been considered to contain some degree of historical, architectural, or cultural significance (or combinations thereof). Such significance, however, ranges from the national importance of Colonial Williamsburg to very small and very modest neighborhoods; these latter frequently have been designated on the basis of very local considerations of "significance." In their totality, however, these districts large and small, elegant and humble, old and not-so-old, constitute a priceless inventory of our national heritage.

The Historic District program has become a major element in the historic preservation movement in the U.S. At the same time, however, these Districts offer delightful opportunities for the adventuresome traveller and are rich in raw material for history buffs and the professional scholar. Whatever your interests may be, I hope you will enjoy America's Historic Districts.

USE OF THE GUIDE

There are three levels of entry, each organized alphabetically: State, City, and Historic District(s). If a District is not actually located within a city or town, it is listed under the nearest community and carries the notation "Vicinity."

Because many interesting Districts are not generally known, it is advisable to consult this Guide when planning travel in the region. You might choose to pick out interesting Districts from the Guide, and then lay out your route. Or, you may prefer to plan your basic route, then consult the Guide to see what Districts of interest are in cities along your way. From personal experience I have found that just a little pre-planning has alerted me to Districts I otherwise might have driven past without knowing of their existence. This applies particularly to travel on inter-state highways.

In touring Districts, I strongly recommend that upon arrival you obtain a local self-guided tour map or brochure whenever they are available. To cite from personal experience again, I have found that even residents of a known District may have little or no information about the District; but a self-guided tour map generally contains solid historical information and is helpful for navigating around an unfamiliar neighborhood.

Also recommended are a pair of binoculars, useful for picking out architectural details from a distance, and a handy architectural reference book. For example, the Preservation Press of the National Trust for Historic Preservation, 1600 H St., Washington D.C., publishes a very helpful paperback, *What Style Is It?*

My first priority in compiling this Guide has been to identify those cities and towns with Historic Districts; many Districts carry the name of their city, but there are also many Districts with unique titles, and of course in many cities there are multiple Districts, each with its own title. My next priority has been to provide a brief description of as many

Districts as possible. Information also is provided on the following when available: where to obtain a self-guided tour map or brochure; whether guided tours are offered; annual open-house tours or other major Special Events.

Definitions of abbreviations and terms used in this Guide are as follows:

1. A "Historic District" (**HD**) is a geographic area of historic, cultural, or aesthetic importance which either is listed in the National Register of Historic Places or is protected by a local preservation ordinance (I have included a very limited number of "districts" which are not based on these criteria, but which are neighborhoods I judge to have special interest or charm).

2. The National Register of Historic Places is maintained by the National Park Service, Department of the Interior. Established by the 1966 Historic Preservation Act, the Register (updated annually) contains "districts, sites, buildings, structures and objects significant in American history, architecture, archeology and culture ...."

3. **N H L** - A National Historic Landmark is a building, site, structure, district or object judged by the Department of the Interior to be of "national significance." The **N H L** entry at the end of a District description means the entire District is a national historic landmark. The **N H L** entry within a district description refers to a structure within that District.

4. **H A B S** - The Historic American Buildings Survey, begun in 1933 within the National Park Service, is a comprehensive cooperative program to record America's historic buildings, with the cooperation of the American Institute of Architects and the Library of Congress. A **HABS** designation indicates a building possesses particular architectural or historical significance. A **HABS** designation is included in the description of a Historic District when at least one property in the District has been documented by the Survey.

5. **H A E R** - In 1969, the Historic American Engineering Record (**HAER**) was established as a companion program to H A B S to document structures of technological and engineering significance. Like **HABS**, it functions through the cooperation of several institutions: the National Park Service, the American Society of Civil Engineers, and the Library of Congress. A **H A E R** designation means the property has been recognized and recorded as an important example of Am-

erican engineering. A **H A E R** designation is included in the description of a District when at least one property in the District has been documented by the Record.

6. Local Historic District - Any District which is not listed in the National Register but has been listed in this Guide is marked with the symbol (L) after the name of the District.

One final word of advice: if your interests are broad and general, you probably will find the most interesting Districts to be those classified as "National Historic Landmarks" (N H L). These Districts have been judged to be of national significance and generally contain structures of outstanding architectural importance (designated by the **H A B S** symbol). Another approach would be to explore those Districts which contain at least one building designated as a National Historic Landmark (NHL).

Huger-Douglas House

ALABAMA

ATHENS

Athens State College HD

1842–1935 – Eight buildings, and oak-shaded original campus. Focal point is massive Founders Hall (1842–1845, Greek Revival). *General Information*: Athens Chamber of Commerce, 101 S. Beatty St., POB 150, Athens AL 35611, telephone (205)-232-2600; Limestone County Historical Society, 200 Christine St., Athens AL 35611.

Robert Beatty HD

1820–1930's – Excellent collection of nearly 100 residences in such styles as Federal, Italianate, Greek Revival, Colonial and Spanish Revival. An extremely cohesive district, with houses in good to excellent condition. *Annual Homes Tour*: Contact Mrs. Don Axford, 301 9th St., Athens, GA 35611. *General Information*: Athens Chamber of Commerce.

AUBURN

Auburn University HD

1860–1951 – Campus district of 9 red-brick buildings, 19th – 20th C. Earliest section of Auburn University (established 1883); focal point is Sanford Hall, High Victorian style.

Old Main and Church Streets HD

No information available at this time.

BIRMINGHAM

Downtown HD

1880's–1920's – Commercial district, approximately 100

buildings, core of Birmingham's boom period beginning in the 1880's. Of note: McAdory Building (1888), Calwell-Milner Building (1887), and Steiner Building (1890, Richardsonian Romanesque). *Map, Self-Guided Tours*: Convention and Visitors Bureau, Commerce Center, 2027 First Ave. North, Birmingham AL 35203, telephone (205) 252-9825; Historical Society, 142 22nd. St., Birmingham AL 35205, telephone (205) 254-2138.

Five Points South HD

1890-1930 - Early "street car suburb" reflecting architectural styles popular throughout the U.S., 1880-1931; styles include Queen Anne, Craftsman, and Classical Revival. Of note: Lathrop House (1901, Classical Revival), McCants House (1888, Second Empire), and Robertson House (c. 1900, Queen Anne). *Map, Self-Guided Tours*: See **Downtown District**.

Forest Park HD

1906-late 1920's - More than 600 substantial residences and cozy cottages nestled along winding, tree-shaded streets. Many were designed by leading local architects, with styles including Beaux-Arts, Georgian Revival, and Tudor Revival. *Map, Self-Guided Tours*: See **Downtown District**.

Fourth Avenue HD

1908-1941 - Numerous brick buildings, 1 and 2 stories; area was center of black achievement during "Jim Crow" years. Styles include Beaux-Arts, Renaissance Revival, Art Moderne. *General Information*: Birmingham Historical Society, 142 22nd St. South, Birmingham AL 35205, telephone (205) 254-2138.

Glen Iris Park HD

1902-1920 - A virtually intact early 20th C. upper-class restricted community of 16 2-story homes. Styles include Colonial Revival, Romanesque Revival, and Spanish Colonial Revival.

Highland Avenue - Rhodes Park HD

1880's-1910 - Residential district containing the city's first planned upper-class boulevard. Nearly 200 homes, illustrating popular turn-of-century architecture, including Bungaloid and Revival styles. *General Information*: See **Downtown District**.

Morris Avenue HD

1887–1917 – City's only remaining concentration of late 19th C. warehouse architecture; primarily 2 to 4–story brick structures, some with cast–iron trim, ornamental brickwork. Area was city's major wholesale food center from mid–1880's to 1950's. *General Information*: See **Fourth Avenue HD.**

BREWTON

Brewton Historic Commercial District

Late 19th to early 20th C. – Approximately 35 structures, mostly 1 and 2–story brick commercial buildings. Of note: Bank of Brewton, beautifully detailed with terra–cotta tile (Renaissance Revival).

CAMDEN

Wilcox County Courthouse HD

1840–1930's – Approximately 30 structures, centered on 1859 Greek Revival courthouse. Numerous brick commercial establishments, mostly brick, 1 and 2 stories.

CARLOWVILLE

Carlowville HD

Mid–19th to early 20th C. – Twenty–one interesting buildings, with Greek Revival style predominant. Other styles include Georgian Colonial, Federal, and Victorian cottages, in a tranquil rural setting.

CENTREVILLE

Centreville HD

Late 19th to early 20th C. – Twenty–six governmental and commercial structures; the majority are 1 and 2–story brick buildings. Of note: Kennedy House (1837, Federal), and 1902 Romanesque courthouse which is focal point of district.

CHEROKEE (VICINITY)

Old Natchez Trace HD

Early 1800's - Seven structures on portion of old pioneer path (Natchez Trace Trail) to the Southwest, now part of Natchez Trace Parkway.

CULLMAN

Cullman HD

Mid-1870's-1930's - Residential, approximately 80 period buildings, on 27 blocks. Majority are single-family dwellings reflecting such styles as: Queen Anne, Eastlake, Italianate, and Romantic revivals. Town was a major German immigrant colony, "Die Deutsche Kolonie Van Nord Alabama".

Cullman Downtown HD

Late 19th to early 20th C. - City's commercial center, encompassing several city blocks with 51 interesting buildings, most of brick. Styles include Italianate, Eastlake, and Chicago School commercial. Of note: German Bank Building (Neo-Classical) and the 1908 Esther Opera House.

DECATUR

Albany Heritage Neighborhood HD

Late 1880's-1930's - A well-preserved late 19th C. residential development with nearly 200 properties of interest. A number of larger 2-story Victorian homes, and heavy concentration of typical bungalows. *Map, Self-Guided Tours*: Tourism Bureau, 925 Bank Street NE, Decatur AL 35602, telephone (205) 350-2028. *Annual Homes Tour*: "Christmas in Historic Decatur" (Monday before Christmas); Tourism Bureau, POB 2003, Decatur, AL 35602.

Bank Street - Old Decatur HD

1860's-1940's - Approximately 300 buildings of interest, with commercial and residential sections. Most commercial buildings are brick, with residences of brick, shingles, and clapboard. Styles include elaborate Queen Annes, Shingle, Colonial Revival, and Tudor. *Map, Self-Guided Tours*: See **Albany Heritage Neighborhood.**

DEMOPOLIS

Demopolis Historic Business District

1867-1930's - Town's commercial center, relatively unchanged since 1928. Approximately 55 structures, mostly 1 and 2-stories, brick. Thirty-one buildings date from 1880-1889, many with extravagant Victorian ornamentation.

DOTHAN

Main Street Commercial District

1885-1933 - Six blocks of closely spaced commercial and warehouse structures, mostly 1 or 2-story brick. Approximately 40 buildings of interest, illustrating Dothan's development. Unfortunately, appearance of many buildings has been compromised by attempts at "modernization."

EUFALA

Seth Lore - Irwinton HD

19th-20th C. - Seventy-five residential and commercial buildings, 3 principal styles: Greek Revival, Italianate, Victorian period. Of note: McNab Bank Building (c. 1860, cast-iron and stone), Sheppard Cottage (1837), Shorter Mansion (1906, Neo-Classical Revival). **H A B S** *Map, Self-Guided Tours*: Eufala Heritage Association, Shorter Mansion, 340 N. Eufala Ave., Eufala AL 36027, telephone (205) 687-3793. *Guided Tours*: Contact above. *Annual Homes Tour*: Eufala Pilgrimage (April) Eufala Heritage Association, POB 486, Eufala, AL 36027.

EUTAW

Courthouse Square HD

19th C. - District's focal point is Greek Revival courthouse, reconstructed 1870. Also of note: Eutaw Presbyterian Church; "Kirkwood" Mansion. *Annual Homes Tour*: Fall Pilgrimage (late September), Chamber of Commerce, 260 Prairie Ave., Eutaw AL 35462, telephone (205)-372-9769. *General Information*: City Hall, 116 Main St., Eutaw AL 35462, telephone (205)-372-4212.

Fayette County Courthouse HD
Early 20th C.-1955 - Twenty-six government and commercial structures, many built following fire in 1911 which destroyed 19th C. commercial area. District has retained its early 20th C. character. Of note: Neo-Classical Revival Courthouse (1912), and Fayette County Bank Building (Neo-Classical Revival).

FLORENCE

Sannoner HD
19th to early 20th C. - Finest collection of early and mid-19th C. architecture in this area, highlighted by collection of 25 brick dwellings, 1 1/2 or 2 1/2 stories. Of note: Wakefield House (Federal), Irving Place (1843), and Ashcraft-Dabney House (early Greek Revival). District retains much 19th, early 20th C. character. **H A B S** *Map, Self-Guided Tours*: Mr. Billy Ray Warren, 501 N. Walnut St., Florence AL 35630. *Guided Tours*: See above. *Annual Homes Tour*: Fourth weekend in April; Chamber of Commerce, 104 S. Pine St., Florence AL 35631.

Walnut Street HD
Late 19th to early 20th C. - Fashionable residential area of some 29 dwellings; styles include large frame Victorian and Classical Revival homes, small frame and brick cottages, and bungalows. *General Information*: See **Sannoner HD**.

Wood Avenue HD
1830-1930 - Fifty-five structures include elaborate Queen Anne and handsome Georgian Revival homes, plus modest Victorian, Bungalow, and Revival style houses. An upper and middle-class neighborhood, along one of city's oldest streets. *General Information*: See **Sannoner HD**.

GREENSBORO

Greensboro HD
1821-1925 - Commercial and residential area includes some of the town's major commercial structures and private dwellings, as well as modest cottages. Of note: Greenwood-Moore House (Greek Revival), 1904 Opera House, Georgian Revival courthouse (1908). District has retained much of its 19th C. character. **H A B S**

HAMILTON (VICINITY)

Pearce's Mill HD

1850–1875 - Privately-owned mill complex includes several millsites, stone dam, family house and cemetery, tenant farmhouse, servants' quarters, general store, and related outbuildings.

HUNTSVILLE

Old Town HD

1870–1930 - Middle-class urban residential, with approximately 200 structures of interest. Has retained a high concentration of closely spaced, ornate Victorian homes. District's ambience due in part to rich landscaping, surviving brick sidewalks, and a number of carriage blocks.

Twickenham HD

19th, 20th C. - Center-city residential district with wide variety of architectural styles, 1814 to 1972. Of note are the Fearn-Garth House (Greek Revival, c. 1820), and Second Empire house at 506 Franklin Street. **H A B S**

JEFFERSON

Jefferson HD

1840–1960 - Small village (privately owned), one of oldest communities in Marengo County, is a good example of a plantation community. Village contains 2 churches, store, and a number of 1 and 2-story frame dwellings with vernacular Greek Revival elements.

LAFAYETTE

Chambers County Courthouse Sq. HD

Late 19th to early 20th C. - Noted for virtually unaltered courthouse and for its concentrated collection of small town commercial buildings (many with original storefronts). Forty-five structures of interest, mostly brick, 1 and 2 stories. *Map, Self-Guided Tours*: City Clerk's Office, City Hall, Alabama Ave. West, LaFayette AL 36862.

LOACHAPOKA

Loachapoka HD

19th C. - Small-town residential area featuring 17 structures, primarily 1-story frame cottages with Greek Revival elements. Town, due to the railroad, was an important local trading center from 1840's to 1870's.

LOWNDESBORO

Lowndesboro HD

Mid-19th C. - Antebellum village with 14 dwellings, including simple country homes, raised cottages, and several elaborate Greek Revival mansions. Also 5 churches, dating from 1830 to 1888. **H A B S** *Annual Homes Tour*: Lowndesboro Pilgrimage (March), POB 11, Lowndesboro AL 36752, telephone (205)-278-3263.

MARION

Green Street HD

Mid-1830's to present - A well-defined neighborhood of 33 structures; includes 12 significant antebellum examples of transitional Federal-Greek Revival style, and 1 early example of Gothic Revival. **H A B S**

MOBILE

Church Street East HD

19th C. - Downtown area contains government, commercial, and residential structures in variety of 19th. C. styles, reflecting city's antebellum history. District, with considerable open space, has retained strong 19th. C. flavor. Of note: 1836 Greek Revival Presbyterian Church, 1858 Italianate City Hall (NHL), and Barton Academy (1836). **H A B S** *Map, Self-Guided Tours*: Convention and Visitor Dept., Chamber of Commerce, 451 Government St., Mobile AL 36602, telephone (205) 433-6951. *Guided Tours*: Gray Line of Mobile, 607 Dauphin St., Mobile AL 36602, telephone (205) 432-2229. *Annual Homes Tour*: Historic Mobile Homes Tours (2nd week in March), POB 2187, Mobile AL 36652, tele. (205)-433-6951.

DeTonti Square HD.

Mid-19th C. - Downtown district reflecting city's 19th. C. affluence from cotton. Contains residential and office structures, predominantly 1-2 story brick with elaborate cast-iron verandas. Major styles are Federal and Greek Revival, with some frame cottages and a scattering of Victorians. **H A B S** *Map, Self-Guided Tours*: See **Church Street East HD.**

Fort Conde Village HD

19th C. (L) Four-block area adjacent to reconstructed Fort Conde contains buildings representative of 19th. C. architectural styles and building types prominent in Mobile: Federal, Gulf Coast cottage, Neo-Classical, Italianate, and styles of the Victorian era. Of note: Spear House (1857, Italianate), Hall-Ford House (1836, Gulf Coast cottage-Greek Revival). *Map, Self-Guided Tours*: See **Church Street East HD.**

Historic Common Street HD

1890-1920 - Residential neighborhood contains 19 significant structures; styles include vernacular Greek Revival, Italianate, Victorian-era, Neo-Classical, and Bungalow.

Lower Dauphin Street HD (Old Dauphin Way)

Late 19th C. - Residential district, primarily of simple frame cottages which were homes of carpenters, steamboat pilots, and commission merchants. Also several sections of grander homes, in styles of late Victorian era. Of note: unique 3-block grouping of shotgun cottages on Caroline Ave., the Kimball Cottage (c. 1870, Carpenter Gothic), and the Protestant Childrens Home (1845). *Map, Self-Guided Tours*: See **Church Street East HD.**

Oakleigh Garden HD (Washington Square)

19th, early 20th C. - Residential area near center city contains variety of 19th. C. styles. Focal point is Washington Square with its large oak shade trees and fountain. Numerous buildings of historic and architectural significance, including 1831-1832 Greek Revival Oakleigh House, and outstanding Queen Anne house at 950 Government Street. **H A B S** *Map, Self-Guided Tours*: See **Church Street East HD.**

MOBILE (VICINITY)

Springhill Neighborhood HD

19th C. - Nine buildings in a district established in mid-1820's as a resort-refuge from yellow fever plagues in Mobile, 6 1/2 miles to the east. Structures include 4 large country homes (2 are fine examples of Greek Revival), 3 summer cottages, and several religious buildings.

MONTEVALLO

University of Montevallo HD

1823-1977 - Sixteen structures on approximately 25 acres in heart of the campus. Established in 1896 as the Alabama Girls' Industrial School. **H A B S**

MONTGOMERY

Cloverdale HD

1910-1930 - Approximately 300 residential structures, with good examples of most early 20th C. styles including Neo-Greek Revival, Tudor, Spanish Mission, Bungalow, and Arts and Crafts. Picturesque landscaping, typical of designs popularized by Frederick Law Olmstead.

Cottage Hill HD

Early 19th-20th C. - A downtown middle-class neighborhood, predominantly late 19th C. Developed for merchants and clerks after 1880, it is only surviving neighborhood of its type in Montgomery. Majority of structures are modest frame buildings, plus some large-scale Victorian dwellings and commercial buildings. *Annual Homes Tour*: Jubilee Open-House (May), Fall Open-House; contact Ms. Eleanor Davis, 426 Martha St., Montgomery AL 36104.

Court Square - Dexter Ave. HD

Map, Self-Guided Tours: Visitor Information Center, 310 Hull St., Montgomery AL 36104.

Garden HD

1890-1930 - Approximately 750 structures, featuring fine 19th and early 20th C. homes, many designed by noted local architects. Styles include Greek Revival, Queen Anne, Colonial Revival, Spanish Mission, Arts and Crafts, and Tudor.

Lower Commerce Street HD
Late 19th to early 20th C. - A superb collection of some 55 period warehouses and wholesale stores. Most are brick, with a rich variety of decorative materials. Finest such grouping in Alabama.

North Lawrence - Monroe St. HD
1860-1890 - Six brick buildings, with significant associations with the growth of black-owned, managed, and supported businesses in Montgomery.

Ordeman-Shaw HD (Old North Hull Street)
Mid-19th C. - Residential district containing numerous mid-19th C. houses, outbuildings; some earlier buildings have Greek Revival details, with fancy porches and bracketed cornices common on later houses. Of note: Ordeman-Shaw House (c. 1842, Italianate), and antebellum brick slave quarters structure (museum). *Map, Self-Guided Tours*: Landmarks Foundation, 310 Hull St., Montgomery AL 36104. *Guided Tours*: Daily; contact above.

Perry Street HD
Early to mid-19th C. - Primarily antebellum, this residential area (near the downtown) contains numerous 1 and 2-story brick and frame structures in a variety of 19th C. styles reflecting the city's history. Of note: the Cody House (1830, Federal-Greek Revival), Lomax House (1847, Greek Revival), and the Greil House (1854, Italianate) **H A B S** *Map, Self-Guided Tours*: See **Ordeman-Shaw HD**

South Perry Street HD
1836-1925 - Fifteen commercial buildings whose storefronts reflect downtown Montgomery's architectural development. Includes examples of Federal, Queen Anne, Neo-Classical and Art Deco.

MONTROSE

Montrose HD
Late 19th C. - Residential district has retained an unusual concentration of vernacular Creole Cottages, 1 1/2 stories, frame. Community laid out in a grid pattern with large lots, wide tree-lined streets, and occasional views of Mobile Bay. Neighborhood has retained much of its 19th C. character.

MOORESVILLE

Mooresville HD

Mid-19th C. - A village primarily of 19th C. dwellings, 1 - 2 1/2 story, brick and frame, many set off by white picket fences. Of note: Church of Christ (Greek Revival), and the Woodruff House (Federal and Greek Revival). One of the older incorporated towns in Alabama (1818), this village has retained much of its mid-19th C. character. **H A B S**

NORTHPORT

Northport HD

Mid-19th to early 20th C. - Over 100 structures, commercial and residential, covering 20 blocks. Significant for its high concentration of simplified vernacular interpretations of prevailing national styles. Features tree-lined streets and numerous 1-story wooden cottages.

OPELIKA

Railroad Ave. District

1872-1930 - Historic commercial core of this important east Alabama trade center. Contains approximately 73 structures; many are 1 and 2-story brick commercial or warehouse buildings. Of note: Courthouse, First United Methodist Church, and Old First National Bank, all Neo-Classical or Classical Revival. *General Information*: Chamber of Commerce, South 7th St., POB 2366, Opelika AL 35121, telephone (205)-745-4861.

PHENIX CITY

Phenix City

Special Events: Ice Cream Social and Street Fair; contact Phenix City Historic Preservation Society. *General Information*: Chamber of Commerce, 1107 Broad St., POB 1326, Phenix City AL 36867, telephone (205)-298-3639; Phenix City Historic Preservation Society.

Brownsville - Summerville HD
Late 19th to mid-20th C. - Residential and commercial. Majority of houses are late Victorian workers cottages, while commercial centers are characterized by small units scattered throughout the neighborhood. Styles include Greek Revival, Victorian period, Neo-Classical, and Bungalow.

Girard HD
Late 19th to early 20th C. - Residential and commercial, significant for its shotgun houses, Victorian homes, and turn-of-the-century commercial buildings. Of note: Citizen's Bank (1909, Renaissance Revival), Collins Scott House (1850, Greek Revival, with c. 1870 Victorian additions).

Kid Alley HD
Early 20th C. - A block of 12 Victorian-era homes; single-family residences, frame, ranging from large cottages to small shotguns. The yards are landscaped and each house is painted one or two colors, giving the feeling of a Victorian neighborhood.

Lower 20th St. HD
Early 20th C. - Residential streetscape of Victorian-era cottages and shotguns, 1-story, single family.

U. H. Smith HD
Late 19th C. - Six single-family dwellings, all wood frame; includes 2 shotguns and a variety of Victorian Cottage styles, some with Greek Revival influence.

Snow Valley HD
Late 19th C. - One of 2 surviving Victorian neighborhoods left in the Girard area; 10 houses of interest along this dirt road. All are detached, single-family, 19th C. residences; most have gingerbread bargeboards and turned porch columns.

Upper 20th St. HD
c. 1900 - Nine single-family dwellings, shotguns and bungalows. A well-preserved microcosm of city's residential development, 1880-1930.

PRATTVILLE

Daniel Pratt HD
1880-1920 - Over 200 properties, including commercial, in-

dustrial, residential, and institutional architecture. Encompasses 19th C. nucleus of the modern town, with core of district formed by 2 groups of industrial buildings: pre-Civil War Bush Hog/Continental complex and the former Pratt cotton textile mills (late 19th C.). Strong historical associations with New Hampshire-born industrialist Daniel Pratt, who championed industrialization in the South. *Map, Self-Guided Tours*: Chamber of Commerce, 1002 E. Main St., PO Drawer O, Prattville AL 36067, telephone (205)-365-7392. *Annual Homes Tour*: Autauga County Heritage Association, 135 First St., Prattville AL 36067, telephone (205)-361-0961.

ST. CLAIR SPRINGS

St. Clair Springs HD

Late 19th to early 20th C. - Developed as a health resort in the 1870's, the town declined after 1900 but has retained much of its 19th C. character. Includes 21 frame, clapboarded cottages, 1 and 1 1/2 stories, in Greek Revival and late-Victorian-era styles. Of note: 1849 Keith House, 1886 Betty Montgomery House, and 1894 Fort-Rathburn House.

SCOTTSBORO

College Hill HD

1890-1930's - A quiet neighborhood of well-kept houses, on tree-shaded streets. Thirteen period homes in various styles, including Vernacular, Bungaloid, Classical Revival, and Neo-English Cottage. A significant concentration of buildings reflecting development of residential architecture in Scottsboro.

Public Square HD

1870-present - Twenty-six commercial and civic buildings, mostly 1 and 2-story brick or block construction. Their lack of ornamentation and detailing reflects late 19th - early 20th C. architectural choices of Alabama's poorer rural communities. Courthouse is significant as site of the first of the internationally famous "Scottsboro Boys" trials: a 1930's rape case with racial overtones which eventually went to the U.S. Supreme Court.

SELMA

Old Town HD

19th to early 20th C. - One of largest historic districts in Alabama, this residential and commercial district covers nearly 60 city blocks with some 600 structures. Of note: Phillips-Hobbs-Joyce House (1837, Greek Revival), Weaver House (1868, Gothic Revival), and Shanks-Noah House (c. 1900, Victorian red brick). *Map, Self-Guided Tours*: Chamber of Commerce, 513 Lauderdale St., PO Drawer D, Selma AL 36701, telephone (205)-875-7241. *Guided Tours*: Groups only, 2 weeks notice; contact above. *Annual Homes Tour*: Historic Selma Pilgrimage (4th weekend in March), POB 586, Selma AL 36702; Holiday Tour of Homes (mid-December), contact Chamber of Commerce.

Water Avenue HD

1860-1880 - Waterfront area with 21 noteworthy commercial structures, of brick and stone, 1-3 stories, some with cast-iron verandas and decorative Italianate elements. Of note: Dallas Feed and Seed Co., 1118-1120 Water St., S & P Furniture and Men's Shoes, 1217-1221 Water Ave. Selma developed rapidly after the mid-19th C. construction of the Alabama and Tennessee Railroad and was an important Confederate military depot; its later prosperity was based on cotton. **H A B S** *Map, Self-Guided Tours*: See **Old Town HD.**

SHEFFIELD

Nitrate Village No. 1 HD

1917 - A nitrate plant plus workers' village, built by U. S. Government as part of World War I defense effort. Village consisted of 85 stucco houses, school, and officers' barracks, all laid out in shape of Liberty Bell (when viewed from the air). Scarcely occupied in World War I, village sat vacant until TVA was established in 1930's. In 1949, the properties were auctioned off to private owners. Most of the c. 1917 cottages have survived. *General Information*: City Offices, Sheffield AL 35660; or Tennessee Valley Historical Society, POB 149, Sheffield AL 35660.

STEVENSON

Stevenson HD

1850's-1911 - A 19th C. southern railroad town, with its charm surprisingly well preserved. Contains 34 buildings, several historic sites/ruins. Historical associations with "Great Locomotive Chase" during Civil War.

SUMMERFIELD

Summerfield HD

19th C. - A small rural town, formerly an important educational center, with present population of approximately 200. A number of important 19th C. dwellings scattered along meandering gravel roads, and a concentration of significant buildings along the 3 blocks of Main Street. Major styles are Federal, Greek Revival.

TALLADEGA

Courthouse Square HD

Late Victorian - District, centered around the courthouse square, features numerous brick commercial and civic structures, 1 to 4 stories, with a variety of Victorian details. City has been the county seat since 1836; most of the structures in the district were erected during economic boom, 1870's to early 20th C. *Annual Homes Tour*: April in Talladega, Chamber of Commerce, 210 East St., PO Drawer A, Talladega AL 35160, telephone (209)-362-9075. *General Information*: Chamber of Commerce.

Silk Stocking HD

Late 19th to early 20th C. - One hundred and twenty significant structures in area developed in 1880's as town's finest residential neighborhood. Styles include Federal, Greek Revival, Gothic Revival, Queen Anne, and Eastlake. **H A B S** *General Information*: See **Courthouse Square HD**.

TROY

College Street HD

Late 19th to early 20th C. - A virtually intact residential community from late 19th to early 20th C. built by the town's civic and social leaders. Of note: Wood-Spahn House (Queen Anne), Henderson-Denison House (Queen Anne, Eastlake), and the Folmar-Easton House (modified Prairie-style).

TUSCALOOSA

Audubon Place HD

1912-1939 - A single, tree-lined cul-de-sac street with 37 well-designed middle income homes, most built in 1920's. Styles include Spanish and Colonial Revival, English Cottage, and Bungalow.

Caplewood Drive HD

1920's to mid-1930's - A long narrow lane with approximately 45 variations of modest bungalows and cottages; centrally situated between downtown and University of Alabama campus. An early example of a planned neighborhood, using quality materials and workmanship.

Druid City HD

19th to early 20th C. - Residential district, approximately 50 dwellings; styles include late Georgian/Federal, Gothic Revival, Queen Anne, and Neo-Classical Revival. Of note: Collier-Overby-Boone House (1820's), Dearing-Swain House (1835, Greek Revival), and Harrison-Laseter House (1856, Italianate). Neighborhood's development, halted by Civil War, was resumed after 1900; has retained much of its early 20th C. character. **H A B S** *Guided Tours*: Tuscaloosa County Preservation Society, 28th Ave. and University Blvd., POB 1665, Tuscaloosa AL 35401, telephone (205)-758-2238. *Annual Homes Tour*: Tuscaloosa Heritage Week (March or April), contact Heritage Week, Box 1665, Tuscaloosa AL 35403. *General Information*: Chamber of Commerce, 2200 University Blvd., POB 430, Tuscaloosa AL 35402, telephone (205)-758-3072.

Gorgas-Manly HD. (University of Alabama)

19th C. - Eight buildings in heart of university campus, featuring Greek and Gothic Revival styles. University was chartered in 1819; is is a 520-acre campus in the town of University which is near Tuscaloosa. Of note: 1829 Gorgas House with Greek Revival elements (by architect William Nichols, who planned the campus), and Clark Hall (1886, Gothic Revival). **H A B S** *Map, Self-Guided Tours*: University Infor., Center, University AL 35486, tele. (205)-348-6063.

TUSCUMBIA

Colbert County Courthouse Square HD

19th C. - Central section of the city, containing 22 significant structures, a mix of government, commercial, religious, and residential buildings. Of note: Episcopal Church (1852, Gothic Revival), 1881 Court House (with elaborate Neo-Baroque clock tower), and the 7 structures comprising Commercial Row. **H A B S** *Annual Homes Tour*: Historic Tour; contact Chamber of Commerce, 110 N. Main St., Tuscumbia AL 35674. *General Information*: See above.

Tuscumbia HD

1825-1941 - Contains 639 properties, with a diversity of residential, commercial, institutional, and recreational buildings. Styles include Greek Revival, Queen Anne, Folk Victorian, Bungalow, and Beaux Arts.

TUSKEGEE

Main Street HD

19th to early 20th C. - A concentrated collection of excellent examples of residential and commercial architecture. Of note is a grouping of 20 mid-19th C. houses, including the Bledsoe House (1835). Styles represented include Federal-Greek Revival, Greek Revival, Gothic Revival, and Romanesque Revival.

North Main St. HD

1835-1920's - These 8 houses are among city's best examples of Federal, Greek Revival, and Queen Anne styles, in a very picturesque and park-like setting.

UNION SPRINGS

Bullock County Courthouse HD

19th to early 20th C. - Predominantly 19th C. commercial, with 47 significant structures; included are a 3-story Italianate county courthouse, jail, library, and numerous churches. Reflects town's history; founded in 1835, prospered during mid-19th C. following its designation as county seat and coming of the railroad.

FLORIDA

APALACHICOLA

Apalachicola HD

19th to early 20th C. A remarkable concentration of residential and commercial buildings from the 19th to the early 20th C., reflecting town's history as major Gulf Coast cotton center (1830–1860), and seafood and lumbering center (1870–1930). Of note: neighborhood along Sixth St. with numerous pre-Civil War dwellings. *Map, Self-Guided Tours*: Chamber of Commerce, 45 Market St., Apalachicola FL 32320, telephone (904)-653-9419. *Special Events*: Florida Seafood Festival, 1st Saturday in November. *General Information*: Apalachicola Area Historical Society, POB 75, Apalachicola FL 32320.

ARCADIA

Arcadia HD

1883–1930. Government, commercial and entertainment buildings, churches, schools, and residences. Styles include Victorian Gothic, Queen Anne, Classical and Mediterranean Revival. Of note: monumental courthouse (1912 Classical Revival) and 18-block commercial sector developed between 1904 and the late 1920's. District has retained much of its 19th C. character. *Map, Self-Guided Tours*: Downtown Association, 20 N. Polk Ave., POB 1943, Arcadia FL 33821, telephone (813)-993-1410; De Soto Chamber of Commerce, POB 149, Arcadia FL 33821, telephone (813)-494-4033. *Special Events*: Arcadia Rodeo (April, July).

BRADENTON

Braden Castle Park HD

1924–1929. Remarkably complete assemblage of trailer sites,

small frame cottages, and communal buildings laid out in 1924 as a seasonal campground ("tin can campers"). Contains approximately 200 cottages and sites for about 90 trailers. Park still flourishes, functioning much as it did when first conceived by Camping Tourists of America, an offshoot of Tin Can Tourists of America. *General Information*: Manatee County Historical Commission, 604 15th St. E., Bradenton FL 33508, telephone (813)-747-9664.

ESTERO

Koreshan Unity Settlement HD

1894. State museum facility contains a community complex of 20 surviving buildings: residences, dormitories, post office, bakery, store, machine shop. Most buildings are frame, with tin roofs; landscaping is exotic and tropical. Founded by Koreshan Unity, communal sect based on theories emphasizing education, culture, landscaping. Sect declined after death of founder Cyrus Teed in 1908. *Guided Tours*: Three daily Park Ranger Tours; see Park Office for schedule, fee. Koreshan State Hispanic Site, Estero FL 33928, telephone (813)-992-0311.

FERNANDINA BEACH

Fernandina Beach HD

19th - 20th C. Commercial and residential, developed during city's post-Civil War industrial and tourist boom. Of note; Fairbanks House (High Victorian Italianate), Humphrey and Bailey Houses (Queen Anne), and County Courthouse. District still reflects its 19th century prosperity.

FORT MYERS

Downtown Fort Myers

1890's - 1920's (L). Mostly commercial, plus civic structures and several residences. Traditional business core of this riverside Gulf Coast city; numerous brick Victorian-era and 1920's - Spanish Colonial Revival buildings provide strong period flavor despite modernizations. Of interest: 1880's Gardner House, 1898 Murphy-Burroughs Home, 1898 Heitman Building, 1923 ACL Railroad depot (Spanish Mission style, now museum), 1940 Edison Theater (Art Deco). Focus of city's downtown renewal program. *Map, Self-Guided Tours*:

For sale, Ft. Myers Historical Museum, ACL Depot, 2300 Peck St., Fort Myers FL 33901, telephone (813)-332-5955.

GAINESVILLE

Northeast Gainesville Residential HD

1880's - 1920's. One of city's oldest residential neighborhoods, covering 63 blocks. Majority of houses are Queen Anne but district also reflects spectrum of many styles popular in late 19th and early 20th C. *Map, Self-Guided Tours*: Historic Gainesville, Inc., (Thomas Center), 306 NE 6th Ave., POB 466, Gainesville FL 32602. *Annual Homes Tour*: Spring Pilgrimage (March); contact above.

JACKSONVILLE

Riverside HD

1871 - 1935. Large residential neighborhood contains over 30 subdivisions and 3 major parks; approximately 2,000 significant buildings, the majority reflecting middle and upper-income taste in residential architecture. Styles include Bungalow, Prairie School, Colonial and Mediterranean Revival. Bungalow predominates (60% of total), most are 1 story, gable roof, frame.

KEY WEST

Key West HD

19th, early 20th C. United States naval station established in 1825, and city incorporated in 1828. Homes and public buildings built by settlers from eastern U.S., Cuba, Europe, and Bahamas. Oldest buildings are wood, with Bahama-style dwelling (built by ship carpenters) most common. Houses simple in exterior design, frequently with lacy woodwork, carved porch spindles, etc. **H A B S**

LAKELAND

Florida Southern College Architectural District

1937 - 1955. Campus planned by Frank Lloyd Wright, and 7 of the 13 buildings designed during his "organic" period. Structures are steel-frame, with concrete, glass, cypress, and coquina. Of note: Annie Pfieffer chapel, Ordway classroom complex. Campus is only realized example of Wright's planning concepts as idealized in his "Broadacre City" plan involving interrelation of built elements. **H A B S**. *Map, Self-Guided Tours*: Admissions Office, Lakeland FL 33802, telephone (813)-680-4131.

MCINTOSH

McIntosh HD

Mid-1880's - 1930. Variety of structures over 38 blocks, including citrus packing houses, churches, residences. Most are frame, 1 to 2 stories, with Frame Vernacular the predominant style. Other styles are Gothic Revival, Queen Anne and Bungalow. District largely unaltered from the 1930's and has retained much of its architectural integrity. *Annual Homes Tour*: 1890 Festival (usually October); contact Friends of McIntosh, Inc., PO Box 1890, McIntosh FL 32664, telephone (904)-591-1180. (zip code?????????????) *General Information*: Mrs. Margie T. Karow, c/o Friends of McIntosh.

MIAMI BEACH

Miami Beach Architectural District

1920 - 1945. One hundred twenty-five-block area with largest concentration in U.S. of resort architecture of 1920's - 1930's era. More than 800 architecturally significant buildings, especially the beachfront series of hotels on Ocean Drive; these are in Moderne Style, made famous in the Chicago and New York World Fairs, 1933 and 1939. *Guided Tours*: Saturdays, 10:30 a.m. - 12:30 p.m. or by appointment; Miami Design Preservation League (MDPL), 1236 Ocean Dr., Miami Beach FL 33139, telephone (305)-672-2014. *Special Events*: Art Deco Weekend (January); Summerfest (July-August); contact MDPL. *General Information*: Contact MDPL.

MICANOPY

Micanopy HD

Late 19th to early 20th C. Grew into prosperous market town during second half of 19th C. Center of early orange-growing industry, was hard hit by freeze of 1894-95; has retained small-town atmosphere with additional character from open green spaces, ancient oaks, other native trees. Contains a number of period buildings, especially from 30-year period before and after 1900. *Map, Self-Guided Tours*: Town Hall, also Old Ice Cream Parlor, both on Cholokka Road, Micanopy FL 32667. *Special Events*: Micanopy Fall Harvest Festival.

MONTICELLO

Monticello HD

19th C. District includes area within original town plan of 1828, with 42 structures from 19th C. and a number of outbuildings. Still largely intact 19th C. community, with outstanding Florida examples of such styles as Greek and Classic Revival, Italianate, and Stick. Of note: Bailey-Brinson House (Italianate), Budd-Braswell House (1840's), and Christ Church (Stick Style).

OCALA

Ocala HD

1880 - 1930. Extensive residential area with concentration of well-preserved homes on shaded streets with numerous live oaks. Earliest development dominated by Queen Anne style, with Florida land boom of the next two decades exemplified by revival-style residences on large sites (see Fifth Street). *General Information*: Historic Ocala Preservation Society, (904)-351-1861 or (904)-732-2023; POB 3123, Ocala FL 32678; also City Planning Office, Ocala FL 32671.

PALATKA

Palatka North HD

Late 19th - early 20th C. Residential neighborhood covers 11 city blocks, with Queen Anne, Colonial and Mediterranean Revival, and Bungalow-style homes set along tree-shaded streets. Of 76 pre-1930 buildings, some 30 erected in 19th C. Of note: Ft. Shannon Officers Quarters (1840, Greek Revival), massive Bronson-Mulholland House (Greek Revival), and pre-Civil War St. Mark's Episcopal Church (Gothic Revival).

Palatka South HD

1852 - 1930. Twenty-three-block neighborhood contains approximately 180 buildings predating 1930, with half from city's "Golden Age" of late 19th C. Once the city's most fashionable residential area, it contains Queen Anne, Colonial and Mediterranean Revival styles; district is significant for the concentration and quality of its architecture. Of note: ornate Blanchard House (1897), Conant House (1886 Queen Anne), and William Tilghman House (c. 1884, Georgian Revival).

PENSACOLA

Naval Air Station HD

1865 - 1918. Site of one of the Navy's earliest bases (established 1824), and the Navy's first pilot training center. Covers 82 acres, with 55 structures, mostly brick or frame. Buildings include residences, octagonal 1854 Armory and Chapel, and 6 historic metal seaplane hangers (1916-1918). **N H L - H A B S.** *General Information*: Pensacola Visitors Information Center, 1401 E. Gregory St., Pensacola FL 32501; also, Naval Aviation Museum, and Public Affairs Office, Bldg. 45, NAS, Pensacola FL 32508.

North Hill HD

1870's - 1930's. Early residential suburb for upper-middle class, covering 80 blocks. Contains wide range of styles, including fine examples of Queen Anne, Classical, Spanish, and Colonial Revival, and Moderne. Earliest houses, 1870-1910, primarily frame; later periods, 1910-1930, feature brick and stucco. District has retained its original character, a major factor being the shaded, heavily-planted effect from the several parks, and the mature trees and shrubs around homes.

Pensacola HD (also Seville Square)

18th, 19th C. City was settled in 18th C., serving as capital of W. Florida during British occupation (1763-1781), and the last Spanish period (1781-1821). Became a fishing, shipping, and transportation center, with structures within district illustrating those prosperous times. Dwellings all date from 19th C., in variety of styles: Gulf Coast or Creole cottages, Greek Revival, Victorian-era. **H A B S**. *Map, Self-Guided Tours*: Visitor Information Center, 1401 E. Gregory St., Pensacola FL 32501, telephone (904)-434-1234, or 1-(800)-874-1234. *General Information*: Historic Pensacola Preservation Board, (904)-434-1042; Pensacola Historical Museum, (904)-433-1559.

QUINCY

Quincy HD

1840 - 1920. Of interest because of remarkable concentration of buildings erected over nearly 100 years. Approximately 145 residential and commercial structures in 16 city blocks. First tobacco boom, 1840-1860, produced number of elegant Classic Revival homes. Second boom, late 1880's to 1920, left several late-Victorian homes. Of note: Gibbs House (c. 1850's, Classic Revival), Quincy Women's Club (c. 1852), and the Quincy Academy (c. 1850, Georgian - Federal).

SANFORD

Sanford Commercial HD

1887 - 1910. District covers approximately 11 city blocks, and includes 25 structures, majority of which are Victorian with Italianate elements, 1 and 2 stories. Of note: those buildings associated with the Plant Investment Co., an. important transportation organization.

SARASOTA

Burns Court HD

1924 - 1925. Small residential district of 15 concrete-block and masonry 1-story bungalows, stucco-finished, in Mediterranean Revival style. Built as a cooperative subdivision by Owen Burns, prominent developer, and designed by Thomas Reed Martin, Sarasota. District is remarkably intact, including original sidewalks, 1-car garages in 5 outbuildings, and walled enclosure. *Map, Self-Guided Tours*: Sarasota County Archives, 701 Plaza de Santo Domingo, Sarasota FL 33577, telephone (813)-365-1000, ext. 2329.

Caples - Ringlings Estates HD

1911 - 1920's. One hundred fifty-acre district composed of contiguous former estates of 3 of city's most prominent citizens: Ralph Caples, John Ringling, Charles Ringling. Caples residence (now used by New College) was built in late 1920's in Mediterranean Revival style. Charles Ringling house features Italian Renaissance style. Most elaborate and distinctive building in district is John Ringling residence, "Ca' d' Zan", designed in Venetian Gothic by Dwight James

Baum (museum). Ringling estate also contains Ringling Museum of Art, designed by John Phillips in Italian Renaissance style.

Palm Avenue HD

1920's (L). Began in late 1880's, developing into beautiful residential area. Now contains many commercial structures and aging hotels but has retained considerable atmosphere. Includes numerous Mediterranean Revival buildings. Of note: El Verona Hotel (1925), Karl Bickel residence (1925), Frances-Carleton Apartments (1924). See also S. H. Kress Store (1932), city's finest example of Art Deco. *Map, Self-Guided Tours*: See **Burns Court HD.**

ST. AUGUSTINE

Abbott Tract HD

19th C. - 1930. Largest concentration of 19th C. buildings in city, and some of the city's finest examples of Victorian-era architecture; residential district covers 17 blocks and contains 136 pre-1930 buildings. Of note: Beach Cottage (1839), Joyner House (1840), and Abbott House (c. 1861). Area relatively free of modern intrusions and many of the period buildings have retained their architectural integrity. *General Information*: See **Walled City HD.**

Model Land Co. HD

1885 - 1934. Neighborhoods known collectively as "the Model Land Co. tract" are the finest developments in city from the Flagler era, with fine examples of late-19th and early-20th C. buildings. District has 245 pre-1930 buildings, 60 from Flagler era, 1885-1904; other notable buildings reflect the 1914-1930 boom. Of note: Hotel Ponce de Leon (now Flagler College), Grace United Methodist Church, and Markland Residence (1839). *General Information*: See **Abbott Tract HD.**

Walled City HD

17th - 19th C. St. Augustine was founded in 1565 as Spanish military base and is oldest continuously occupied European settlement in continental U.S. District, adjacent to historic Fort "Castillo de San Marcos" (National Park Service) contains original residences (31 of which have above-ground portions predating 1821), plus several reconstructions and restorations. *Map, Self-Guided Tours*: Chamber of Commerce,

Visitor Information Center, 10 Castillo Drive, St. Augustine FL 32084. *Guided Tours*: National Park Service at Castillo de San Marcos fort; Florida State Museum, San Augustin Antiguo Village; St. Augustine Sightseeing Trains, 3 Cordova St., St. Augustine FL 32084, telephone (904)-829-6545. *General Information*: Historic St. Augustine Preservation Board, POB 1987, St. Augustine FL 32084.

TALLAHASSEE

Calhoun Street HD

1840 - 1940. One of city's oldest and most important residential neighborhoods, presenting spectrum of architectural styles, 1840-1940. Added feature of area is the canopy of large live oaks. Of note: Bloxham House (1844, only surviving 19th C. townhouse), Chesley House (1895, Queen Anne), and Richard Shine House (1907, Colonial Revival).

Magnolia Heights HD

1899 - 1934. City's first 20th-C. suburb, with 40 buildings. Styles include simple Frame Vernacular, Bungalow, Colonial Revival, and Queen Anne. Except for some apartment complexes, district characterized by modestly scaled frame houses of 1 and 1 1/2 stories.

Park Avenue HD

1830 - 1912. A series of neighborhoods which evolved along a 9-block street of public parks. District offers rich historic panorama of residences, churches, public, and commercial structures reflecting city's development, 1825-1936. Buildings primarily from 2 periods of city's growth: 1830-1860 and 1880-1912.

TAMPA

Hyde Park HD

1886 - 1933. Oldest and best preserved of Tampa's early residential neighborhoods, with approximately 1,600 buildings. Most are wood frame, reflecting American architectural tastes during late 19th C. and first 3 decades of 20th C. House types range from shotgun houses to high-style masonry mansions. District has retained much of its original ambience, with its older houses, unaltered streetscapes, and tree-lined avenues.

General Information: Historic Tampa Preservation Board, 452 W. Kennedy, Tampa FL 33606, telephone (813)-272-3843.

West Tampa HD

1890's to early 1930's. Contains a variety of residential, commercial, social, and industrial buildings. Excellent examples of frame vernacular and bungalow-style housing, late 19th, and early 20th C. The most important buildings are 11 cigar factories, 3-story brick. District is historically significant due to associations with cigar industry, the Latin American community, and individuals involved in Tampa's early development. *General Information*: See **Hyde Park HD**.

Ybor City HD

1880's - 20th C. Once the center of U.S. cigar industry, employing hundreds of Cuban and other immigrant workers. Primarily commercial with a few residences; contains numerous brick and stone structures, many with Spanish-style elements. Of note: old Ybor Factory, Centro Espanol, and El Pasaje Hotel. *Map, Self-Guided Tours*: Ybor City State Museum (old Perlita Bakery), 9th Ave. near 18th St., also at local merchants. *Special Events*: Contact Ybor City Chamber of Commerce, 1513 8th Ave., Tampa FL 33605, telephone (813)-248-3712; also Tampa Preservation, Inc., (813)-254-3194.

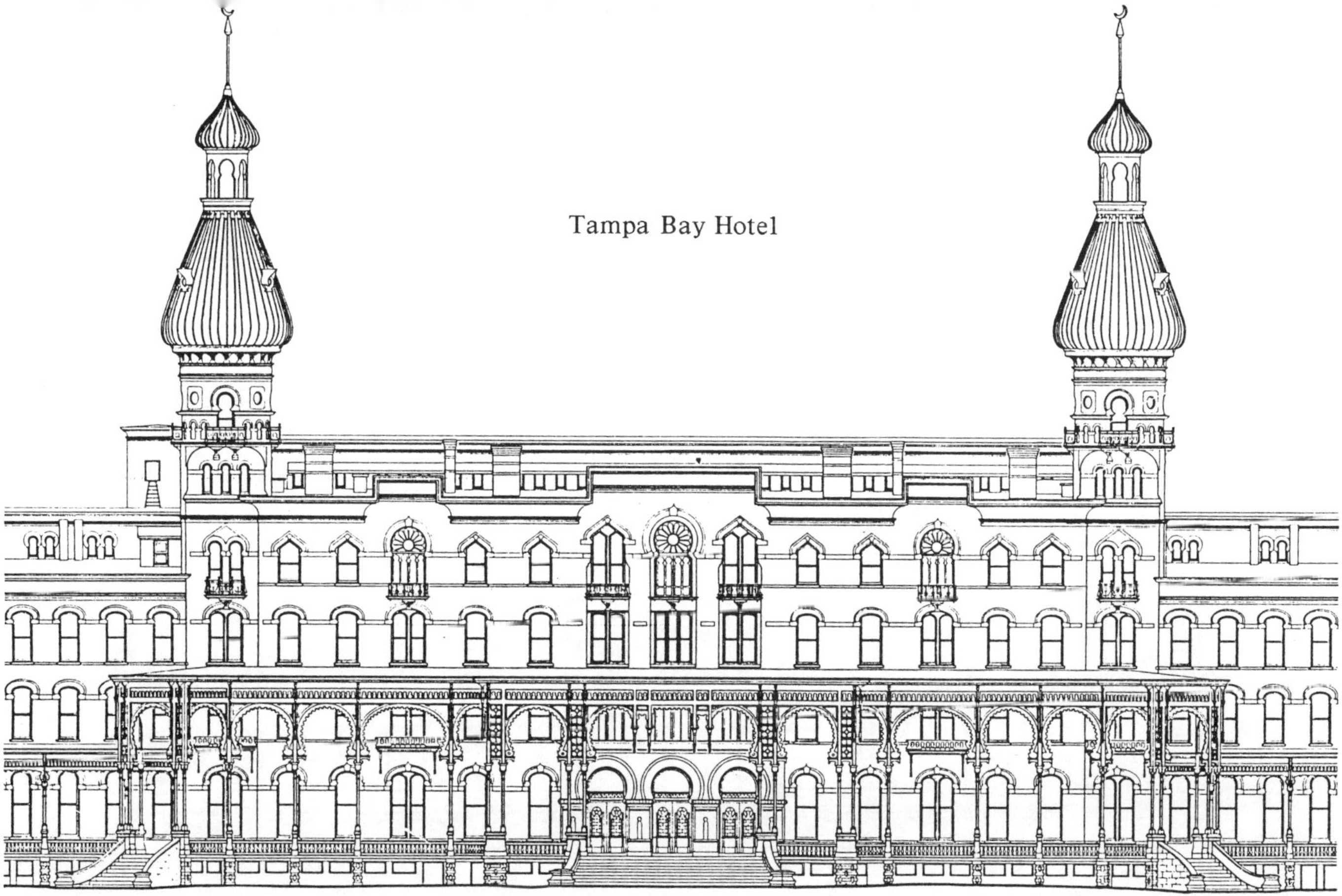

Tampa Bay Hotel

William Remshart row houses

GEORGIA

ALBANY

Albany Railroad Depot HD

1857–c. 1917 - Three major railroad buildings and a wide brick street. Buildings are 1913 Union Depot, the 1857 depot, and a Railway Express Agency structure from World War I.

AMERICUS

Americus HD

1850's–1900 - Residential-commercial, with 25 significant buildings of frame or masonry, 1 and 2 1/2 stories. Styles include Greek and Gothic Revival, Romanesque Revival, Queen Anne, Stick, Eastlake, and Neoclassical Revival. Has retained much of its 19th C. character. *Map, Self-Guided Tours*: Chamber of Commerce, 400 W. Lamar St., POB 724, Americus GA 31709, telephone (912)-924-2646; also Sumter Historic Preservation Society, POB 1416, Americus GA 31709.

ATHENS

Bloomfield St. HD

Late 19th to early 20th C. - A densely-developed in-town residential neighborhood. Styles include Victorian Eclectic, American Foursquare, and Bungalow/Craftsman. Extensive landscaping, limited modern intrusions.

Boulevard HD

Late 19th to early 20th C. - A streetcar suburb with 1 and 2-story houses, ranging from simple vernacular cottages to large mansions, mostly of wood. Styles include Greek Revival, Victorian Eclectic, American Foursquare, Neoclassical, and Bungalow. Extensive landscaping, few modern intrusions.

Cobbham HD

19th-20th C. - Densely populated in-town neighborhood of single and multi-family dwellings (with increasing commercial and institutional intrusions). Structures range from Greek and Gothic Revival to styles popular in late 19th, early 20th C. *General Information*: Historic Cobbham Foundation, 573 Hill St., Cobbham GA 30606.

Dearing Street HD

Mid to late 19th C. - Residential, 60 structures, primarily frame, two stories, in Greek Revival and Italianate. Area originally part of land grant for University of Georgia. Has retained much of its 19th C. character. *Map, Self-Guided Tours*: Welcome Center, 280 E. Doughtery Street, Athens GA 30601, telephone (404)-546-1805; Athens-Clarke Heritage Foundation, Fire Hall #2, 489 Prince Street, Athens GA 30601, telephone (404)-353-1801. *Guided Tours*: City tour by reservation; contact Convention and Visitors Bureau, (404) 549-6800; POB 948, Athens GA 30603. *Annual Homes Tour*: Athens/Clarke Tour of Homes (April); Upstairs/Downtown Tour (October). Contact Athens-Clarke Heritage Foundation.

Downtown Athens HD

Late 19th to early 20th C. - Primarily commercial, plus governmental and religious structures, hotels, warehouses, and railroad-related structures.

Milledge Ave. HD

1850's-1900's - Residential, with houses predominantly 2 stories, large in scale. Styles include Greek Revival, Queen Anne, Neoclassical, Colonial and Tudor Revival, American Foursquare, and Craftsman/Bungalow. Of note: A. P. Dearing House (1856, Greek Revival), and the Hamilton-Phinizy - Segrest House (1857).

Milledge Circle HD

1910-1930's - Residential, primarily modest 1 or 2-story brick. Styles include American Foursquare, Neoclassical, and Bungalow.

ATLANTA

Ansley Park HD

Early 20th C. - A suburban residential district of 275 acres, with approximately 600 houses. Developed between 1904 and 1930, remains virtually unchanged. Displays a wide range of eclectic and period architectural styles.

Atlanta Underground HD

Late 19th to early 20th C. - A 2 1/2-block business district, composed of multi-storied brick buildings with stone, iron, sheet metal, and terra cotta details. Generally Victorian in style, with some examples of Neoclassical and Functional design.

Atlanta University Center District

1869-20th C. - Includes the campuses and related historic structures of the institutions comprising the Atlanta University Center, 2 churches, University Homes residential development, and residential areas associated with development of the educational complex. Buildings of interest include: Gaines (Old North) Hall (1869, Italianate); Fountain (Stone) Hall (1882, Queen Anne); and the Morris Brown College Administration Building (1905, Georgian Revival).

Brookwood Hills HD

Early 1920's - A suburban residential development of approximately 90 acres with 255 residences, large recreation area, and 2 distinctive bricked and landscaped entranceways to the subdivision. District incorporates major architectural, landscape, and planning elements of suburban development of the early 1920's in America.

Cabbagetown HD

c. 1891 - Textile-mill district within city of Atlanta; 300 frame, clapboarded, 1 and 2-story structures. Principal style is Vernacular Victorian. Of note: two of three original mill buildings, the Reinhardt Street Row, and the shotgun houses on Kirkwood Avenue. One of earliest factory-supported villages in South, district has retained much of its 19th C. character.

Castleberry Hill HD

1890's-1930's - A densely developed commercial district of about 40 acres, with 108 buildings. Includes 1 and 2-story brick retail/commercial buildings with modest late Victorian and Early 20th C. Commercial-style detailing, and solid rows of 2 and 3-story warehouses (the majority built in 1920's).

Druid Hills Parks (and Parkways) HD

1900–1915 - Includes notable residences by local architect Nell Reid, in wealthy suburb of Druid Hills, and series of small parks and parkways. Landscape architects were Frederick Law Olmstead, Sr. and John C. Olmstead. One of few examples of Olmstead's work in Southeast.

Emory University HD

1915 - Neoclassical Revival university complex includes classroom, library, and administration buildings, primarily of reinforced concrete faced with multicolor marble slabs and terra cotta decoration. Of note: law school and theology buildings designed by Edward Tilton, and Glenn Memorial Church designed by firm, Hentz-Adler-Shutze. University originally established to promote Christian education and endowed by Asa Griggs Candler from his Coca-Cola fortune.

Fairlie-Poplar HD

1890's-1920's - Commercial, with styles ranging from Victorian to Art Deco, providing relatively unaltered glimpse into Atlanta's evolution from a pioneer railroad town to modern city. Features a number of early skyscrapers. Of note: Asa Candler Building (1906, 17 stories), Rhodes-Haverty Building (1929, 21 stories), Flatiron Building (1897, 11 stories), and Old Federal Courthouse (1911, Second Renaissance Revival). *Map, Self-Guided Tours*: Atlanta Convention and Visitors Bureau; Atlanta Preservation Center, 84 Peachtree Street NW, Atlanta GA 30303, telephone (404)-522-4345. *Guided Tours*: Contact Preservation Center, for guided tours, April - October.

Fox Theatre HD

Early 20th C. - Three major buildings (Fox Theatre, Georgian Terrace Hotel, and Ponce de Leon Apartments), occupying 3 of the 4 corners of the intersection of 2 of city's major traffic arteries (Peachtree Street and Ponce de Leon Avenue). Area had declined but restoration-revival of Fox Theatre by Atlanta Landmarks, Inc. has sparked renewal plans.

Georgia Institute of Technology HD

Late 19th C. - Twelve buildings on the old 9-acre original campus. An attractively landscaped cluster of classroom, dormitory and administrative buildings. These red brick structures are shaded by 100-year old trees.

Grant Park HD

Late 19th to early 20th C. - Covers some 430 acres of rolling terrain, and centers around Grant Park, 131 acres. Majority of structures are residential but district also contains school buildings, churches, and commercial clusters that have served this large, old neighborhood. Residential structures range in size from large 2-story mansions to more modest 2-story modified Queen Anne frame dwellings and 1-story Victorian cottages and Craftsman bungalows. Of note: Cyclorama, large circular painting of the "Battle for Atlanta", in c. 1920 Classical Revival building at park's center.

Grant Park North HD

Late 19th to early 20th C. - A very small and cohesive city neighborhood characterized by late Victorian-era houses. Most are 1-story; many have retained the Victorian trim on their porches as well as such elements as stained and leaded glass. Well shaded by oak trees, with sections of original brick or octagonal concrete-paven sidewalks.

Inman Park District

19th-20th C. - Suburban residential, with large number of period houses in wide variety of styles: High Victorian Gothic and Italianate, Queen Anne, Stick, Neoclassical Revival, and Bungaloid. Atlanta's first planned suburb, with picturesque street pattern, large trees, and green areas. *Map, Self-Guided Tours*: See **Fairlie-Poplar HD.** *Guided Tours*: See **Fairlie-Poplar HD.**

Martin Luther King, Jr. HD

19th-20th C. - Commercial/residential neighborhood, including birthplace and gravesite of Reverend Martin Luther King, Jr. Also the Ebenezer Baptist Church and numerous shotgun row houses (typical of those rented to blacks in 1920's). District has retained much of its original character. **N H L**

Sweet Auburn HD

c. 1890-1940 - Commercial, public, and religious structures, of brick or stone, in range of 19th-20th C. styles. Of note: Odd Fellows Building, Atlanta Life Insurance Co. District was center of thriving black economy, providing base for a rising black middle class in Atlanta, early 20th C. **N H L.** *Map, Self-Guided Tours*: Mayor's Office, City Hall, 68 Mithcell St. SW, Atlanta GA 30303; Atlanta Preservation Center see **Fairlie Poplar HD.**

Techwood Homes HD

1935-1936 - Multiple housing complex of 2-story row houses,

3-story apartment buildings, store, garages, etc. Designed by Burge and Stevens, architects, was an early Public Works Administration (PWA) project. Replacing a slum, complex was an early Federal effort at low-income housing.

AUGUSTA

Broad St. HD

1820's-1930's - City's oldest historic area, and historic downtown commercial center. Fine examples of late-Federal and Greek Revival buildings, Italianate storefronts, Richardsonian Romanesque structures, and Art Moderne facades.

Greene Street HD

Early 19th to early 20th C. - A linear district on both sides of a magnificent avenue, with some 55 significant buildings, most of them residential. Almost all are 2 to 3 stories with a common setback, frequently creating impressive streetscapes. No modern intrusions.

Historic Augusta Canal and Industrial District

1845-1900 - Industrial, with 9-mile canal constructed 1845-46 (enlarged 1877), gates, spillways, etc., and 4 textile mill buildings erected in 1870's-1880's. Sibley Mill unusually colorful, architecturally unique. Entire complex symbolizes Southern determination to industrialize after Civil War; outstanding surviving example of a major engineering system. **N H L**

Laney - Walker North HD

Mid-19th to early 20th C. - Large residential district, with scattered churches and commercial clusters. Majority of houses are 1-story wood-framed with weatherboard siding. Modest Victorian Eclectic detailing very common, plus some Greek Revival, Colonial Revival, and Bungalow/Craftsman detailing. Front porches very prevalent. Strong historical associations with 3 of Atlanta's historic minority populations - Irish, Chinese, and blacks.

Pinched Gut HD

Late 19th to early 20th C. - Fifty-one city blocks of residential structures, 2 large cemeteries, 11-acre city park. A large group of houses built pre-1916, other area built up 1916-1930. A wide variety of architectural styles and types.

Summerville HD

Early 19th to early 20th C. - Approximately 80 city blocks of mostly suburban residential development; a wide variety of detached, single-family house types and styles, including Federal, Greek Revival, Gothic Revival, Italianate, Queen Anne, and Neoclassical. District also contains a few commercial buildings, an arsenal, college campus, and a large resort hotel.

BACONTON

Baconton Commercial HD

Early 20th C. - Approximately 12 brick structures, 1 and 2 stories, situated beside the railroad tracks. Typical commercial architecture found in South Georgia towns, with arched windows, cast-iron storefronts, and sheet metal canopies over the sidewalks.

South Railroad HD

c. 1900-1927 - Small district of 7 houses and one service station, facing the railroad tracks. Most houses are designed with modest late-Victorian or Craftsman/Bungalow features.

Walton St. - Church St. HD

Late 19th to early 20th C. - Some 18 homes, offering the town's largest concentration of significant residential architecture. Styles represented include late Victorian Eclectic, Neoclassical, Bungaloid, Spanish Mission, and Georgian Revival.

BOWERSVILLE

Bowersville HD

Late 19th C.-1925 - Historic residential and commercial resources of this small town, flanking both sides of the railroad track which cuts through the area. Commercial buildings date from 1889-1907, 1908-1910; residences are wooden, primarily 1-story. The more elaborate homes have Victorian Eclectic detailing.

BRUNSWICK

Brunswick Old Town HD

Late 19th to early 20th C. - Business, residential, with strong turn-of-the-century appearance. Styles include Queen Anne, Eastlake, Gothic and Jacobean Revival, and Italianate. Of note: Old City Hall (c. 1888, Queen Anne), Mahoney/McGarvey house (1891, unusually fine Victorian Eclectic), and H. Haffner residence (c. 1900, Neoclassical Revival). Town laid out in 1771, became Port of Entry in 1789; has modern port and active fishing industry. *Map, Self-Guided Tours*: For sale by the Old Town Brunswick Preservation Association, c/o Old City Hall, Mansfield and Newcastle Sts., Brunswick GA 31520 (irregular hours). *General Information*: Chamber of Commerce, 4 Glynn Ave., POB 250, Brunswick GA 31520, telephone (912)-265-0620.

CAMILLA

Camilla Commercial HD

Late 19th to early 20th C. - Downtown, and the adjacent Art Deco-style Mitchell County Courthouse. Styles represented in commercial buildings include simple Victorian Eclectic, Early 20th C., Commercial/Utilitarian, and Art Deco.

CANON

Canon Commercial HD

Late 19th to early 20th C. - An intact area of historic commercial buildings in town's center. The buildings are simple 1 and 2-story brick structures; features include corbeled cornices and cast-iron columns. Of note: W. F. Bowers Building, built in early 1890's.

CANTON

Canton Commercial HD

Late 19th to early 20th C. - A relatively intact group of commercial buildings covering 1 1/2 blocks. Most are of brick, 1 to 3 stories; styles include Victorian Eclectic, Beaux-Arts, and Art Moderne.

CARROLLTON

South Carrollton Residential HD

Late 19th to early 20th C. An in-town neighborhood; includes a range of house types from modest cottages to large homes of prominent families. Styles include Victorian Gothic, Queen Anne, Eclectic, and Neoclassical. Majority of houses are wood-framed with weatherboarded siding.

CAVE SPRING

Cave Spring Commercial HD

Late 19th to early 20th C. - A relatively dense group of 1 and 2-story brick buildings in town's historic downtown. Decorative brick detailing is noteworthy, as is use of wood in imitation of cast-iron storefronts.

Cave Spring Residential HD

Late 19th to early 20th C. - Several intact blocks of housing, and two churches. Houses are detached, wood-framed, single-family residences. Styles include Greek Revival, Gothic Revival, Italianate, Victorian Eclectic, and Queen Anne. Has retained much of its original atmosphere.

Georgia School for the Deaf HD

1849-1947 - Four historic buildings, landscaped yard, and sidewalks, driveways, and paved courtyards. Buildings are brick, with the largest, Fannin Hall, dating from 1849 (but with substantial alterations).

Rolator Park HD

19th C. to early 20th C. - City's largest public park and preserve, containing 1851 Baptist Church in Greek Revival style and two turn-of-the-century Neoclassical academy buildings.

CLARKESVILLE

South Washington Street HD

Late 19th to early 20th C. - A linear district of approximately 12 structures, primarily residential. Good example of a modest "streetcar suburb", with representations of plain style, Victorian Eclectic, Queen Anne, Georgian Revival, and Bungalow.

Washington - Jefferson St. HD
Early 19th to early 20th C. - Approximately one dozen houses, including some of city's finest residences. Contains a large antebellum farmhouse, 2 excellent examples of Gothic Revival style, an impressive Georgian Revival house, and a rare 19th C. servants' house.

CLARKESVILLE (VICINITY)

Woodlands - Blythewood HD
1840's - Two outstanding examples of the picturesque and romantic early Victorian cottage. Neighboring houses, "Woodlands" and "Blythewood", built in early 1840's as summer residences for Savannah families. Both homes are extremely well preserved (private).

CLERMONT

Clermont Residential HD
Early 20th C. - Contains a variety of popular early 20th C. styles, including Victorian Eclectic, Georgian Revival, Neoclassical, and Bungalow/Craftsman. Houses are primarily 1 and 2-story wood-framed, with porches, roof dormers.

CLINTON

Old Clinton HD
19th C. - Residential, early 19th C. houses, several sites, and a church. Buildings largely frame with clapboarding, several attributed to builder-architect Daniel Pratt. Town boasted one of country's largest antebellum cotton gins, and one of first female seminaries. **H A B S**

COLBERT

Colbert HD
1890's-1920's - Small rural town 10 miles east of Athens, on S.R. 72. District contains a commercial block, depot, hotel, 3 blocks of wood-framed houses and an impressive late-Victorian farmhouse. Relatively untouched by modernization.

COLQUITT

Colquitt Town Square HD

General Information: Colquitt City Hall, Colquitt GA 31737.

COLUMBUS

Columbus HD

Early 19th C. - City was surveyed and laid out in 1828. District consists of 29 city blocks, with approximately 600 structures. Styles range from simple Georgian cottages to large Greek Revival and Gothic Revival homes. *Map, Self-Guided Tours*: Convention and Visitors Bureau, POB 2768, Columbus GA 31902, telephone (404)-322-1613; Historic Columbus Foundation, 700 Broadway, POB 5312, Columbus GA 31906, telephone (404)-322-0756. *Guided Tours*: Wednesdays, Saturdays; contact Welcome Center, (404)-571-7455, or Historic Columbus Foundation. *Annual Homes Tour*: Salisbury Fair (first weekend, May); contact Historic District Preservation Society, POB 263, Columbus GA 31906 or Historic Columbus Foundation.

Historic Riverfront Industrial District

1844-1900 - Chattahoochee River drops 125 feet within 2.5 miles at Columbus, producing tremendous power potential. District consists of city's three oldest dams (1824, 1844, 1900) and five industries associated with river power (City Mills, 1828, Eagle and Phenix Mills, 1850, Columbus Iron Works, 1853, Muscogee Manufacturing, 1868, Bibb Manufacturing Co., 1900). Rare examples of early technologies, and the mills have both historic and architectural significance. Columbus Iron Works has been converted into a Convention and Trade Center, recipient of 1981 Honors Award, National Trust for Historic Preservation. **N H L.** *General Information*: Convention and Visitors Bureau (404)-322-1613.

COVINGTON

Floyd Street HD

19th to early 20th C. - Small residential district which catered to city's prominent families. Majority of dwellings are either Greek Revival or Neoclassical Revival. Of note: Swanscombe Property (1830, Greek Revival), and Porter-

Rogers-Tuck House 1903, Neoclassical Revival). *Map, Self-Guided Tours*: Chamber of Commerce, 1121 Floyd Street, POB 168, Covington GA 30209, telephone (404)-786-7510.

CULLODEN

Culloden HD

19th to early 20th C. - A very small community 30 miles west of Macon. Approximately one-half dozen commercial buildings of brick, 2 blocks of in-town housing, and a string of residences and farmhouses to the southwest. District also contains a historic public well and wellhouse at intersection of College Street - Thomaston Road.

CUMBERLAND ISLAND (NATIONAL SEASHORE)

Dungeness HD

High Point - Half Moon Bluff HD

c. 1930 - A former hotel and 9 outbuildings; originally a resort complex on this largest of the "Golden Isles", now a private estate. Closest mainland town is St. Marys.

Plum Orchard HD

19th C. - Seventeen structures, a small cemetery, ruins of an antebellum home and an archeological site. Major structure is Plum Orchard Mansion (1898 Neoclassical Revival) designed by Boston firm, Peabody and Stearns.

Stafford Plantation HD

No further information available at this time.

CUTHBERT

Cuthbert HD

Mid to late 19th C. - Primarily residential, with number of frame dwellings, 1 1/2 and 2 1/2 stories; outstanding examples of Greek Revival, Late Gothic Revival, and Eastlake. Of note: three small Greek Revival law offices, c. 1830's; Pulaski Barnes house (1880); County Courthouse (1885).

DAHLONEGA

Dahlonega Commercial HD

19th–20th C. – Town, established in 1833, was once center of active gold mining area. Downtown core contains number of buildings from late Victorian era and early 1900's. Of note: Old Lumpkin County Courthouse (1836, now Gold Museum), Price building (c. 1897), Hall's Block (1883), and Hall House (1881). *Map, Self-Guided Tours*: Chamber of Commerce, Public Square, POB 2037, Dahlonega GA 30533, telephone (404)-864-3711.

DALTON

Crown Mill HD

1884 to early 20th C. – An exceptionally well-preserved cotton factory complex and mill village. Industrial structures are predominantly brick, while village consists of several dozen modest frame houses plus company store, school, recreation areas, and mill owner's house.

DARIEN

Vernon Square – Columbus Square HD

Mid-19th to early 20th C. – Homes, 5 churches, and an armory (now city hall) on a bluff overlooking Darien River. Majority of historic buildings are wood-framed with weatherboard siding. Styles represented include Greek and Gothic Revival, Victorian Eclectic, Colonial Revival, and Craftsman/Bungalow.

DILLARD (VICINITY)

Hambidge Center HD

19th – 20th C. – A small rural district 3 miles west of Dillard in the Betty's Creek area of north Georgia mountains. Strong historical associations with arts and crafts, through Jay Hambidge Arts Foundation (founded in mid-1930's) and conception of folklore magazine, *Foxfire*, in 1960's. Structures include an 1830's log cabin, an 1890's log lodge, a 1920's rock farmhouse, a 1930's gristmill, and 1940's arts and crafts buildings.

EAST POINT

East Point Industrial District

Late 19th to early 20th C. - District is comprised of 5 industrial complexes: White Hickory Wagon Works; Blount Carriage and Buggy Works; Couch Brothers Cotton Mills; Atlanta Utility Works; and, the Oak Knitting Mills Buildings. Wagon Works, now a textile warehouse, was constructed in 1884; buggy works built c. 1907, as was Couch Brothers Mills. Extensive non-historic additions and major modern intrusions.

EATONTON

Eatonton HD

19th to early 20th C. - Extensive district containing about 100 residential and commercial structures. Most are frame, one or two stories, with numerous outstanding examples of such styles as Greek Revival, Georgian Revival, and those of Victorian era. Of note: Wilkins-Cooper-Jenkins House (1817), Slade-Dunn House (c. 1850, Greek Revival), Abercrombie-Rosser Hood House (c. 1818, Federal) and the 1905 Georgian Revival Courthouse. Has retained much of its 19th C. character. *Map, Self-Guided Tours*: Chamber of Commerce, 105 Sumter Street, POB 656, Eatonton GA 31024, telephone (404)-485-7701; also Historical Society, 206 N. Madison Ave., Eatonton GA 31024. *Annual Homes Tour*: Spring Tour of Homes (early May); contact Chamber of Commerce.

ELBERTON

Elberton Commercial HD

Late 19th to early 20th C. - Several blocks of densely grouped brick structures; styles include Romanesque, Renaissance, Neoclassical, and Victorian Eclectic. Details include cast-iron columns in storefronts, and stone, terra cotta, and pressed-metal ornamentation.

Elberton Residential HD

19th to early 20th C. - Intact in-town neighborhood of single-family dwellings. Styles include Greek Revival, Gothic Revival, Victorian Eclectic, Eastlake, Queen Anne, Neoclassical, Colonial Revival, and Bungalow/Craftsman. Few intrusions mar district's cohesive historic residential character.

FLOWERY BRANCH

Flowery Branch Commercial HD

Late 19th to early 20th C. - Town's central business district, with a collection of period commercial buildings constructed of brick or rusticated concrete block with number of decorative features.

FORSYTH

Downtown Commercial HD

Late 19th to early 20th C. - Town incorporated in 1823, prospered from post-Civil War cotton industry. The Old Courthouse Square has been described in local tourism leaflet as "a picture postcard arriving a century late." Of note: Empire Cotton Warehouse (c. 1868, Italianate elements), Pye's Opera House (1870), and Citizen's Bank (c. 1905, Neoclassical Revival). *Map, Self-Guided Tours*: Chamber of Commerce, Courthouse Square, POB 811, Forsyth GA 31029, telephone (912)-994-5171; Historical Society, c/o Whistle Stop Antiques, Old Depot, E. Adams and E. Johnston Street, Forsyth GA 31029. *Annual Homes Tour*: Contact Christ United Methodist Church, North Drive, Forsyth GA 31029 (912)-994-1232.

FORT GAINS

Fort Gains HD

1850's to early 1900's - Residential, commercial, institutional, and industrial. Commercial buildings primarily brick, from 1880's to early 1900's. Residences range from antebellum Greek Revival to Gothic Revival and Queen Anne.

FORT OGELTHORPE

Fort Ogelthorpe HD

c. 1900-1910 - Some three dozen buildings and several large landscaped areas, once an army cavalry base (decommissioned after World War II). Includes a number of clapboarded Queen Anne-style residences, also stables, chapel, officers' club, bandhouse, and bandstand.

GAINESVILLE

Brenau College District

1878-1920 - College and surrounding residential structures; most significant date from 1878-1920 and include examples of Queen Anne, Second Empire, and Neoclassical Revival styles.

Chicopee Mill and Village HD

1927 - Planned industrial town located 3.5 miles from downtown Gainesville. Industrial complex dominated by the historic textile mill, an enormous 1-story rectangular structure. Mill village consists of some 220 houses, the majority 1-story bungalows veneered with tapestry brick, and finished with Craftsman detailing.

Green Street HD

Late 19th to early 20th C. - Residential, approximately 30 dwellings, primarily frame, 2 and 2 1/2 stories. Of note: Newman-Quinlan-Jones House (Neoclassical Revival) and Smith-Palmour-Estes House (Queen Anne). Area prospered from 19th C. cotton marketing and has retained much of its late 19th C. character, including fine examples of Georgian Revival.

GILLSVILLE

Gillsville HD

Late 19th to early 20th C. - A linear district along State Route 52, in this small town; comprised of residential and commercial buildings and one antebellum residence. Residential structures are primarily 1-story, wood-framed, plain style vernacular or Victorian Eclectic. Commercial town center contains grouping of several attached 1-story brick structures. Of interest: antebellum Garrison House, 2-story Greek Revival.

GREENSBORO (VICINITY)

Penfield HD

c. 1833-1900 - Residential, 7 miles north of Greensboro on GA 5925. Approximately 30 brick or frame houses, 1 and 2-stories; predominant styles are Greek Revival and Vernacular.

Of note: Dr. Masey house (raised cottage), Iverson Brooks house (full-height tetrastyle portico), and brick-shingle Presbyterian Church. District developed around Mercer Institute and University (early 19th C. Baptist school), and has retained much of its 19th C. character.

GRIFFIN

Old Medical College Historical Area

1850's - Two buildings with Greek Revival/Victorian elements. (Private, not accessible to public).

GUYTON

Guyton HD

Mid-19th to early 20th C. - Residential and business, with approximately 20 blocks containing 100 structures of significance. Numerous homes from the mid-to-late 1800's, and four churches of interest: United Methodist, 1846; Antioch Christian, 1875; New Hope AME, 1886; New Providence Baptist, 1891. *Map, Self-Guided Tours*: City Hall, Second Street, POB 99, Guyton GA 31312, telephone (912)-772-3353. *Annual Homes Tour*: Christmas Tour, Gala and Cotillion (second Tuesday, December); contact City Hall.

JEKYLL ISLAND

Jekyll Island Club HD

19th-20th C. - Resort complex and self-sufficient millionaires' community centered around a luxurious frame-and-brick Victorian clubhouse (1887). Features large private residences, chapel, shops, stores, in a variety of late 19th, early 20th C. styles. Typical of this once-exclusive resort is the Rockefeller Cottage, 1892, Shingle Style, 2 1/2 stories (museum). N H L. *Map, Self-Guided Tours*: Visitors Welcome Center, (912)-635-3400; also, Macy Cottage, Millionaires' Village. *Guided Tours*: Daily; contact Macy Cottage, (912)-635-2727.

JEWELL

Jewell HD

1840's to late 19th C. - Significant as the remains of an early Georgia mill village, with architectural features from the 1840's and latter half of 19th C. Nearby are sites of a textile mill, gristmill, and iron foundry. Twelve miles east of Sparta.

JONESBORO

Jonesboro HD

19th C. - Residential, commercial, with antebellum cottages, Greek Revival and Victorian-era dwellings, and brick commercial buildings. *Map, Self-Guided Tours*: Local merchants, and Historic Jonesboro, c/o Mrs. Betty Woodward, 177 Spring Street, Jonesboro GA 30236, telephone (404)-478-6277. *Guided Tours*: Holiday Inn-South, 6288 Old Dixie Highway, Jonesboro GA 30236, telephone (404)-968-4300. *Special Events*: Fall festival (mid-October); Tara Harvest Ball; contact Historic Jonesboro, POB 922, Jonesboro GA 30236.

KENNESAW

Big Shanty Village HD

c. 1900 - Historic downtown area consists of 2 blocks of turn-of-the-century brick commercial buildings, railroad depot, cotton gin/museum and warehouse. Also several blocks of Victorian and c. 1900 cottages and houses. Contemporary intrusions include mobile home and used car lot.

Cherokee Street HD

Late 19th to early 20th C. A significant intact collection of Victorian cottages, farmhouses, and tenant-type dwellings.

North Main Street HD

Mid-19th to early 20th C. An intact residential area consisting of modestly scaled homes; types range from plantation plain to Neoclassical, with a predominance of late 19th C. hip- and gable-roofed Victorian cottages.

Summers Street HD

Late 19th C. Consists of several town residences from late

19th C. and a single farmhouse. Houses are modest 1 and 2-story frame with detailings in Queen Anne, Eastlake, and Craftsman styles.

LAGRANGE

LaGrange HD

1840's-1920's - Residential, with number of outstanding antebellum homes, many in Greek Revival style. Of note: Heard-Dallis House (1830's, 1842), "Bellevue" (1854), and former Presbyterian Church (1846). Town dates from 1828. *Map, Self-Guided Tours*: Chamber of Commerce, 221 Bull St., POB 636, LaGrange GA 30241, telephone (404)-884-8671; Troup County Archives, 136 Main Street, LaGrange GA 30240, telephone (404)-884-1828.

Vernon Rd. HD

Early 19th to early 20th C. - A linear residential district along Vernon Road, comprised of single-family residences. Styles range from antebellum Greek Revival through post-Civil War Victorian Eclectic to Neoclassical and Georgian Revival, Bungalow, and English Tudor.

LAVONIA

Jones Street Residential HD

Late 19th to early 20th C. - An intact neighborhood of 14 historic residential structures, primarily wood-framed single-family. A cohesive streetscape with a distinct Victorian-era character.

Lavonia Commercial HD

Late 19th to early 20th C. - Encompasses city's historic central business district, dating from 1878. Most buildings are brick, 1 or 2-stories, some featuring considerable brick ornamentation; also a dense grouping of brick structures with cast-iron columns, on Grogan Street. District's focal point is old Lavonia Depot.

Vickery St. Residential HD

Late 19th to early 20th C. - A 4-block residential area, primarily detached wood-framed single-family residences. Styles include Queen Anne, Gothic Revival, Victorian Eclectic, Georgian Revival, Renaissance Revival, and Bungalow. A number of the homes feature elaborate detailing, primarily Gothic Revival.

West Ave. - Roberts St. Residential HD
Late 19th to early 20th C. - Two dozen houses and a city park on approximately 20 acres of land. Houses consist primarily of wood-framed, weatherboarded Victorian cottages, and Craftsman-style bungalows of brick. District has a definite neighborhood character, with no major intrusions.

LEXINGTON

Lexington HD
Mid-19th to early 20th C. A few 18th C. structures, a considerable number of mid-19th C. residential and commercial buildings,and several late 19th C. civic buildings (including county Courthouse). Contains several imposing Greek Revival houses.

LINTON

Linton HD
1858-1894. Residential, approximately 20 one and two-story brick and frame structures, with numerous examples of Greek Revival and Italianate styles. Of note: Dr. John Stone House, c. 1850, and Boyer house, c. 1860's, both Greek Revival. Town is a substantially intact 19th C. village, built as a support community for Washington Institute, an early Baptist school.

LULA

Lula Residential HD
Late 19th to early 20th C. - An intact area of vernacular houses, with such Victorian-eclectic elements as porches, bracketed posts, and chimneys with decorative brick detailing.

LUMPKIN

Lumpkin Commercial HD
Late 19th to early 20th C. - City's historic center of commerce and government, with courthouse square (with its Con-

federate monument) as focal point. A series of architecturally significant Victorian commercial properties on 2 sides of the square, primarily 1 story, with cast-iron facades. Other significant buildings include Beddingfield Inn (Greek Revival) and the Courthouse (early 20th C., Classical Revival).

East Main Street Residential HD

Late 19th C. - A very small but cohesive grouping of dwellings: a Plantation Plain - style cottage; 2 Victorian cottages; and a Queen Anne house. Fine examples of those styles.

Pigtail Alley HD

Early 19th to early 20th C. - A fine collecton of houses, ranging from small cottages to relatively large plantation houses. Styles include Plantation Plain, Greek Revival, Victorian-era, and Classical Revival. A high level of craftsmanship is represented in these homes.

Uptown Residential HD

Mid-19th to early 20th C. - Several intact blocks of housing, and 2 churches. Styles represented include Greek Revival, Victorian-era, Classical Revival, and Bungalow. Greek Revival homes show exceptional craftsmanship, while all the houses display a high level of quality. Has retained the appearance of a rural downtown residential neighborhood.

MACON

Macon HD

19th-20th C. - Contains much of city's original downtown, with numerous commercial, civic, and residential structures in wide variety of styles, especially those of Victorian era. Of note: City Hall (1836, Greek Revival), and the College Hill neighborhood with numerous Greek Revival mansions. *Map, Self-Guided Tours*: Middle Georgia Historical Society, Inc., 935 High Street, Macon GA 31201, telephone (912)-743-3851. *Guided Tours*: See above; also Convention and Visitors Bureau, Inc., 200 Coliseum Drive, Macon GA 31298, telephone (912)-743-3401. *Annual Homes Tour*: Christmas Tour of Homes: contact above; Spring Homes Tour, contact Wesleyan College, Macon GA 31297.

Cherokee Heights HD

c. 1900-1940's - Planned residential suburban community

covering approximately 12 blocks. Styles include Georgian Revival, English Tudor, Spanish Mission, and Craftsman/Bungalow. Very few modern intrusions.

Vineville HD

1830's-1930's - Primarily residential, with some 700 properties. Predominant house types are late 19th C. Victorian, turn-of-the-century Neoclassical, and early 20th C. Bungalow. Also includes early 19th C. homes.

MADISON

Madison HD

19th C. - Residences and other buildings in various 19th C. styles, including several fine Greek Revival houses and homes of the Victorian period. Town, which developed as a center for surrounding cotton-growing counties, was known for beautiful homes and gardens; little change has occurred in 20th C.

MARIETTA

Northwest Marietta HD

1840's-1900 - Residential, commercial; primarily 1.5 and 2.5-story structures of frame or brick, some clapboarded. Of note: McNeel-Hawkins-Hamrick house (Georgian Revival), and Brumby-Wallace-Dennington house (Eastlake). Has retained much of its 19th C. character. *Map, Self-Guided Tours*: Welcome Center, 265 Church Street, Marietta GA 30060, telephone (404)-429-1115.

MARSHALLVILLE

East Main Street Residential District

c. 1900 - A small district, primarily of smaller, plainer homes. A cohesive neighborhood, representative of town's middle class in the 19th C. Of note: Baptist Church, and Craig House (only remaining major Greek Revival). Some intrusion by modern ranch-style houses.

Marshallville Commercial District

Late 19th C. - Small 2-block collection of commercial buildings, all of brick, 1 and 2 stories. Bisected by railroad line, with Victoria-era railroad depot. A cohesive group of Victorian commercial buildings, well preserved.

West Main Street Residential District
c. 1840–1890's – Still the most fashionable residential area of this small rural town, district contains early Greek Revival residences, Victorian-Eclectic homes, and a Gothic Revival Church. Features large lots, tree-shaded streets.

MAYFIELD (VICINITY)

Camilla-Zack Community Center HD
Late 19th–20th C. – Complex of stone and log structures which.once included a community center, cooperative store, health center, school, church, and cottages. Begun shortly after Civil War to serve needs of local freed blacks; became active regional center for rural blacks during Great Depression, and was active through 1950's.

MAYSVILLE

Maysville HD
1870's–1920's – Town's commercial center, surrounding residences (mostly 1-story frame with modest Victorian detailing), and a Victorian-Eclectic church. Commercial buildings are brick, mostly in Victorian Eclectic style. An extremely intact district.

METCALFE

Metcalfe HD
1887–1920 – Residential and commercial, containing some 35 significant structures representative of the late Victorian era. Focal point is Metcalfe Depot, 1887–1888, of native long leaf yellow pine. Many of the structures possess features of either the Queen Anne or Eastlake style.

MIDWAY

Midway HD
18th C. – Small, rural, featuring Midway Church (1792 meeting-house with belfry), its cemetery surrounded by brick

wall, a section of Old Sunbury Road of 1790, and a 1959 museum building designed as an 18th C. Gulf cottage. A once-influential area that declined with Civil War. *General Information*: Midway Historical Museum, POB119, Midway GA 31320, telephone (912)-884-5837.

MILLEDGEVILLE

Milledgeville HD

19th C. - Residential, commercial, and collegiate buildings in town planned in 1803 as state capital. Many fine Greek Revival residences, business district of two and three-story brick Italianate buildings, and late 19th C. Georgian Revival buildings, e.g., Atkinson Hall, Georgia College. A well-preserved 19th C. city, conceived to serve as state capital (moved to Atlanta in 1868). **H A B S**. *Map, Self-Guided Tours*: Chamber of Commerce, 130 S. Jefferson Street, Milledgeville GA 31061, telephone (912)-452-4687. *Guided Tours*: Tour Trolley, Tuesday and Friday, c/o Chamber of Commerce. *Annual Homes Tour*: Tour of Homes (Old South Week, April); Christmas Candlelight House Tour (December), Chamber of Commerce, Tourism Division, POB 751, Milledgeville GA 31061.

MONROE

East Church Street HD

Late 19th to early 20th C. - Residential area, with majority of buildings either Neoclassical or bungalows, most built of wood. A fine collection of homes from several socio-economic classes, including Monroe's largest collection of Victorian-era-style structures.

East Marable St. HD

Late 19th to early 20th C. - A relatively small residential area composed generally of modest 1-story frame homes. Area developed in the late 1800's as a middle-class segregated neighborhood.

McDaniel Street HD

1830's-1930's - Residential area which as neighborhood for Monroe's wealthy citizens. Offers a number of popular period architectural styles, and several very large and fine houses. Styles include Neoclassical, Classical and Colonial Revival.

Monland Place HD

Early 20th C. - A planned middle class neighborhood, made up of 1 and 2-story frame (and some brick) buildings constructed from 1906 to the 1930's. While the earliest houses have a certain degree of Victorian detailing, later homes are simple and straightforward. Wide streets, uniform lot size, and uniform set-back give the area a planned character.

Monroe and Walton Mills HD

1890's to early 1900's - Primarily an industrial complex composed of two large brick textile mills and supporting worker mill housing of wood construction. Also associated commercial and religious structures from early 1900's.

Monroe Commercial District

Late 19th C. - Monroe is a small city approximately 40 miles east of Atlanta. Historic commercial area is turn-of-the-century with 1 and 2-story brick buildings exhibiting Victorian qualities. Major structures are the Walton County Courthouse, Walton Hotel.

North Broad St. HD

Turn-of-the-Century - Residential area, primarily of middle and upper-middle class. Classical and Colonial Revival styles predominate, but some very fine Greek Revival and Victorian-era structures. Considerable historic preservation work reportedly in progress.

South Broad St. HD

Mid-19th to early 20th C. - A small residential neighborhood, with house sizes ranging from small to quite large. Architectural styles reflect Monroe's changing tastes over a span of some 80 years, and include Plantation Plain, American Gothic, and Neoclassical.

South Madison Ave. - Pannel Rd. HD

1880's-1930's - A small collection of late 19th and early 20th C. houses built at what was an important country crossroads. This hamlet was later absorbed by town's growth. Most of the buildings are 1 and 2-story frame.

NEWNAN

Greenville Street - LaGrange Street HD
19th to early 20th C. - Residential, including cottages, bungalows, and mansions. Styles include antebellum Greek Revival, Victorian Gothic, Queen Anne, Neoclassical, and Colonial Revival.

Northwest Residential HD
1829-1900's - Number of fine antebellum homes. Of note: magnificent Willcoxen-Arnold Home (1852), Sargent-Bryant Rosenzweig Home (c. 1840, Greek Revival), and the Parrott-Camp Home (described in local tourism leaflet as an "extraordinary example of Victorian architecture"). *Map, Self-Guided Tours*: Chamber of Commerce, 1 Savannah Street, POB 1103, Newnan GA 30263, telephone (404)-253-2270; also Newnan/Coweta Historical Society, POB 1101, Newnan GA 30264. *Annual Homes Tour*: Hospitality Tour of Homes (second weekend, October); contact Historical Society.

NORCROSS

Norcross HD
1870 to early 20th C. - Historic core of this small community, containing residential and commercial properties of architectural and historical significance to this town's development.

OXFORD

Oxford HD
Mid to late 19th C. - Residential, commercial, and Oxford College (private junior college affliated with United Methodist Church). Residential structures primarily frame, 2 1/2 stories, with gabled and hipped roofs; styles include Federal, Greek Revival, and Neoclassical. Town, an early 19th C. planned community, has retained much of its original character. **H A B S**. *Map, Self-Guided Tours*: Registrar, Oxford College, Oxford GA 30267; Oxford Lions club.

PHILOMATH

Philomath HD
19th C. - A fine collection of 19th C. buildings, particularly of

Greek Revival and Plantation Plain styles. Of note: Drake-Arnold-Armour House (1845, Greek Revival); the Daisy Nash House (c. 1860, modified raised cottage).

PLAINS

Plains HD

Late 19th to early 20th C. - Primarily commercial, residential, institutional, and church buildings of late 19th - early 20th C. Commercial downtown area contains 8 brick buildings, 1 and 2 stories, with metal awnings. Houses comprise a mixture of Queen Anne, Neoclassical, Late-Victorian and Bungalow/Craftsman styles. A good example of a small southwest Georgia town.

QUITMAN

Quitman HD

Mid-19th to early 20th C. - Wide variety of historic residential, commercial, industrial, and institutional buildings. Neighborhoods contain Greek Revival cottages c. 1860, late Victorian Eclectic and Neoclassical structures, and 1920's bungalows. Of note: Baum House (1860, Greek Revival), Courthouse (1864), and Stanley Bennet house (1905, Eastlake). *Map, Self-Guided Tours*: Chamber of Commerce, 900 E. Screven Street, Quitman GA 31643, telephone (912)-263-4841.

ROME

Between the Rivers HD

1870's-1930's - City's oldest section, with commercial, residential institutional, and industrial areas. Typical Victorian and Neoclassical commercial buildings, of brick. Of note: Masonic Temple, in Second Empire style. Residential styles include Queen Anne, Gothic, Eastlake, and Romanesque.

East Rome HD

Late 19th to early 20th C. - A neighborhood with residential, commercial, and institutional structures. Residential section notable for lot sizes plus styles and scale of the houses; architectural styles include Queen Anne, Second Empire, Georgian Revival, and Bungalow/Craftsman.

Lower Avenue A HD

Late 19th to early 20th C. - A small district of 9 houses, all modest frame structures of one story (with one exception). Houses, built from the 1880's to the 1920's, all have porches.

Mt. Aventine HD

Late 19th to early 20th C. - A small residential area, one of city's first suburbs. Majority of houses are large 1 and 2-story frame structures with late-Victorian detailing: stained and leaded glass, turned balusters, and decorative scrollwork.

South Broad Street HD

Late 19th to early 20th C. - A residential area which developed after 1870. Contains large brick and frame houses featuring turrets, stained and leaded glass, and porches with brackets. Also smaller Bungalow/Craftsman homes. District is remnant of once-larger neighborhood.

Upper Avenue A HD

1880-1920. - A residential neighborhood which began as a separate suburban village on west bank of the Oostanaula River. Majority of homes are solid 1 and 2-story frame structures. Larger homes feature such late-Victorian details as decorative shingling, large porches with brackets, and stained glass.

ROSWELL

Roswell HD

1837-20th C. - Early planned community centered around town square, with many brick and frame late-Georgian and Greek Revival dwellings. Planned by Roswell and Barrington King in the 1830's as a village to contain an "unrivalled group of temple houses." Of note: Barrington Hall (1839-1842), Bullock Hall (c. 1840), and Mimosa Hall. Has retained much of its 19th C. character. *Map, Self-Guided Tours*: Chamber of Commerce, 950 Mansell Road, POB 846, Roswell GA 30077, telephone (404)-993-8806; Roswell Historical Society, POB 274, Roswell GA 30077, telephone (404)-992-1665.

ROYSTON

Royston Commercial HD

Late 19th to early 20th C. - Encompasses the intact portion of town's historic commercial center. Majority of buildings are 1 and 2-story brick structures with party walls; they are modest Victorian and Early 20th C. Commercial-style, with eclectic detailing drawn from Gothic, Romanesque, Classical Revival, and Craftsman styles. Of note: extremely intact Dorough Building (Carter Hardware), and the P.C. Scarboro Building, a finely-detailed early Ford dealership.

RUSSELL

Russell Homeplace HD

1912-1967 - Family compound containing four residences, family cemetery and memorial garden, and five historic outbuildings. (Private.)

SASSER

Sasser Commercial HD

c. 1900-1912 - A 2-block downtown area on Main Street, on either side of the railroad tracks. Buildings mostly 1 and 2-story brick, in early 20th C. commercial vernacular. Details include cast-iron columns, plate-glass windows, and store awnings.

SAVANNAH

Ardsley Park - Chatham Crescent HD

c. 1910 - Large residential area developed as two adjacent planned subdivisions. Majority are single-family wood-framed buildings; sizes range from grand, 2 1/2-story structures to modest 1-story cottages. Styles include every Revival style from early 20th C., and many eclectic variations. Uniform setbacks, fine detailing, and few modern intrusions contribute to district's ambience.

Savannah HD

18th to early 19th C. - Significant because it has retained much of Ogelthorpe's innovative 1732 city plan (with parks or "squares" as key feature), and includes many buildings (1816-

1822) of architectural merit by English architect William Jay. His Owens-Thomas House illustrates English Regency style, while the Green-Meldrum House is early example of Gothic Revival. Also of note: a number of fine churches and public buildings, and extensive restorations. **N H L; H A B S.** *Map, Self-Guided Tours*: Savannah Visitors Center, 301 W. Broad Street (1860 railroad station), Savannah GA 31401, telephone (912)-233-6651. *Guided Tours*: See above for half-dozen options. *Annual Homes Tour*: Savannah Tour of Homes and Gardens, March or April each year. Contact Advance Order Department, 18 Abercorn Street, Savannah GA 31401 (or Historic Savannah Foundation, Inc., POB 1733, Savannah GA 31402, telephone (912)-233-7787); Annual Christmas Tour of Homes, second weekend in December, contact Downtown Neighborhood Association, 117 East Jones Street, Savannah GA 31401, telephone (912)-232-5935. *Special Events*: For schedules of numerous events throughout the year, see "Savannah Happenings" brochure, Visitors Center, 301 Broad Street, Savannah GA 31401.

Savannah Victorian HD

1870-1897 - Predominantly residential, with approximately 450 frame or brick structures featuring various elements of Victorian styles. Buildings are set along tree-lined streets on a grid pattern, with brick sidewalks. Area has undergone considerable restoration, and has retained much of its Victorian-era character. *General Information*: See **Savannah HD**.

SHELLMAN

Shellman HD

1890's-1920's - A dense grouping of modest late Victorian-style commercial structures, several residential areas with Victorian Eclectic-style predominant, plus depot, churches, and modest workers' houses. Many of commercial buildings have intact storefronts, including cast-iron columns.

SOCIAL CIRCLE

Social Circle HD

19th to early 20th C. - Mixed-use, containing residential, commercial, and industrial areas. Styles represented include Plantation Plain, Greek Revival, Gothic Revival, Queen Anne,

Second Empire, Italianate, Victorian Eclectic, and Bungalow. Considerable downtown renovation in recent years.

SPARTA

Sparta HD

18th-20th C. - Village with numerous 18th and 19th C. dwellings and commercial structures. Focal point is courthouse square with 1831 Second Empire courthouse. Of note: Rossiter-Little House (18th C.), and Sayre-Shivers House (Federal, Greek Revival). Community has retained much of its 19th C. appearance.

ST. MARYS

St. Marys HD

1787 to early 20th C. - Residential, commercial, and religious buildings, dating from late 18th to early 20th C. Of note: the waterfront area, Oak Grove Cemetery, c. 1787. Town was first county seat, and an important early port. *Map, Self-Guided Tours*: Chamber of Commerce, Orange Hall, St. Marys GA 31558. *Guided Tours*: See above. *Annual Homes Tour*: April; contact Kiwanis Club, 605 Osborne Street, St. Marys GA 31558.

TALBOTTON

LeVert HD

1828-1900. Residential, with 22 frame, clapboarded, 1 and 2 1/2-story dwellings. Styles include Greek Revival, Eastlake, Queen Anne. Town developed because of cotton farming; was also important 19th C. educational center.

THOMASVILLE

Thomasville

Map, Self-Guided Tours: (For entire city) Chamber of Commerce, 430 S. Broad St., POB 560, Thomasville GA 31799, telephone (912)-226-9600. *Guided Tours*: Chamber of Commerce, Monday - Saturday. *Group Tours*: Thomasville Landmarks, Inc., PO Box 1285, Thomasville GA 31799. *Annual Homes Tour*: Rose Festival Tour of Homes (April);

Candlelight Tour of Homes (3rd Saturday in December); contact Chamber of Commerce or Thomasville Landmarks.

Dawson St. Residential District

1830's-1930's - A large and varied area of in-town historic housing, primarily of wooden construction. Houses range from simple cottages in the black settlement to multi-story mansions along North Dawson street. Architectural styles represented include Greek Revival, Victorian Eclectic, Neoclassical, Georgian Revival, and Bungalow/Craftsman. District also contains a number of churches, pecan orchards associated with several of the homes, and two historic cemeteries, one for whites and one for blacks. Of interest: the "Big Oak", a 300-year old landmark live oak tree.

East End District

Late 19th C. - A 2-block residential area containing approximately 24 modest, wood-framed structures, 1 or 2-story. Styles represented include Second Empire, Plantation Plain, late-Victorian, and Bungalow/Craftsman.

Fletcherville HD

1850's-c. 1900 - A substantial residential neighborhood, composed primarily of modest 1-story wood-framed structures. Oldest houses, dating from 1850's and 1860's, are on South College Street and Fletcher Street facing the square. Architectural styles represented include Greek Revival, Victorian Eclectic, and Bungalow/Craftsman.

Gordon Ave. HD

c. 1900 - A group of 5 relatively large houses, 1 1/2 and 2-stories, wood-framed, on large lots. Dwellings reflect late-Victorian, Neoclassical, and Colonial Revival styles.

Paradise Park District

Late 19th to early 20th C. - Composed of landscaped park and historic residential properties bordering the park. Houses include large wood-framed structures in Victorian Eclectic, Neoclassical, Colonial Revival, and Bungalow/Craftsman. Park features a gazebo, and landscaping includes a thick stand of pine trees, oaks with Spanish moss, palm trees, and magnolias.

Tockwotton - Love Place District

1850's-1920's - A residential area, primarily of single-family houses; most are imposing 2- and 3-story high-style houses with elaborate detailing. Architectural styles represented include Greek Revival, Victorian Eclectic, Neoclassical, and Bungalow/Craftsman.

THOMSON (VICINITY)

Thomas Carr HD

Early 1800's - Very small farm/residential district of six frame or brick dwellings, 1 1/2 and 2 1/2 stories. Of note (many with Federal or Greek Revival elements): Simpson House, Bohler house, and Alexandria house (with massive rear chimneys). Land originally owned by Thomas Carr, a major figure in the Yazoo land frauds (1795, leading to a landmark U.S. Supreme Court decision in 1810).

TYBEE ISLAND

Fort Screven HD

Late 19th to early 20th C. - A turn-of-the-century federal coastal defense military installation and late 19th C. Tybee Light, located 15 miles east of Savannah. Fort complex is remarkably complete, with massive gun emplacements, officers' housing, barracks, and parade ground.

VALDOSTA

Fairview HD

1880-1915 - A prime residential area featuring imposing homes built for city's prominent families. Styles include Queen Anne, Prairie, and Bungaloid. Contains small 1-story cottages, the vernacular 1-story Georgian plan, and massive 2-story homes.

North Patterson St. HD

c. 1899-1919 - A 2-block area containing 14 large 1 and 2-story houses, with sizes ranging from medium-sized to very large "mansions". Styles include Victorian Eclectic and Neoclassical.

Valdosta Commercial HD

Late 19th to early 20th C. Historic commercial center of the city since 1860, with commercial and civic buildings. Styles represented include Victorian Eclectic, Queen Anne, Renaissance Revival, and Beaux-Arts. Major buildings include 1906 County Courthouse and 1908 City Hall.

WARM SPRINGS

Warm Springs HD

19th-20th C. - Resort and therapy complex with numerous structures, including administration building, two dormitories, outdoor dance pavilion, chapel, private cottages, and therapy facilities. President Franklin Delano Roosevelt frequently occupied the "Little White House" here while being treated in the springs for polio. Major buildings are the work of Henry Toombs, architect and planner. **N H L**

WASHINGTON

East Robert Tombs Avenue HD

Late 18th to early 20th C. Residential and churches, featuring 2-story frame structures in Greek Revival style. Of note: Dunwoody-Norman house (1830-1840, 1860's, Greek Revival), and the Episcopal Church (c. 1895, Victorian Eclectic). Area has retained much of its 19th C. character, with dense foliage and tree-lined streets. *Map, Self-Guided Tours*: Chamber of Commerce, 25 City Square, POB 661, Washington GA 30673, telephone (404)-678-1396; also, Washington-Wilkes Historical Foundation, 308 E. Robert Tombs Avenue, Washington GA 30673, telephone (404)-678-2105. *Annual Homes Tour*: April of each odd-numbered year; contact Washington Womens' Club, or Kiwanis Club.

North Washington HD

1780-1910 - Primarily residential; numerous 2 and 2 1/2 story brick and frame houses and 1 and 1 1/2 story frame cottages in Greek Revival and other 19th C. styles. District dominated by the Gilbert-Alexander House (1808, Federal), and The Cedars (original c. 1793, modified Victorian Eclectic). *General Information*: See **East Robert Tombs HD.**

West Robert Tombs Avenue HD

1790-1900 - Residential neighborhood, featuring sophisticated frame houses, 2 and 2 1/2 stories, in Greek Revival and a variety of later 19th C. styles, a few commercial buildings, and a row of small, late 19th C. cottages. Of note: Tupper-Barnett House (c. 1860, Greek Revival), Hill-Harris House (late 19th C., Queen Anne), and the Barksdale-Burt House (1893, Eclectic). Despite some commercial intrusions, this district has retained much of its late 19th C. character. *General Information*: See **East Robert Tombs HD**.

WATKINSVILLE

South Main Street HD

19th to early 20th C. - Residential, contains 38 structures. Styles represented include Greek Revival, Plantation Plain, Gothic Revival, Queen Anne, Eastlake, Victorian Eclectic, and Bungalow. Of note: Methodist Church (1893, Gothic Revival). Has retained much of its turn-of-the-century atmosphere.

WAYCROSS

Waycross HD

1870's-1890's - Residential, approximately 250 dwellings, primarily frame, clapboarded, 1 1/2 and 2 1/2 stories, gabled. Styles include Queen Anne, Eastlake, Stick, Bungaloid, Neoclassical Revival. Has retained much of its 19th C. character.

WEST POINT (VICINITY)

Long Cane HD

1829-1850's - Small agricultural/residential district includes five frame buildings, 1 1/2 and 2 1/2 stories; predominantly Vernacular Greek Revival. Community developed into a post office and stagecoach stop, but declined because of Civil War and soil exhaustion.

WINDER

Broad Street Commercial HD

Late 19th to early 20th C. - Commercial and governmental buildings, covering one full block and parts of three others. Most commercial buildings are brick, 2 stories; courthouse is also brick, in Neoclassical style.

Jackson St. Commercial District
Late 19th to early 20th C. - Downtown commercial, covering parts of 4 blocks. Most buildings are 2-story brick, a few with metal storefronts.

North Broad St. Residential HD.
19th-early 20th C. - Surviving portion of an in-town neighborhood; includes small frame Victorian cottages, bungalows, and Neoclassical residences.

YOUNG HARRIS

Young Harris College HD
1897-1945 - Center of the main college campus, containing two oldest surviving structures, Susan B. Harris Chapel (1892, brick) and Sharp Hall (1912, brick), landscaped grounds, and a row of historic cedar trees. East of U.S. Highway 76, in Towns County.

KENTUCKY

ANCHORAGE

Anchorage HD

1880's–1890's - Town first settled in 1783; the modern residential areas were laid out in 1880's–1890's, per design of Frederick Law Olmstead for a "garden community." Was summer retreat for residents of nearby Louisville, away from threat of yellow fever and malaria. *Annual Homes Tour*: Historic Open House Tour (early December); contact Anchorage Independent School PTA, Anchorage KY 40223.

ASHLAND

Bath Avenue HD

Mid-19th to early 20th C. - City's most prestigious residential neighborhood since c. 1854 and beginnings of iron-industry prosperity. Offers a variety of 19th C. architectural styles popular with industrial owners-managers. Of note: Poage-Russell House (1875), McGown House (1892, Eastlake), and Hugh Means House (c. 1885). *Map, Self-Guided Tours*: Tourism Center, 1300 Winchester Avenue, POB 187, Ashland KY 41101, telephone (606)-329-1007.

ATHENS

Athens HD

No further information at this time.

AUGUSTA

Augusta HD

1830's–1930 - Primarily residential, some 145 structures; 18 are pre-1850, 38 from 1851–1877, 46 from 1877 to 1900. A unique and cohesive collection of brick and frame structures, with almost no modern intrusions. *Map, Self-Guided Tours*: City Offices, 218 Main Street, Augusta KY 41002. *Guided Tours*: See above. *Annual Homes Tour*: Heritage Days (early September); Heritage Days, POB 85, Augusta KY 41002.

Augusta Residential District.

No further information at this time.

Water Street HD (Riverside Drive)

c. 1790's–1890's - Residential, approximately 25 brick, frame, and log dwellings. Of note: early 19th C. Federal rowhouses between Main and Parkview Streets, and Marshall House (c. 1819, Federal). Town has retained much of its 19th C. character. *Map, Self-Guided Tours*: See **Augusta HD.**

BARBOURVILLE

Barbourville Business District.

No further information at this time.

Barbourville Commercial District.

No further information at this time.

BARDSTOWN

Bardstown HD

Late 18th - 19th C. Residential, plus civic and religious structures. Residences include frontier-era log structures (clap-boarded), Georgian homes, and fine examples of Federal and Greek Revival. *Map, Self-Guided Tours*: Chamber of Commerce, Courthouse Square, POB 296, Bardstown KY 40004, telephone (502)-348-9545. *Guided Tours*: (a) Free tourmobile trips, June–Labor Day, from Information Center; (b) step-on guides for tour buses, c/o Chamber of Commerce. *Annual Homes Tour*: Candlelight Tours (November), c/o Chamber of Commerce.

St. Joseph Cathedral and College HD

No further information at this time.

BENHAM

Benham HD

No further information at this time.

BOWLING GREEN

College Hill HD

No further information at this time.

Downtown Bowling Green HD

No further information at this time.

St. Joseph's HD

No further information at this time.

Upper East Main St. HD

No further information at this time.

BURLINGTON

Burlington HD

No further information at this time.

BURNSIDE

Burnside HD

No further information at this time.

CAMPBELLSVILLE

Historic Commercial District.

1880–1910 - Compact, diversified core of business area, 1880–1910. Most buildings brick, Italianate; many with original iron or stone facades. Of note: County Clerk's Office (1865, Federal details), Baptist Church (1889, Gothic), and the George L. Mesher Block of cast-iron storefronts.

CARROLLTON

Carrollton HD

1800's–1930 - More than 25 blocks and 350 buildings, including residential and commercial areas. Majority of structures are late 19th C., with styles of late Victorian era. One of most intact of state's early 19th C. Ohio River towns; contains many structures of outstanding architectural merit, and has retained much of its 19th C. character. *Map, Self-Guided Tours*: Carroll County Community Development Corp., County Courthouse, POB 334, Carrollton KY 41008, telephone (502)-732-8204. *Guided Tours*: Free cassette tape, Information Center, Old Stone Jail, Courthouse Square, June–September. *Annual Homes Tour*: June; contact Carroll County Community Development Corporation.

CARROLLTON (VICINITY)

Hunter's Bottom HD

Early 19th to early 20th C. - Rural residential, including 14 large-scale 19th C. houses, with outbuildings, cemetery, church, and a 1913 distillery. Of note: Cornelius DeWeese house (1845), Owen Miller house (1870), and Richwood Plantation, each with Italianate elements.

CLOVERPORT

Cloverport HD

No further information at this time.

COVINGTON

Covington Main Street HD

No further information at this time.

Downtown Commercial District.

No further information at this time.

Licking Riverside HD

1846–1900 - Primarily residential, with numerous detached and rowhouses of masonry, 2 1/2 and 3 stories. Styles include Greek and Gothic Revival, Second Empire, Queen Anne, Neo-Classical and Georgian Revival. Of note: Collins and Lee houses (Italianate), Appel House (Second Empire), and United Methodist Church (Gothic Revival). Has retained much of its 19th C. character, as an upper middle-class community.

Mutter Gottes HD

No further information at this time.

Ritte's Corner Commercial District.

No further information at this time.

Riverside Drive HD

No further information at this time.

Seminary Square HD

Early 19th to early 20th C. - Mostly residential, with approximately 130 buildings on 18 acres. Features brick 19th C. townhouses, with lots defined by elaborate iron fences. Three exceptional townhouses are John Fisk House, W. E. Ashbrooke House, and the Harriet Albro House. Directly across Ohio River from Cincinnati, OH; has retained much of the atmosphere of a small community.

Wallace Woods Residential District.

No further information at this time.

Westside/Main Strasse HD

No further information at this time.

CUMBERLAND GAP

Cumberland Gap HD

No further information at this time.

CYNTHIANA

Cynthiana Commercial District.

No further information at this time.

DANVILLE

Constitution Square HD

Late 18th-19th C. - Residential and commercial, surrounding Constitution Square State Park. Buildings primarily late 18th-

19th C. brick or frame. Square was site of 1785–1792 state constitutional conventions, leading to separation of Kentucky from Virginia. *Map, Self-Guided Tours*: Chamber of Commerce, 2nd and Walnut, Danville KY 40422, telephone (606)-236-2361; Historical Society, Constitution Square, Danville KY 40422, telephone (606)-236-4376.

Todd–Montgomery Houses HD

1837–1842. Four brick or stuccoed 2-story Greek Revival dwellings: Todd-Cheek House, Montgomery-Rodes House (with prominent Ionic tetrastyle portico), Proctor-Rowland House, and Bowman-Anderson House.

DOE RUN CREEK

Doe Run Creek HD

No further information available at this time.

EAST NEWPORT

East Newport HD

No further information available at this time.

ELIZABETHTOWN

Courthouse Square HD

19th C. Residential-commercial-civic core of the town, dating from c. 1779; focal point is the 1873 Courthouse. Of note: Jonathan Hills House (c. 1824, half-timber and brick nogging), LaRue house (1830), Brown-Pusey house (1825 Georgian), and 1834 brick Baptist Church. *Map, Self-Guided Tours*: Chamber of Commerce, 23 Public Square, Elizabethtown KY 42701, telephone (502)-765-4334; Visitors & Information Commission, 23 Public Square, Elizabethtown KY, telephone (502)-765-2175.

EMINENCE

Eminence Commercial District.

No further information available at this time.

FALLS OF ROUGH

Falls of Rough HD

No further information available at this time.

FALMOUTH

Central Falmouth HD

No further information available at this time.

FLEMINGSBURG

Flemingsburg HD

No further information available at this time.

FORT THOMAS MILITARY RESERVATION

Fort Thomas Military Reservation District.

No further information available at this time.

FRANKFORT

Corner in Celebrities District HD

18th-20th C. - City's oldest residential section, named for unusually large number of notable residents. Of note: Liberty Hall (1796, Georgian), Orlando Brown house (1835, Greek Revival), John Bibb house (1857, Gothic Revival), and Thomas Todd house (1812, Federal). Area's character enhanced by walled gardens, overhanging trees. **H A B S**

Frankfort Barracks HD

1871 - Six brick multiple dwelling units, built to house Federal occupation troops after Civil War. Structures, 1 and 1 1/2 stories, have had only minor alterations; rare example of post-bellum military architecture.

Frankfort Commercial District.

No further information available at this time.

Old Statehouse HD

No further information available at this time.

South Frankfort Neighborhood HD
1833–1925 – Large, predominantly residential area with approximately 660 buildings, many from late 19th and early 20th C. Contains a variety of building types and styles, including small vernacular homes, large and stylish Victorian-era residences, and Craftsman Bungalows. Dramatically sited on south side of Kentucky River, with few modern intrusions.

FRANKLIN

Franklin Downtown Commerical District.
No further information available at this time.

GEORGETOWN

East Main Street Residential District.
1814–1920 – Town's heart, with approximately 50 residences, two churches, two public buildings. Frame and brick structures of various styles, including Federal-Georgian, Greek Revival, Victorian-era, and Neo-Classic. Of note: James Emison House (1820), Presbyterian Church (c. 1865, Gothic Revival), and Shropshire House, oldest building in the district.

Georgetown College HD
No further information available at this time.

Lane's Run HD
No further information available at this time.

Main Street Commercial District.
1869–1891 – A remakably intact concentration of 39 cast-iron and brick buildings, primarily 2 and 3 stories, with Victorian facades. Principal styles are Italianate, Second Empire, and Romanesque Revival. Of note: Wells House (1869, Italianate), Allgaire Building (1869) and Rankins and Webb Building (c. 1876).

GHENT

Ghent HD
Early to mid-19th C. – A well-preserved Ohio River village with approximately 80 structures; majority are single-family residences. Principal architectural style is vernacular, with

unusual prevalence of small-scale hall parlors. Has retained an unhurried, quiet village ambience.

GLASGOW

Cave City Commercial District.
No further information available at this time.

North Race St. HD
No further information available at this time.

S. W. Glasgow Residential District.
No further information available at this time.

GREENVILLE

Greenville Commercial District.
No further information available at this time.

North Main St. HD
No further information available at this time.

South Cherry St. HD
No further information available at this time.

GUYN'S MILL

Guyn's Mill HD
No further information available at this time.

HARRODSBURG

College Street HD
No further information available at this time.

Harrodsburg Commercial District.
No further information available at this time.

Morgan Row HD
No further information available at this time.

HAWESVILLE

Hawesville HD
No further information available at this time.

HENSLEY SETTLEMENT

Hensley Settlement HD
No further information available at this time.

HOPKINSVILLE

East Seventh Street HD
No further information available at this time.

Hopkinsville Commercial District.
No further information available at this time.

Hopkinsville Residential District.
No further information available at this time.

Hopkinsville Warehouse District.
No further information available at this time.

LANCASTER

Lancaster Commercial District.
No further information available at this time.

LEBANON

Lebanon Historic Commercial District.
No further information available at this time.

LEXINGTON

Bell Court Neighborhood HD
c. 1900 - A cohesive middle-class residential area with 157 buildings. Styles vary from elegant Queen Anne and Richardsonian Romanesque to Arts and Crafts houses. Of note: Clay Villa (c. 1846, Italianate), and Bell Place (c. 1890,

eclectic). Most houses are intact, and large, handsome shade trees line the sidewalks.

Constitution HD
No further information available at this time.

Downtown Commercial District.
No further information available at this time.

Elsmere Park HD
1891-1913 - Residential, planned upper-middle-class neighborhood of 29 single-family dwellings; 1 1/2 and 2 1/2-story masonry houses derived from turn-of-the-century pattern-book designs, primarily Queen Anne and Neo-Classical Revival. Of note: Giovanelli-Clay house with elaborate formal gardens, the four Buckner houses, and the John Bruckner House (1891, Queen Anne).

Government Block Building HD
No further information available at this time.

Gratz Park HD
18th-20th C. - Residential, close to city's center, with homes bordering park. Features 2 and 2 1/2-story brick dwellings in variety of 19th-20th C. styles. Of note: Hunt-Morgan House (1814, Federal), and Public Library (1904, Neo-Classical Revival).

Maxwell St. Houses HD
No further information available at this time.

North Broadway/Short Street District.
No further information available at this time.

North Limestone Commercial District.
No further information available at this time.

Northside HD
No further information available at this time.

Society Hill HD
No further information available at this time.

Southeast Residential - Commercial District.
No further information available at this time.

South Hill HD
Early 19th to early 20th C. - Urban, approximately 200 structures in variety of styles and house types, including early log-and-frame houses (now clapboarded), Federal and Greek Revival townhouses, Victorian cottages, and mansions. A pocket of urbanity notable for location, historic value to the community, and rich architectural variety.

Victorian Commercial Block District.
No further information available at this time.

West High Street HD
18th-19th C. - Three blocks of houses with architectural styles spanning nearly 100 years. Of note: Breckinridge House (c. 1784), Brobston House (c. 1786), John Leiby House (c. 1805), Richardson House (c. 1832), and Hill Street Church (c. 1828-1831).

Western Suburb HD
1830's-1840's - Residential, approximately 60 significant structures of log, frame, or brick, incorporating elements of a variety of 19th C. styles. Has retained many characteristics of a 19th C. middle-class community of prosperous tradesmen and craftsmen. Of interest: girlhood home of Mary Todd Lincoln.

Woodlands HD
No further information available at this time.

Woodward Heights Neighborhood District.
No further information available at this time.

LITCHFIELD

Court Square HD
No further information available at this time.

LOUISVILLE

Belknap Campus HD
1872-1974 - Approximately 31 educational and residential structures of brick, frame, or stone. Site of three important institutions: Louisville House of Refuge, and Louisville Industrial School, 1859-1924; and, University of Louisville

since 1924. Campus plan by noted architect Jens Frederick Larson, with elements of a comprehensive plan by Allied Architects of Kentucky. *General Information*: See **Old Louisville.**

Butchertown HD

c. 1832-1900 - Residential and commercial, primarily brick-frame 19th C. buildings, and Bourbon Stockyards (early economic core of community). Vernacular Greek Revival and Italianate elements widespread. Of note: 1868 home of Thomas A. Edison, typical of the area's many shotgun and camel-back style houses. *Map, Self-Guided Tours*: Preservation Alliance, 716 W. Main Street, Louisville KY 40202, telephone (505)-583-8622.

Cherokee Triangle Area Residential District

19th to early 20th C. - Approximately 900 frame or masonry, 2 and 3-story dwellings; many architectural styles, including Gothic Revival, Queen Anne, Italianate, Georgian Revival, Beaux-Arts. Of note: Hilliard House (Gothic Revival), Weikel House (Queen Anne), Highland Presbyterian Church (Gothic Revival), and Hugh Mevin house (Neo-Classical Revival). Area, developed as a middle-class late 19th C. streetcar suburb, has retained much of its integrity. *Map, Self-Guided Tours*: See Butchertown.

Clifton HD

No further information available at this time.

Crescent Hill HD

c. 1890-1920 - Middle-class residential neighborhood; includes fine churches and schools, small commercial area. Displays a rich collection of late 19th - 20th C. architectural styles including Queen Anne, Craftsman, Classical and Colonial Revival, American Four-Square. *General Information*: See **Butchertown** HD

First Street HD

No further information available at this time.

Highlands HD

No further information available at this time.

Limerick HD

No further information available at this time.

Lower W. Market Street HD
No further information available at this time.

Marlow-Place Bungalow HD
No further information available at this time.

North Old Louisville District No. 1.
No further information available at this time.

North Old Louisville District No. 2.
No further information available at this time.

Oakdale HD
No further information available at this time.

Old Louisville Residential District.
1870's-1900 - Developed after Southern Exposition of 1883, becoming a popular area for city's successful businessmen. Houses primarily 2 and 3-story, in frame, brick, and stone. Of note: Landwald house (elegant Italianate, with gardens designed by Olmstead Associates), Theophilus Conrad mansion (Richardsonian Romanesque), Edwin Hite Ferguson house (1903, Beaux-Arts). Neighborhood has retained much of its 19th C. character. *Map, Self-Guided Tours*: Preservation Alliance, 716 W. Main Street, Louisville KY 40202, telephone (502)-583-8622. *Guided Tours*: Contact above. *Annual Homes Tour*: Derby Week House Tours, 1340 South Fourth, Louisville KY 40208, telephone (502)-635-5244.

Olmstead Park System HD
No further information available at this time.

Parkland HD
No further information available at this time.

Phoenix Hill HD
No further information available at this time.

Portland HD
19th C. - Originally an independent river port town, annexed by Louisville in 1852. Founded in 1814 by French group, and by 1819 had become major residential area and commercial port. Of note: Portland Cemetery (1830's), Our Lady Church (c. 1839), and c. 1850 mansions on Portland Avenue. Area has retained a rich French and Irish heritage. *Map, Self-Guided Tours*: See **Old Louisville Residential District**.

Rauchfuss Houses HD
No further information available at this time.

Russell HD
No further information available at this time.

St. James-Belgravia HD
Late 19th to early 20th C. - Residential area developed on site of Southern Exposition (1883-1889), from 1890's to World War I. Styles include Victorian-era, Georgian and Jacobethan Revival; types include rowhouses, duplexes, and freestanding houses, of limestone, brick, stucco, or frame. Location of first large-scale installation of Edison's newly-invented incandescent light. *General Information*: See **Old Louisville O H D.**

Southern Heights-Beechmont HD
No further information available at this time.

West Broadway HD
No further information available at this time.

West Main Street HD
1870-1890 - Approximately 200 commercial buildings in 3-block riverfront area. Majority are 3-5 stories, of brick, cast-iron, and wood construction; many of facades used cast-iron elements selected from catalogs, and decorative stone. *General Information*: See **Old Louisville O H D.**

LUDLOW

Central Ludlow HD
No further information available at this time.

MARROWBONE

Marrowbone HD
No further information available at this time.

MAYFIELD

Downtown Commercial District.

19th to early 20th C. - This 9-block area, running north and east from 1888 City Hall block, comprised original community. *Map, Self-Guided Tours*: Chamber of Commerce, 902 West Broadway, POB 468, Mayfield KY, telephone (502)-247-6101. *Annual Homes Tour*: Early December; contact Laurel Oak Garden Club, c/o Chamber of Commerce.

MAYSVILLE

Courthouse Square and Mechanics Row HD

1816-1850's - Fifteen dwellings, three county offices, church, and county courthouse; structures mostly brick, 2 and 2 1/2 stories. Of note: January-Duke House (1838, Greek Revival), Mason County Courthouse (temple-form, 1844), and the Hord-Cartmill house (1816-1822, with Second Empire remodeling and notable cast-iron decoration). Town established because of Ohio River commerce; Creole-style influences from river trade with New Orleans. *Map, Self-Guided Tours*: Chamber of Commerce, 115 E. Third St., Maysville KY 41056, telephone (606)-564-5534. *Guided Tours*: Mrs. Harriet Cartwell, 18 W. Third St., Maysville KY 41056, telephone (606)-564-3431.

Maysville Downtown HD

No further information available at this time.

West Fourth Street HD

c. 1840-1849. Group of 5 brick structures featuring simple Greek Revival elements and stepped gable ends, reflecting influence of building techniques of German immigrants. Private, not accessible to public. *General Information*: See Chamber of Commerce.

MIDDLESBORO

Downtown Commercial District.

1880-1930 - One of finest late 19th - early 20th C. commercial districts in eastern Kentucky coalfields region. Includes commercial, civic, and religious buildings, town square, and old city canal. Of note: Campbell Building (1890), Old People's Bank Building, Cato Building, and First Presbyterian Church (1889, 1912). Retains much of its 19th C. character.

MIDWAY

Midway HD

c. 1870 to early 20th C. - Approximately 180 buildings, including town's business core and a fashionable residential street. Purposely located midway between Lexington and Frankfort along the Lexington and Ohio Railroad, town became site of many fine residences after 1870, plus several notable religious and educational institutions. Appears relatively unchanged from the 1890's.

MILLERS RUN

Millers Run HD

No further information available at this time.

MILLERSBURG

Millersburg HD

No further information available at this time.

MILTON

Third St. HD

No further information available at this time.

MONTICELLO

Monticello Historic Commercial District.

No further information available at this time.

MORGANFIELD

Morganfield Commercial District.

No further information available at this time.

MOUNT ST. JOSEPH

Academy HD
No further information available at this time.

MT. STERLING

Mt. Sterling Commercial District.
No further information available at this time.

MT. VERNON

Mt. Vernon Commercial District.
No further information available at this time.

NAZARETH

Sisters of Charity-Nazareth College HD
No further information available at this time.

NERINX

Loretto Motherhouse HD
No further information available at this time.

NEWPORT

Mansion Hill HD
Late 19th to early 20th C. - Residential, approximately 400 buildings, ranging from workers' dwellings to 20-room mansions of exceptional design. Features architectural styles and trends unique to the Cincinnati area; spans period from just before Victorian era, to just after. An extremely cohesive neighborhood displaying high quality of workmanship; has retained much of its 19th C. ambience.

NICHOLASVILLE

Nicholasville HD
No further information available at this time.

NICHOLASVILLE (VICINITY)

Jessamine Co. District.
No further information available at this time.

OLD EDDYVILLE

Old Eddyville HD
No further information available at this time.

OWENSBORO

Historic Commercial District.
19th-20th C. - Three blocks reflecting city's development as manufacturing, trade, and transportation center. Of note: Smith-Werner Building (1850), with outstanding cast-iron front added (c. 1880), Oddfellows Lodge Hall (1895, Romanesque Revival), and Bates Building (1895, Moorish Revival). *Map, Self-Guided Tours*: Downtown Owensboro, Inc., 224 Allen Street, Owensboro KY 42302, telephone (502)-683-2060.

OWENTOWN

Central Owenton HD
No further information available at this time.

North Main - North Adams HD
Special Events: Homecoming Festival (last Saturday in April); contact Historical Society. *General Information*: Owen County Historical Society, c/o County Library, Owenton KY 40359, telephone (520)-484-3450.

OWINGSVILLE

Owingsville Commercial District.
No further information available at this time.

OXFORD

Oxford HD

No further information available at this time.

PADUCAH

Jefferson Street - Fountain Avenue HD

1890-1920 - Residential, prestigious showcase neighborhood since turn-of-the-century; wide range of styles, from late Victorian era through 1920's. Most are of very high quality and craftsmanship. Area was an early expansion of Paducah, stimulated by installation of streetcar lines, c. 1889.

Lower Town Neighborhood District.

No further information available at this time.

Paducah Downtown Commercial HD

No further information available at this time.

Paducah Market House HD

No further information available at this time.

PARIS

Courthouse Square HD

1788-1939 - A mix of public, commercial, and residential buildings highlighted by courthouse square. Of note: Duncan Tavern (1788, Georgian), Ewalt Building (c. 1840, Greek Revival), Memorial Building (1859), and Bourbon County Courthouse (1902-05, Beaux-Arts). A fine collection of buildings arranged in a notable town-square plan.

PARIS (VICINITY)

Paris Pike HD

No further information available at this time.

PERRYVILLE

Perryville HD

18th-20th C. - A virtually unaltered 19th C. agricultural community with residences dating from 1790's to 20th C.; earliest are of log construction, clapboarded. Also several institutional buildings and a row of 15 frame commercial structures, 1 and 2 stories, built pre-1864.

PIKEVILLE

College Street HD
No further information available at this time.

Commercial District.
No further information available at this time.

Huffman Avenue HD
No further information available at this time.

North Main St. HD
No further information available at this time.

Pikeville High School HD
No further information available at this time.

Scott Ave. HD
No further information available at this time.

South Courthouse Square HD
No further information available at this time.

Third Street HD

PLEASANT HILL

Shakertown At Pleasant Hill HD
19th C. - Museum district of 23 structures, brick and frame, 2 and 3 1/2 stories, built 1809-1859. Simplified Shaker styles with Federal and Greek Revival elements. Of note: 1820 Meetinghouse with elaborate interior truss system, 1839 Trustees' Office, and the large East and West Family Dwelling Houses (1817, 1821). One of the largest colonies established by the United Society of Believers in Christ's Second Appearing (Shakers). **N H L; H A B S**

RICHMOND

Downtown Richmond HD

19th C. - Mostly commercial, with Greek Revival courthouse as focal point. Majority of structures are brick, 2 and 3 stories, with a variety of stone and metal Italianate and Victorian-era decorative details. *Map, Self-Guided Tours*: Richmond Tourism, 321 N. Second Street, Richmond KY 40475, telephone (606)-623-0759; Chamber of Commerce, 101 Irvine Street, POB 876, Richmond KY 40475, telephone (606)-623-1720. *Group Tours*: contact Richmond Tourism.

Eastern Kentucky University HD

No further information available at this time.

West Richmond HD

No further information available at this time.

RUSSELLVILLE

Russellville HD

19th C. - Fifty-block mix of residential and commercial structures, 1 1/2 and 2 1/2 stories, brick and frame. Was home of many VIPs, including nine state governors. Styles include Greek, Gothic, and Renaissance Revival, Italianate, Queen Anne, Eastlake, Neo-Classical Revival. Of note: Breathitt-Morehead House, John J. Crittenden House, and the Nimrod Long Bank. Has retained much of its 19th C. character.

SHELBYVILLE

Courthouse - Main St. Commercial District.

No further information available at this time.

Seventh St. HD

No further information available at this time.

West Shelbyville HD

No further information available at this time.

SMITH'S GROVE

Smith's Grove HD
No further information available at this time.

SOMERSET

Downtown Commercial District.
No further information available at this time.

Harvey's Hill HD
No further information available at this time.

West Columbia St. HD
No further information available at this time.

SOUTH UNION (AND VICINITY)

Shakertown HD
1822-1917 - Museum, with two Shaker support complexes, including community center (1822-23, Georgian), and a commercial area with 1-story brick store and Post Office (1859), and 2-story brick hotel-tavern (1869). Founded in 1807, to encourage westward spread of Shaker beliefs. Open May 1 - October 1. *Special Events*: The Shaker Festival (July, 10 days); Christmas Open House. *General Information*: Shaker Museum, Shakertown at S. Union, South Union KY 42283, telephone (502)-542-4167.

SPRINGFIELD

Springfield Commercial District.
No further information available at this time.

ST. MARY'S (VICINITY)

St. Mary's College HD
No further information available at this time.

STANFORD

Baughman's Mill & L and N RR HD
No further information available at this time.

VERSAILLES

Downtown Versailles HD
1847–1965 - Commercial, 36 structures, predominantly brick and cast-iron, 2 and 3 stories. One of oldest towns in central Kentucky, incorporated 1792; styles include Greek Revival, Italianate, Neo-Classical, and Romanesque Revival. Of note: Brown House (c. 1847), Masonic Hall (1881), Woodford Hotel (c. 1889).

Morgan Street HD
Late 18th to early 20th C. - One of town's oldest, most desirable residential areas, with large number of homes notable for architectural quality and historical associations. District displays an unusual variety of styles, with a number of outstanding Federal style buildings. Of note: J. C. Carter House (1792, Federal), David Thornton and William Barr Houses (c. 1821, exeptional Federal designs), and the Thomas Paine Porter House (1850's, Gothic Revival).

Rose Hill HD
No further information available at this time.

WARSAW

Warsaw HD
1800–1930 - River town, 118 significant properties reflecting every style and period from 1820 to 1930. Most buildings date from 19th C.; 18 commercial structures, three churches, 96 residences, one courthouse. One of best-preserved 19th C. Ohio River towns in Kentucky, with strong flavor of the 1880's.

WASHINGTON

Washington HD
18th–19th C. - A little-altered, early 19th C. Kentucky town. Houses and public buildings span nearly 100 years of local ar-

chitecture. Of note: Broderick's Tavern (1794), Albert Sindy Johnson House (c. 1797), the Paxton Inn (1818), and Methodist Church South (1848). **H A B S.** *Map, Self-Guided Tours*: Old Washington, Inc., POB 225, Washington KY 41096, telephone (606)-759-7843; Maysville Chamber of Commerce, 115 E. Third St., POB 507, Maysville KY 41056, telephone (606)-564-5534. *Guided Tours*: Old Washington, Inc.

WHEELWRIGHT

Wheelwright Commercial District.
No further information available at this time.

WINCHESTER

Downtown Commercial District.
1830's-1920's - One of the most remarkable collections of late 19th C. commercial architecture in Kentucky, 2 1/2 blocks by 1 1/2 blocks, with 1855 Greek-Temple-form courthouse as focal point. Majority of the 114 structures are 2 or 3-story brick, built during last two decades of 19th C. or in early 20th C. Of note: Woods Building (c. 1886), Citizens National Bank (Richardsonian), fraternal lodge (1907, Classical Revival). A high concentration of landmark buildings, relatively unaltered over the years.

Cabildo Alley

LOUISIANA

ABITA SPRINGS

Abita Springs HD

c. 1900-1930 - Residential-commercial, numerous shotgun houses with Eastlake and Colonial Revival elements. Also more substantial buildings, featuring Queen Anne and Colonial Revival styling. Buildings widely spaced, in a heavily-forested environment; district is typical turn-of-the-century community that served as a weekend and summer resort for New Orleans. Has retained much of its original atmosphere.

BATON ROUGE

Beauregard Town HD

1806-1930 - Mostly residential (plus small warehouse area, "Catfish Town"), approximately 400 structures. Typical houses are modest 1 or 2-stories; 4 basic styles are Eastlake, Queen Anne, shotgun and bungalow. Of note: 1923 Courthouse (Neo-Classical Revival), the Old Governor's Mansion (1930), two early-20th C. eclectic Gothic churches. Extensive restoration since early 1970's; has become a fashionable area of city. *Map, Self-Guided Tours*: Foundation for Historical Louisiana, 900 N. Boulevard, Baton Rouge LA 70802, telephone (504)-387-2464. *Guided Tours*: See above.

Roseland Terrace HD

1911-1930 - Residential, 18 blocks, approximately 346 structures, most of them frame bungalows, 1 and 2 stories. Earliest homes reflect Queen Anne and Colonial Revival influences. An excellent example of an early-20th C. residential neighborhood; has retained much of its original "garden suburb" atmosphere.

Spanish Town HD

Late 1800's-1930's - Approximately 250 significant buildings, oldest house dating from 1823. Several fine examples of Greek Revival, and large numbers of Queen Anne, shotgun, and small Creole houses. Of note: Pino House (c. 1823, Classical Mode), Stewart-Doutherty House (1854, Classical Revival), and Grace-Persac House (c. 1830). City's oldest neighborhood, laid out in 1805. Narrow intimate streets, irregular block layout, and high concentration of old buildings give it a special character. *Guided Tours*: See **Beauregard Town HD.**

BROUSSARD

Main Street HD

1876-1910 - The Broussard Multiple Resource Area (MRA) consists of 10 individual buildings, and a 5-building Main Street HD. District contains 3 large frame Queen Anne residences and 2 late Italianate commercial buildings. Ten other significant buildings scattered throughout this small semi-rural crossroads community.

CLINTON

Courthouse and Lawyers Row HD

1840-1860 - Small district features brick, 2-story courthouse designed by J. S. Savage, architect. Opposite it are 5 law-office buildings which, combined with courthouse, form a harmonious Greek Revival complex. **N H L; H A B S**

CONVENT (VICINITY)

St. Michael's Church HD

c. 1875-20th C. - Small rural district set behind a Mississippi River levee, with 8 buildings and a cemetery. St. Michael's Church (1833-1870's) is a large and handsome Victorian, blending Romanesque and Gothic styles. Adjacent rectory, 1875, Greek Revival, Other buildings include 2 late 19th C. cottages, a large c. 1900 schoolhouse.

COVINGTON

District of St. John HD

c. 1880-1930 - Residential-commercial, 20 blocks, approximately 170 structures. Residential section contains mostly 1 and 2-story wooden structures built without architects; local types include shotgun, raised cottage and the North Shore House (indigenous to north shore of Lake Ponchartrain). Stylistic influences include Eastlake, Queen Anne. An outstanding historic environment, with tree-lined streets, relatively unchanged commercial area. Significant in history of urban planning, for early use of squares held in common ("ox lots"). *Map, Self-Guided Tours*: Covington Chamber of Commerce, PO Box 1179, Covington LA 70434, telephone (504)-892-3216.

CROWLEY

Crowley HD

1887-1931 - Residential-commercial, approximately 300 significant structures. Styles include Queen Anne, Eastlake, Colonial Revival, and Bungaloid. Of note: Acadia Parish Courthouse (Art Deco), Grand Opera House (1900), and dozens of outstanding examples of Queen Anne residences. Residential areas cover 40 blocks, set off by shade from mature live oaks.

DE RIDDER

De Ridder Commercial District

1900-1933 - Three blocks, 42 structures, most of brick, 1 and 2 stories. Of note: 2 exceptional examples of the Neo-Classical and Beaux-Arts influence in an isolated rural location - Lumberman's Bank and Trust (1913), and First National Bank (1920). District contains a significant collection of period commercial buildings reflecting town's importance as trading center since turn of the century.

DONALDSONVILLE

Donaldsonville HD

1865-1933 - Commercial-residential, approximately 635 structures, closely packed in 50 blocks. Well-preserved working class housing (shotgun houses, cottages, bungalows), a number of pretentious residences in Queen Anne and Eastlake styles, and a number of Italianate commercial buildings. Of note: Ascension Catholic Church (1875-1895), the Lemann Store (3-story Italianate with cast-iron gallery), and the landscaping of Crescent Park and Louisiana Square. *Map, Self-Guided Tours*: Chamber of Commerce, 430 Railroad Ave., Donaldsonville LA 70346, telephone (504)-473-4814. *Group Tours*: Ascension Heritage Association (ASHA), c/o Main Street Program, POB 460, Donaldsonville LA 70346, telephone (504)-473-4814. *Annual Homes Tour*: Sunshine Festival (mid-October); Christmas Tour (second Sunday in December); contact Ascension Heritage Museum, 204 Nichols, Donaldsonville LA 70346, telephone (504)-473-1070.

FISHER

Village of Fisher HD

c. 1900 - Eighty-one buildings constructed as company lumber town. Probably best-preserved turn-of-the-century townscape in Louisiana, with 90 percent of its original buildings, most of the original dirt streets, and original wooden fences. Of note: the Commissary (1900 - 1914) with Baroque front, the Queen Anne-Colonial Revival railroad station, and the Victorian Gothic church. An excellent example of a sawmill town of its era. *Guided Tours*: By appointment; contact Mayor's Office, POB 148, Fisher LA 71426, telephone (318)-256-2913, *Special Events*: Sawmill Days (4th weekend in May); contact Mayor's Office for brochure, details.

FRANKLIN

Franklin HD

1830-c. 1930 - Residential-commercial, about 400 significant structures. Fine commercial buildings on Willow, Main Streets; residential area contains a number of outstanding Greek Revival homes. Of note: Shadowlawn, 2-story frame antebellum mansion; old open-air city market with truss roof. *Map, Self-Guided Tours*: Chamber of Commerce, Hwy 182, POB 38, Franklin LA 70538, telephone (318)-828-5608; also Franklin Historic District Commission, City Hall, 319 Willow St., Franklin LA 70538. *Annual Homes Tour*: Victorian Christmas; Tour of Homes. Contact St. Mary Chapter, Louisiana Landmarks Soc., POB 400, Franklin, LA. 70538.

GRAND COTEAU

Grand Coteau HD

1830-1930 - Rural town includes impressive St. Charles College (1909) with adjoining Acadian cottages and frame shops, a mid-19th C. Renaissance Revival church (with unusual Second Empire roof), and Academy of the Sacred Heart (begun in 1821), with fine Federal, Greek Revival details. Approximately 20 cottages reflecting a significant Creole architectural heritage; lengthy shaded avenues of old live oaks.

GRETNA

Gretna HD

c. 1845-1935 - Mostly residential (with commercial sector near the river), approximately 757 structures covering 53 blocks. Most buildings are 1-story; predominant types are Creole cottages, shotgun houses, and bungalows. Styles include Greek Revival, Italianate, Eastlake, Colonial Revival. Local landmarks include: David Crockett Fire Hall (1859, Italianate), Old Courthouse (1907, Renaissance-Baroque), and Texas-Pacific Railroad Station (1910). Impressive for its size, its rich architectural fabric, and the focus provided by the flamboyant Courthouse set amidst the town green.

HAMMOND

Hammond HD

c. 1880-1930 - Commercial, covering 15 blocks; most buildings are 2-story brick, many with elaborate detailing on facades. Of note: Boos Building, the newspaper offices (1895), and the railroad depot (c. 1900, Queen Anne-Gothic). The town enjoyed considerable prosperity in early 20th C. from its fresh strawberry industry. A cohesive historic district, with a strong unity of architectural style. *Map, Self-Guided Tours*: Hammond Chamber of Commerce, 2 W. Thomas St., POB 1458, Hammond LA 70404, telephone (504)-345-4457; also, Tangipahoa Parish Tourist Commission, 1535 Highway 51 Bypass, Hammond LA 70404, telephone (504)-542-7520. *Annual Homes Tour*: Hammond Heritage Day, contact Central Business District Association (CBDA), POB 2415, Hammond LA 70404, telephone (504)-345-3356.

HOUMA

Houma HD

c. 1890–1933 - A central business district centered around a courthouse square landscaped with live oaks, and two related residential areas. Most of the 118 buildings are from 1890 to 1933. Residences are unpretentious, primarily shotgun houses, bungalows, or cottages. Majority were associated with workers in seafood processing industry; area still a major producer of shrimp, oysters.

INDEPENDENCE

Independence HD

1905–c. 1930 - Commercial, approximately 40 brick commercial buildings which still convey appearance of a prosperous small town of early 20th C. Of note: Old Independence Theatre, railroad station, and Independence Bank. District records the prosperity resulting from the "strawberry boom", and also influx of Italian immigrants.

JACKSON

Jackson HD

1815–c. 1930 - Commercial-residential, encompassing two-thirds of town, approximately 124 structures. Some 30 significant buildings in commercial corridor, many in Federal and Greek Revival styles. Residential types include Greek Revival raised cottages, some Queen Anne homes. Of note: Mill Bank (1835, Greek Revival), Roseneath Townhouse (c. 1832, Greek Revival), and Jackson Town Hall (c. 1906, eclectic with onion dome). Historic area is unusually well-preserved, with an impressive heritage of Greek Revival architecture.

LAFAYETTE

Sterling Grove HD

1890–1934 - Residential, 43 buildings; large and small homes, mostly frame. Styles include Italianate, Eastlake, Queen Anne, Colonial Revival. Of note: Mouton plantation home (1848, Greek Revival), St. Genevieve Church (1925, Romanesque), and 13 major Queen Anne houses. Of special interest: Sterling Street, with large lots, deep setbacks, and live oaks.

LAKE PROVIDENCE

Lake Providence Commercial District

Late 19th to early 20th C. - Thirty-three brick commercial buildings, mostly 1-story. Many have retained original shop fronts, including cast-iron columns. Of note: Masonic Temple (1910), Fisher Hotel (1905), and the Levy Building (1926). A well-preserved turn-of-the-century commercial area.

Lake Providence Residential District

1840-1925 - Fourteen large, pretentious residences, most of them along south shore of Lake Providence. Styles include Greek Revival, Italianate, Queen Anne. Of note: Arlington Mansion (2-story Greek Revival), Bass House (mid-19th C. Italianate villa). District, with its predominant 1 1/2-story-scale, its semi-rural character with large lots, and its architectural quality, represents town's cotton-planter heritage.

MARKSVILLE

Marksville HD

c. 1900-c. 1930 - Commercial, 11 blocks with 57 buildings; mostly 1-story, brick, with simple ornamentation. Of note: 1927 Neo-Classical brick courthouse, Beaux-Arts bank, and the Laborde Buildings with elaborate limestone parapets. A fine example of a rural, early 20th C. business district. *Annual Homes Tour*: Historic Homes of Avoyelles Parish (first Saturday in October), c/o Louisiana Commission des Avoyelles (French), Chamber of Commerce, POB 365, Marksville LA 71351, telephone (318)-253-7568.

NATCHITOCHES

Natchitoches HD

Late 1700's-1890's - Town founded in 1714, and is oldest permanent settlement in Louisiana Purchase Territory. More than 50 significant structures, including early French Colonial, Greek Revival, and Victorian-era. Of note: Roque

House (1790's French Colonial), Ft. Clairborne (1820, raised cottage), Buard-Metoyer Townhouse (c. 1850, Greek Revival), and the Chaplin House (1892). N H L. *Map, Self-Guided Tours*: Natchitoches Parish Tourist Commission, 781 Front St., Natchitoches LA 71457; also Natchitoches Chamber of Commerce. *Annual Homes Tour*: Natchitoches Pilgrimage (2nd weekend in October), POB 2654, Natchitoches LA 71458, telephone (318)-352-4411.

NEW IBERIA

East Main Street HD

c. 1890-c. 1930 - Residential, 71 large and small houses, most of frame construction. Predominant styles are Eastlake, Queen Anne, bungalow, Colonial Revival. Of note: Shadows-on-the-Teche mansion (1834, Creole-Greek Revival, NHL), Georgian Revival post office (1903), and Romanesque synagogue (1903). Town founded by Spanish in 1799 as "Nueva Iberia"; prospered in the era of the river steamboat trade, and district contains the community's grandest residential "rue" of the late 19th - early 20th C. *Map, Self-Guided Tours*: Porters Gifts & Antiques, 446 E. Main St., New Iberia LA 70560, telephone (318)-364-4294. *Annual Homes Tour*: December; contact Ernest Nereaux, 442 E. Main, New Iberia LA 70560, telephone (318)-364-5922.

NEW ORLEANS

New Orleans

Map, Self-Guided Tours: Greater New Orleans Tourist and Convention Center, 1520 Sugar Bowl Drive, New Orleans LA 70130, telephone (504)-556-5011 (for French Quarter); Preservation Resource Center, 604 Julia Street, New Orleans LA 70130, telephone (504)-581-7032 (for New Orleans neighborhoods). *Guided Tours*: Friends of the Cabildo, 701 Chartres St., New Orleans LA 70116, telephone (504)-523-3939 (for French Quarter); National Park Service, 527 St. Ann Street, New Orleans LA 70116, telephone (504)-589-3882 (French Quarter, Garden Districts). *Annual Homes Tour*: Spring Fiesta Association, 826 St. Ann Street, New Orleans, LA. 70116, 581-1367 (1st Friday after Easter); Holiday Home Tour (December), Preservation Resource Center, 604 Julia St., New Orleans LA 70130, telephone (504)-581-7032.

Algiers Point HD

1840-1940 - Residential, with approximately 1,700 buildings, primarily frame, 1-story homes. Styles include Louisiana Colonial, Creole, Greek Revival, Italianate, Gothic, Victorian and Edwardian eras. A self-contained neighborhood which has maintained its turn-of-the-century appearance; an integral part of the community is the Algiers-Canal Street Ferry (operating since 1827), linking the Point to the city proper. *Annual Homes Tour*: early October, sponsored by Algiers Point Development Association; contact Jean McStay, 601 Elmira Ave., New Orleans LA 70114, telephone (504)-366-0704.

Canal Street HD

19th C. - (L) Downtown commercial, including one of city's principal avenues and the side streets leading up to it. Approximately 160 structures, with many styles: Italianate, Greek Revival, Victorian Eclectic. Of note: Boston Club (1844, Greek Revival), U. S. Customs House (1848-1881), Greek Revival), and Bank of America building (1866, Renaissance Revival). This district is one of city's architectural treasures.

Central City HD

c. 1830-c. 1930 - Large district with approximately 4,000 structures, primarily 1-story frame, working-class residences. Predominant styles are Greek Revival, Italianate, Queen Anne, and Eastlake. Majority are either shotgun, or the larger "camelback" house. Of note: St. John the Baptist Church (1872, Renaissance Revival), and a grand Italianate double house at 2103 Baronne St., c. 1850. District was first developed in 1830's; was home for thousands of Irish immigrants, followed by Germans in 1850's.

Esplanade Ridge HD

1830-1930 - Primarily residential, with scattered neighborhood commercial areas. Approximately 4,000 structures predating 1930, most of wood, many painted in a variety of pastel colors. Styles a mix, including Creole cottages, raised villas (with Greek Revival details), and shotguns. Of note: Dufour-Baldwin House (1707 Esplanade Ave.), the Chauffe-Reeves House (2275 Bayou Rd.), and the Spanish Customs House (1300 Moss St.). An area with much character, due especially to French Creole-type homes.

Fauborg Marigny HD

19th to early 20th C. - Dense urban district adjacent to the

Vieux Carre; a variety of structures, including small Creole cottages, residences from Greek Revival through early 20th C. styles, commercial buildings, and warehouses. Of interest: Washington Square, with double row of oak trees. Has retained its diverse character and 19th C. flavor.

French Ouarter HD (Vieux Carre)

1745–1933 - One hundred twenty-block urban district, approximately the original area of the city in 1721. Offers a continuum of architectural styles, including French and Spanish Colonial (1720–1803), early Federal (1803–1825), antebellum (1825–1860), post-Civil War (1850–1900), and modern. Focal point is the great square-originally the Place d'Armes, now known as Jackson Square (NHL). Of note: Ursuline Convent (1748–1752, NHL), the Cabildo (1795, NHL). Approximately 1,000 pre-Civil War buildings, and over 600 Victorian and early 20th C. properties. **N H L; H A B S**

Garden HD

19th–20th C. - Predominantly residential, with numerous dwellings and related community structures, many excellent examples of popular 19th C. styles; includes Egyptian and Greek Revival, Italianate, and Victorian-era, plus many simple shotgun houses. Area enjoys abundant garden space and greenery, has retained much of its 19th C. charm. **N H L**

Irish Channel Area Architectural District

1850–1900 - Extensive residential-commercial area, with approximately 2,300 structures, predominantly brick and frame, 1 and 2 1/2 stories. Of note: Egyptian Revival old courthouse (1836, altered in 1843 and 1890's), the First Presbyterian Church (1856, Greek Revival), and numerous galleried Creole structures. District has strong historical associations with jazz music.

Jackson Barracks HD

1829–1837 - Military, approximately 15 significant early Greek Revival structures around a green commons; majority are brick, 2 and 2 1/2 stories with double-tier wraparound porches. Originally constructed for fear of a slave uprising, but were first used in 1838 during Second Seminole War. State-owned.

Lafayette Square HD

1830's–1880's - (L) Residential, approximately 233 structures, with fine examples of Greek Revival and Italianate. Of note: Julia Row, an intact row of 13 Greek Revival townhouses dating from 1832; monumental Gallier Hall (1845–1850), which served as City Hall until the 1890's; and St. Patrick's Cathedral (1838, Gothic Revival).

Lower Garden HD

19th C. - Urban area with parks, residential and commercial sections. Characterized by contrasting land uses and a variety of building types and styles, including Greek Revival and those from Victorian era. Of note: Coliseum Square with its park and surrounding grand buildings, and the commercial structures on Magazine St., many with 1 and 2-story verandas. Has retained much of its 19th C. appearance, reflecting period affluence.

Picayune Place HD

1833–1900's - (L) Approximately 90 structures, containing perhaps the finest concentration of architecturally-outstanding commercial buildings in New Orleans. Styles include Greek Revival, Italianate, and eclectic. Of note: Greek Revival bank building at 301 Magazine St. (1843), the eclectic Whitney Bank (1888), and Beaux-Arts structure at 211 Camp Street (1900); latter's terra-cotta facade is one of city's finest. Very little intrusion by modern buildings.

St. Charles Avenue HD

19th to early 20th C. - Turn-of-the-century residential, featuring approximately 140 high-style, imposing dwellings in variety of late-Victorian era styles; earlier residences reflect Greek Revival and Italianate details, with later homes in such styles as Second Empire, Queen Anne, and Richardsonian Romanesque. Homes set on spacious grounds, with mature street trees, landscaping. Focal point is St. Charles Ave. streetcar line (on National Register).

Uptown New Orleans HD

c. 1820–1935 - Large urban residential area of about 750 blocks set along the Mississippi River, containing approximately 10,000 structures. Unusually impressive district because of size, range of architectural periods, and quality of examples from each period. Notable for the number of Italianate-style residences, for superb examples of Queen Anne architecture, and for the number, quality, and variety of shotgun houses (50 percent of the district). Of note: Soniat-Dufosset Plantation House (1840's), the Rice House (1866), and the Ferguson-Hellmers House (c. 1870, Gothic Revival).

Warehouse HD
1830's-1911 - (L) Riverfront, approximately 200 commercial and industrial structures. Styles include Greek Revival, Italianate commercial, and Renaissance Revival. Of note: Leeds Iron Foundry (1852, Greek Revival), the Greek Revival warehouse group at 800-844 S. Peters (1852), and the Dixie Art Supply building, 1861 warehouse.

PONCHATOULA

Ponchatoula Commercial District
Early 20th C. - Three streets of commercial buildings, mostly brick, 1-story, ranging from small shops to warehouses built as strawberry packing houses. This district, which prospered from the "strawberry boom" (which ended c. 1931), is considered a superior example of a c. 1900 commercial zone in a small town.

SHREVEPORT

Shreveport Commercial District
c. 1885-1930 - Fifteen blocks with approximately 135 significant buildings; earlier ones mostly 2-story brick with Victorian decorative elements, while c. 1900 buildings are larger and more elaborate, reflecting the boom in oil and lumber. Of note: 1925 Classical-style Courthouse, the 15-story Commercial Bank, and the Slattery Building. An outstanding example of "an old downtown" in Louisiana.

Ledbetter Heights HD (St. Paul's Bottoms)
1880-1934 - Working-class neighborhood of approximately 900 structures, mainly single shotgun houses (1-story frame, 1-room wide, at least 3 rooms deep). The Bottoms developed in the 1880's as a rental neighborhood for blacks employed in city's waterfront warehouses. Houses have little or no styling, some of the streets reportedly are still unpaved; an important example of a working-class neighborhood, with relatively little change.

Texas Avenue HD
Early 1900's - Ten brick commercial buildings, 2 stories, with shop fronts on ground floor. Six are superior examples of Renaissance Revival architecture, with pretensions to high

style. An impressive continuous facade running 2 city blocks; a completely intact vintage commercial streetscape.

ST. FRANCISVILLE

St. Francisville HD

c. 1820-c. 1930 - Commercial-residential, approximately 100 structures, predominantly frame, 1 and 1 1/2 stories, with late-19th C. details. Of note in commercial area: Audubon Hall (1819), the Propinquity store and counting house (1819), and the Old Courthouse (c. 1824). Residential area offers many late-period raised cottages, and bungalows. Relatively unchanged river port, in a village-like setting. *Map, Self-Guided Tours*: West Feliciana Historical Society, POB 338, St. Francisville LA 70775, telephone (504)-635-6330. *Annual Homes Tour*: Audubon Pilgrimage, contact above.

ST. JOSEPH

St. Joseph HD

1830-1930 - Residential-commercial, approximately 75 significant buildings. Twenty-two commercial structures, mostly brick, from late 19th or early 20th C. Residential styles include Greek Revival, Queen Anne, Colonial Revival. Of note: 1850 Post Office (Greek Revival), the Parish Library (an 1850 plantation house), and the 1906 Courthouse on the town green. Of special interest, because of tree-shaded residential neighborhoods and its character as probably the most intact late 19th - early 20th C. river-levee town in Louisiana. In addition, St. Joseph Courthouse Square is significant in black history, for its links with the 1878 race riot in nearby Waterproof.

ST. MARTINVILLE

St. Martinville HD

c. 1820-c. 1910. Commercial-religious-residential; 32 buildings of significance. Two major features: church square in a park-like setting, the surrounding old commercial-residential section. Of note: 1840-Romanesque-inspired church, Greek Revival parish hall, and 6 historic residences, one dating from 1820. An important river port in era of steamboats, district has retained much of its charm and character.

THIBODAUX (VICINITY)

Laurel Valley Sugar Plantation HD

Late 19th C.-1910 - An unusually large sugar plantation complex, approximately 80 buildings on 500 acres. While plantation is pre-1850, the oldest building (the "Big House") is c. 1884; the 45 workers' cottages date from c. 1900. One of largest surviving sugar production and manufacturing complexes in U.S. (museum). *Annual Homes Tour*: Spring Tours; contact Thibodaux Service League, 618 St. Philip, Thibodaux LA 70301. *General Information*: Museum, (504) 446-8111.

WASHINGTON

Washington HD

19th to early 20th C. - Largely residential, approximately 260 structures from 19th and early 20th C. plus 60 modern buildings. Residential areas include workers' neighborhoods (characterized by small Acadian cottages, shotgun houses, and Queen Anne bungalows), and the wealthier sections with their raised Creole houses (featuring Greek Revival, Eastlake, and Queen Anne details). Also a number of commercial buildings, with original late 19th C. ornamental shop fronts.

WINNSBORO

Winnsboro Commercial District

c. 1900-c. 1932 - Thirty-one significant buildings, mostly brick, 1 and 2 stories, with false fronts and conservative decorative detailing. District reflects town's development in connection with Missouri-Pacific Railroad, as prosperous trading center for thriving agricultural community.

Jackson Street HD

1890-1906 - Tiny residential district contains 3 large single-story frame dwellings and 7 outbuildings. Houses are survivors of what was town's prestige neighborhood: Belle Farm (1891, Greek Revival); Scott-Elam House (1906, Queen Anne); Godfrey House (1900, Eastlake elements). Belle Farm also of interest because of its surviving outbuildings: maid's house, barns, smokehouse, shed, and outhouse.

MISSISSIPPI

BAY ST. LOUIS

Beach Boulevard HD
Late 19th-20th C. - One hundred seventy-five-acre district, incorporates a 2-mile strip of Beach Blvd. properties, most of central business core around Main St., and surrounding residential properties. Shotgun and Creole wooden cottages predominant. Contains a number of structures significant to local black history, including St. Augustine's Seminary, St. Rose de Lima Church, and the 100 Men Association Building.

Elmwood HD
c. 1828-1900's - District's buildings record evolution of the area's land use from agricultural to residential, on property once part of the Cowand Plantation. Of note: Elmwood Manor (c. 1828) a fine example of French Colonial style; also, Kimbrough House (c. 1820's), with Queen Anne additions. Most other buildings 1-story frame, with hip roofs and undercut galleries; generally turn-of-the-century eclectic.

Main Street HD
Late 19th to early 20th C. - Small district, a linear row of 1-story vernacular buildings on Main St., all but 1 of frame construction. Included are 2 Creole and 3 shotgun cottages from late 19th C. Have retained much of their original detailing, and are outstanding examples of vernacular house types.

Sycamore Street HD
c. 1860-1920's - Eight residences, 2 commercial buildings; part of remains of a small black settlement (see **Washington St. HD**). Styles include shotgun, Creole cottage, Bungalow, and Queen Anne.

Washington Street HD
1900–c. 1935 - Ten residential, 2 commercial structures; all but one have frame construction, corrugated metal roofs. Vernacular types, predominantly shotgun and Creole cottages dating from c. 1900 to c. 1935. Washington Street together with Sycamore Street HD are what remains of a small black settlement which had developed by 1920's.

BILOXI

West Beach HD
Late 19th to early 20th C. - Residential, approximately 60 significant buildings; Eastlake and Neo-Classical Revival styles predominate. City was a prominent summer resort, late 19th-early 20th C., and most homes in district were developed for wealthy vacationers from New Orleans. Their residences are among the finest to survive on the storm-ridden Gulf Coast. *Map, Self-Guided Tours*: Chamber of Commerce, 1036 Fred Haise Blvd., PO Drawer CC, Biloxi MS 39533, telephone (601)-374-2717. *Special Events*: Spring Pilgrimage (late March); contact Biloxi Council of Garden Clubs, 410 E. Bay View Ave., Biloxi MS 39530, telephone (601)-432-0336.

West Central HD
Mid 19th to early 20th C. - Residential, 70 structures; city's best-preserved middle-to-upper class turn-of-the-century neighborhood. Many large clapboard residences, basically Vernacular, Eastlake, Neo-Classical Revival, or Bungaloid in style. Also smaller homes with interesting Eastlake and Bungalow details. *General Information*: See **West Beach HD**.

BLUE MOUNTAIN

Blue Mountain College HD
1900–1970 - College founded in 1873 by Mark Perrin Lowrey, with leadership by Lowrey family until 1960 (although ownership transferred in 1918 to Mississippi Baptist Convention). Fourteen campus buildings record changing styles in architecture from turn-of-the-century eclectic to the influence of Frank Lloyd Wright.

CANTON

Courthouse Square HD

Mid-late 19th C. - An outstanding Greek Revival courthouse and square surrounded on 4 sides by high-quality, varied commercial buildings. One of the finest such groupings in Mississippi. *Guided Tours*: By horse-drawn surrey, Monday-Thursday-Saturday; contact Chamber of Commerce, POB 202, Canton MS 39046, telephone (601)-859-1606. *General Information*: Madison County Historical Society, 521 S. Lyon, Canton MS 39046.

CARROLLTON

Carrollton HD

Late 19th C. - A remarkably complete, well-preserved example of a prosperous small rural county seat and trading center. Town contains one of the most significant and unaltered assemblages of pre-20th C. architecture in central Mississippi; has retained much of its turn-of-the-century appearance.

COLUMBIA

Keys Hill HD

Early 20th C. - Small residential district composed of town's most architecturally significant collection of early 20th C. homes. Three easternmost houses were built for members of prominent Lampton family; 2 Spanish Colonial Revival residences associated with former Gov. Hugh White. Centerpiece of district is Hugh White Mansion.

COLUMBUS

Central Commercial District

19th-20th C. - Approximately 200 significant buildings in oldest occupied section of Columbus. Of note: Courthouse (1847 Greek Revival, later alterations), Lawyers Row (1840-1860), and First United Methodist Church (1860). *Map, Self-Guided Tours*: Chamber of Commerce, 318 N. 7th St. POB 1016, Columbus MS 39701, telephone (601)-328-4491; also Lowndes County Library, 314 N. 7th St., Columbus MS 39701. *Annual Homes Tour*: Columbus Pilgrimage (first 2 weeks in

April); contact Chamber of Commerce, POB 1016, Columbus MS 39701, telephone (601)-328-4491.

Factory Hill - Frog Bottom - Burns Bottom HD
c. 1885 - 1910 - Primarily residential; 3 distinct neighborhoods reflecting city's historical and architectural evolution. Mostly vernacular cottages dating from late 19th and early 20th C.; representative of city's neighborhoods inhabited by early factory workers. Best surviving and most complete example in this area of a turn-of-the-century mill village.

South Columbus HD
1820's-1930's - Residential district, containing one of greatest concentrations of 19th C. residential structures in Mississippi. Presents a virtually complete record of American building styles from 1820's through 1930's. A cohesive and well-preserved neighborhood, with many significant buildings.

GREENVILLE

Washington Avenue - Main Street HD
Early 20th C. - Residential, with variety of styles including "Four-Square", Colonial Revival, Spanish Colonial Revival, Tudor Revival, and outstanding collection of bungalows. Also contains a unique collection of "high water houses", built prior to flood control on the Mississippi River. Most residences are of fine architectural quality, their grandness reflecting city's early 20th C. prosperity. District has retained much of its original character, and is virtually intact. *Map, Self-Guided Tour*: Chamber of Commerce, 915 Washington Ave., Greenville MS 38702, telephone (601)-378-3141. *Guided Tours*: Offered upon request, with 2 days notice required. Contact above.

GREENWOOD

Cotton Row HD
Late 19th C. - A 3-block district, comprising Mississippi's most important concentration of buildings associated with marketing of cotton and post-Civil War cotton boom. By 1900, Greenwood had become major cotton market in Mississippi. Of the 57 buildings here, 24 have served as cotton offices at one time or another.

Central Commercial and Railroad District
1890-1935 - An important collection of commercial buildings associated with state's post-Civil War cotton boom. Styles include Queen Anne, Romanesque Revival, Neo-Classical Revival, Victorian Gothic, and Bungalow. Howard Street and Carrollton Avenue, two of principal retail streets of downtown, still offer relatively unbroken facade lines characteristic of pre-World War II Greenwood.

Four Corners HD
1908-1930 - A small but architecturally significant concentration of 5 diverse buildings with fine detailing and rich use of materials. These structures, including one of finest domed buildings in the state, illustrate city's post-Civil War cotton prosperity.

Grand Boulevard HD
Late 1890's-1941 - An early planned residential neighborhood featuring avenues shaded by massive oak trees. Contains city's finest examples of Spanish Eclectic, Tudor, Prairie Style, Neo-Classical Revival, and Colonial Revival. A significant district due to overall high quality of its architecture and the beautifully landscaped setting.

River Road and Western Downtown Residential District
1844-1941 - A significant group of architecturally and historically important buildings and sites. Contains fine examples of Queen Anne, Neo-Classical Revival, Prairie, and Italian Renaissance styles. Considerable demolition activity in recent years, and intrusive new construction.

Williams Landing and E. Downtown Residential HD
1890-1935 - Includes site of Williams Landing, point on Yazoo River where the town of Greenwood began as a trading post in 1834. Surviving buildings offer a variety of styles including Queen Anne, Prairie, Neo-Classical Revival, Colonial Revival, and Bungalow. Of note: Whittington House (Neo-Classical Revival brick), and Congregation Ahavath Rayim temple, Frank R. McGeoy, architect. This area has suffered from considerable demolition and modern commercial intrusion.

GULFPORT

Harbor Square HD

c. 1900–1930's - City's original central business district, retaining much of its original character (despite alterations to many buildings). Of special significance: the square comprised by the Durham Buildings (1903), including 3 excellent examples of the Venetian Gothic style. Of note: the N. & F. Hewes Building (1903), Salloum's Toggery (c. 1905), and the Old State Bank Building (c. 1909).

HATTIESBURG

Historic Neighborhood District

1880's–1930 - Residential; city's most architecturally significant neighborhood. Dual significance because of variety of house types and range of styles, and because of its association with many prominent residents. Has retained much of its original character. *Map, Self-Guided Tours*: Chamber of Commerce, 204 W. Front St., POB 710, Hattiesburg MS 39401, telephone (601)-545-3300. *Special Events*: Christmas Candlelight Driving Tour/Open House (weekend before Christmas); contact Historic Neighborhood Association, or Chamber.

Hub City HD

1890's–1930's - Reflects city's evolution from depot stop to regional economic center. Has retained a variety of period building types.

HOLLY SPRINGS

Courthouse HD

1870–1900's - Sixty civic and commercial buildings, of considerable architectural and historical significance for Mississippi. A variety of styles, from the town's most important development periods.

Historic Resources of Holly Springs

1870's–20th C. - Holly Springs is one of state's most significant rural communities, in terms of architecture and history. Four Historic Districts (Southwest Holly Springs, East Holly Springs, Depot-Compress, and North Memphis Street), with wide variety of styles, from folk houses to Greek Revival mansions and Queen Anne cottages. A small but striking collection of high-style 19th C. residences, also Gothic Revival, Italianate. *Annual Homes Tour*: Spring Pilgrimage (April); contact Holly Springs Garden Club, Inc., POB 696, Holly Springs MS 38635.

Mississippi Industrial College HD
1905–1926 - Campus district, illustrating Revival influence as well as Beaux-Arts planning principles popular in early 20th C. Established in 1905 for blacks, college has important associational significance for black history in Mississippi. All key structures from the school's growth period, 1905–1926, have survived.

JACKSON

Belhaven Heights HD
Late 19th to early 20th C. - A cohesive downtown residential neighborhood, with an eclectic blend of period residential architecture. Homeowners have been active against redevelopment, commercial encroachment. *Map, Self-Guided Tours*: "Downtown Jackson Architecture", Convention/Visitors Bureau, POB 1450, jackson MS 39215; Mississippi Museum of Art, 201 E. Pascagoula, Jackson MS 39201, telephone (601)-960-1515.

Farish Street Neighborhood HD
c. 1860–1940's - Economically independent black community, with excellent selection of vernacular building types, majority built between 1890–1930. Area has historical associations with black professionals, businessmen, and craftsmen. *General Information*: See **Belhaven Heights HD.**

Smith Park Architectural District
c. 1840–1940 - Downtown, 16 architecturally significant buildings (stone, concrete), and central public green. Of note: Governor's Mansion (1841, Greek Revival), St. Andrews Episcopal Cathedral (1903, Gothic Revival), and city's first skyscraper, the Lamar Life Building (1924–25). The city's most important group of buildings, in terms of variety and design quality. *General Information*: See **Belhaven Heights HD.**

Spengler's Corner HD
19th-early 20th C. - Commercial, with significant grouping of

period buildings of architectural and historical importance. District has served as a vital center of Jackson since 1840. *General Information*: See **Belhaven Heights HD**.

West Capitol Street HD

Late 19th C.-1920's - Commercial, with earliest intact commercial facades in city, and some of Mississippi's finest Art Deco architecture. An important visual record of this street's turn-of-the-century importance as commercial center and city's growth in the 1920's. *General Information*: See **Belhaven Heights HD**.

LORMAN (VICINITY)

Alcorn State University HD

1870's-20th C. - University created in 1871 as first land-grant school for blacks in U.S. Of note: President's House (Federal style), Chapel (Greek Revival style). 20th C. Colonial Revival buildings designed by prominent Mississippi architects C. H. Lindsay and E. L. Mabovaney.

Rodney Center HD

Mid-19th C. - Interesting and varied rural vernacular architecture. Town was important commercial center along Natchez Trace and Mississippi River, from its 1828 incorporation to its relative abandonment after 1870.

MADISON

Dorrah Street HD

c. 1885-c. 1905 - Only 3 houses, but of local significance as the best interpretations of the Queen Anne vernacular style in Madison. Together, these homes represent town's modest turn-of-the-century prosperity, based on truck farming.

MAGNOLIA

Myrtle Street HD

1881 to early 20th C. - Small cohesive grouping of 5 middle-class homes and 1 church. Styles include Gothic Revival (1881 Presbyterian Church), Queen Anne (1902 Belle Maison), and Greek Revival-inspired (c. 1900 Frith House). Well-preserved residential block, suggestive of turn-of-the-century.

Southtown HD

Late 19th to early 20th C. - Small residential neighborhood, with interesting and significant composition of high-style Queen Anne mansions, formal public buildings, substantial period homes, and 1 Greek Revival cottage. Streets broad and sloping, with profusion of shade trees. An eclectic concentration of late 19th C. residential architecture in a quiet and gracious setting.

MCCOMB

Kramertown-Railroad HD

Early 20th C. - Railroad yard was core of the community's commercial development; in 1911 was site of a National Guard encampment during a nationwide strike by Illinois Central Railroad shop members. Architecturally outstanding, with historical significance.

MERIDIAN

Historic Resources of Meridian

Late 19th C. - Two districts within one-square-mile center of city: central business district; and a smaller depot district composed primarily of industrial buildings. Illustrates postbellum character of a city that owed its beginning and growth to the American railroad system.

NATCHEZ

Cemetery Bluff HD

Primarily park area, significant for its historic use and importance for the city, and the importance of buildings and structures within its boundaries. Features include spectacular view of the Mississippi River, and 2 cemeteries with landscaped open spaces.

Clifton Heights HD

Late 19th to early 20th C. - Residential; contains city's most significant (architecturally, historically) collection of late 19th - early 20th C. residences. They display a high degree of architectural finish. Styles include Shingle, Tudor, Queen Anne, and Colonial Revival. *Annual Homes Tour*: Natchez

Pilgrimage (Spring, Fall), Natchez Tourist Council, POB 347, Natchez MS 39120, telephone (601)-446-6631 and (800)-647-6742; Christmas in Natchez, c/o Natchez Tourist Council.

Natchez Bluffs and Under-The-Hill HD

18th-20th C. - Includes site of early 18th C. fortified French settlement, several brick commercial structures and frame dwellings, the old town square, and original Natchez landing. Originally a frontier post, Natchez became an important transportation center and flourishing cotton market by 1860. Of note: Commercial Bank (1833), Auburn House (1812, NHL), and D'Evereux house (1840, Greek Revival). *Annual Homes Tour*: See **Clifton Heights HD.**

On-Top-Of-The-Hill HD

19th C. - Impressive area composed primarily of 19th C. buildings. City is older than New Orleans and during 19th C. was politically, commercially, and culturally pre-eminent in the region. District boundaries based on the Spanish street grid plan. *Annual Homes Tour*: See **Clifton Heights HD.**

Upriver Residential District

Mid-19th to early 20th C. - Contains one of the most significant (architecturally and historically) collections of mid-19th to early 20th C. residences in Mississippi. Many with a high degree of architectural finish, set in neighborhoods which have retained their architectural integrity. *Annual Homes Tour*: See **Clifton Heights HD.**

NEWTON

West Church Street HD

Early 1900's - Residential neighborhood; architecturally significant in documenting early-1900's prosperity of this small rural railroad center.

OCEAN SPRINGS

Louisville and Nashville (L & N) HD

1827-1890 - Small, residential, with variety of simple structures; contains an 1827 West Indian Colonial-type house (810 Iberville St.) and several late-Victorian houses. Also, 2 houses designed by Frank Lloyd Wright, one for architect Louis Sullivan. This quiet Gulf Coast town was a health resort in 19th C.; with oak tree-lined streets, has retained much of its early atmosphere. *Map, Self-Guided Tours*: Chamber of Commerce, L & N Depot, POB 187, Ocean Springs MS 39564, telephone (601)-875-4424.

Shearwater (Pottery) HD

1928 - Pottery complex established in 1928 by artisan Peter Anderson. Paintings, prints, pastels by brothers James, Walter Anderson on display; also on property are Walter's workshop, home. See Town Community Center, for major display of his murals (Key at Chamber of Commerce).

OXFORD

Courthouse Square HD

Mid-late 19th C. - A cohesive and architecturally significant ensemble of period buildings, public and commercial. Courthouse, focal point for surrounding square, rebuilt after its destruction in Civil War. Author William Faulkner based his legendary Yoknapatawpha County and town of Jefferson on his native Lafayette County and city of Oxford. District typifies early-19th C. principles of town planning.

PASCAGOULA

Front Street HD.

19th C. - Five deteriorated residential structures, 2 stories, frame. Difficult access.

PASS CHRISTIAN

Pass Christian HD

Mid 19th to early 20th C. - Gulf Coast town, called "Newport of the South", contains one of Coast's largest and best-preserved assemblages of noteworthy beachfront houses. Contains 130 residential, commercial buildings; 22 are antebellum, 76 built or remodeled before 1912. District enhanced by a splendid live-oak setting, relatively few intrusions. *Annual Homes Tour*: Fall Tour of Homes (usually October), contact Historical Society, 108 Donlin, Pass Christian MS 39571; Spring Tour (usually March), Garden Club, c/o Chamber of Commerce, POB 307, Pass Christian MS 39571, telephone (601)-452-2252.

PHILADELPHIA

Philadelphia HD

Early 1900's - Residential neighborhood, 42 buildings; significant because it documents the city's "boom time" prosperity of the early 1900's. A fine collection of both stately and modest residences, most built 1905-06. City (pop. 6,500) known nationwide for hosting the annual Neshoba County Fair, an annual summer campground reunion. *Map, Self-Guided Tours*: Chamber of Commerce, POB 51, Philadelphia MS 39350, telephone (601)-656-1742; also at Historical Society, (601)-656-6783.

PHILADELPHIA (VICINITY)

Coldwater Community

No further information available at this time.

Neshoba County Fair HD

1890's-1970's - Mississippi's oldest active county fair, and thought to be oldest and largest campground fair in U.S. Rustic 2-story frame cabins make up 95 percent of district's approximately 470 structures. Cabins painted in various bright shades, with multicolored facades. Decorations include painted tree trunks used as porch posts, colored lights, numerous flags, posters, banners. Fair dates from 1889, includes Mississippi's only licensed horse racing track. Fair season generally in August.

PORT GIBSON

Historic Resources of Port Gibson

Mid-19th C. - An outstanding ensemble of homes and commercial buildings preserved within the context of one of state's most historic towns. Includes a collection of late-Federal and Greek Revival residences and commercial buildings of national significance, and 4 cemeteries of historical interest. St. Mary's Community district is of special note. *Map, Self-Guided Tours*: Chamber of Commerce, POB 491, Port Gibson MS 39150, telephone (601)-437-4351. *Annual Homes Tour*: Spring Pilgrimage (late March or early April), contact Chamber of Commerce.

SHUQUALAK

Central Shuqualak HD

19th C. - A 6-block district; prime example of an early railroad town in rural South. Note: pronounced as "Sugar-Lock".

STARKVILLE

Greensboro Street HD

1860's-1920's - Primarily residential; highly cohesive collection of structures of architectural and historical significance. Contains fine examples of vernacular architecture, and largest concentration of residences of town leaders. A streetscape with well-preserved period ambience. *General Information*: Oktibbeha County Heritage Museum, Starkville MS 39564 and Chamber of Commerce, 322 University Dr., Starkville MS 39759, telephone (601)-323-5783.

VICKSBURG

Main Street HD

Mid 1800's-20th C. - Concentration of well-preserved Greek Revival residences and 19th - 20th C. commercial and public buildings. Low scale of the buildings and amenities such as cast-iron fences and brick-paved streets contribute to its 19th C. character. *Map, Self-Guided Tours*: Warren County Tourist Commission, POB 110, Vicksburg MS 39180, telephone (601)-636-9421; Chamber of Commerce, 2020 Mission 66, POB 709, Vicksburg MS 39180. *Guided Tours*: VDT Headquarters, (601) 638-8888. *Annual Homes Tour*: Pilgrimage of Homes (Fall, Spring), Tourist Commission; (601)-636-9421; out-of-state, (800)-221-3536.

WEST POINT

Central City HD

Mid 19th to early 20th C. - Well-preserved commercial-industrial community, with good examples of commercial architecture. District reflects community's period of greatest growth, from 1870's to early 1920's. Has retained much of its turn-of-the-century character. *Map, Self-Guided Tours*:

Chamber of Commerce, 510 Broad St., POB 177, West Point MS 39772, telephone (601)-494-5121.

Court Street HD

Mid-19th-early 20th C. - Well-preserved residential neighborhood, with excellent examples of period vernacular architecture. Most structures are relatively unaltered, and street has retained much of its period character.

WOODVILLE

Woodville HD

1820-1930 - A distinctive collection of buildings representing a variety of architectural styles, dating roughly from 1820 to 1930. First settled c. 1802, incorporated in 1811.

YAZOO CITY

Town Center HD

Early 19th-20th C. A cohesive and architecturally significant aggregation of civic, commercial, and residential buildings reflecting 150 years of small-scale urban development. Present center of the city, roughly the area of the 1822 town plat, has retained its original sense of place. *Map, Self-Guided Tours*: Chamber of Commerce, 211 E. Broadway, POB 172, Yazoo City MS 39194, telephone (601)-746-1273.

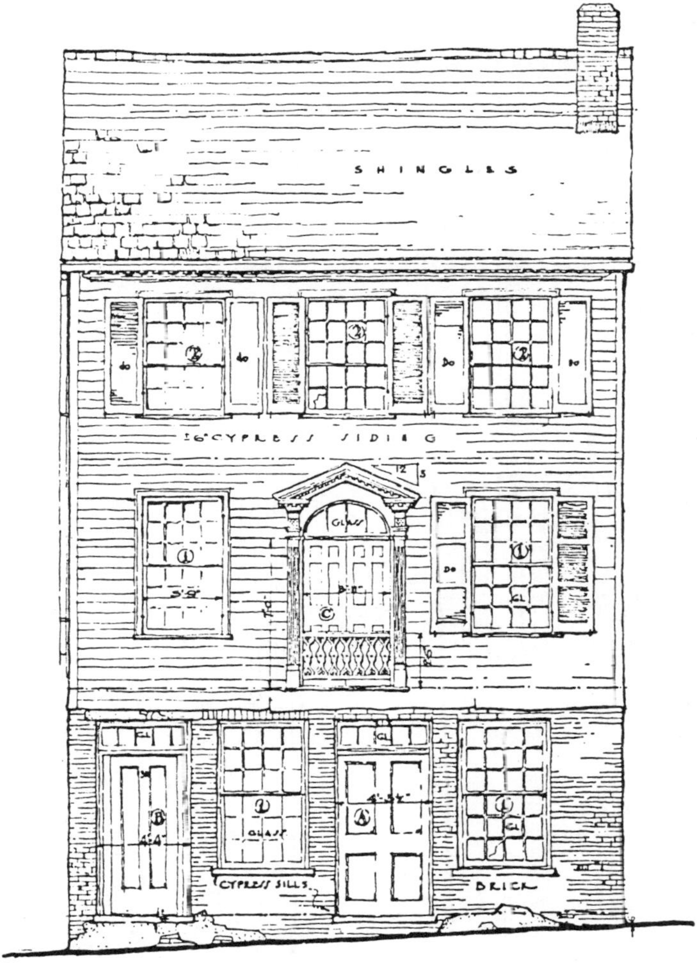

·South Elevation·

311–13 Market Street

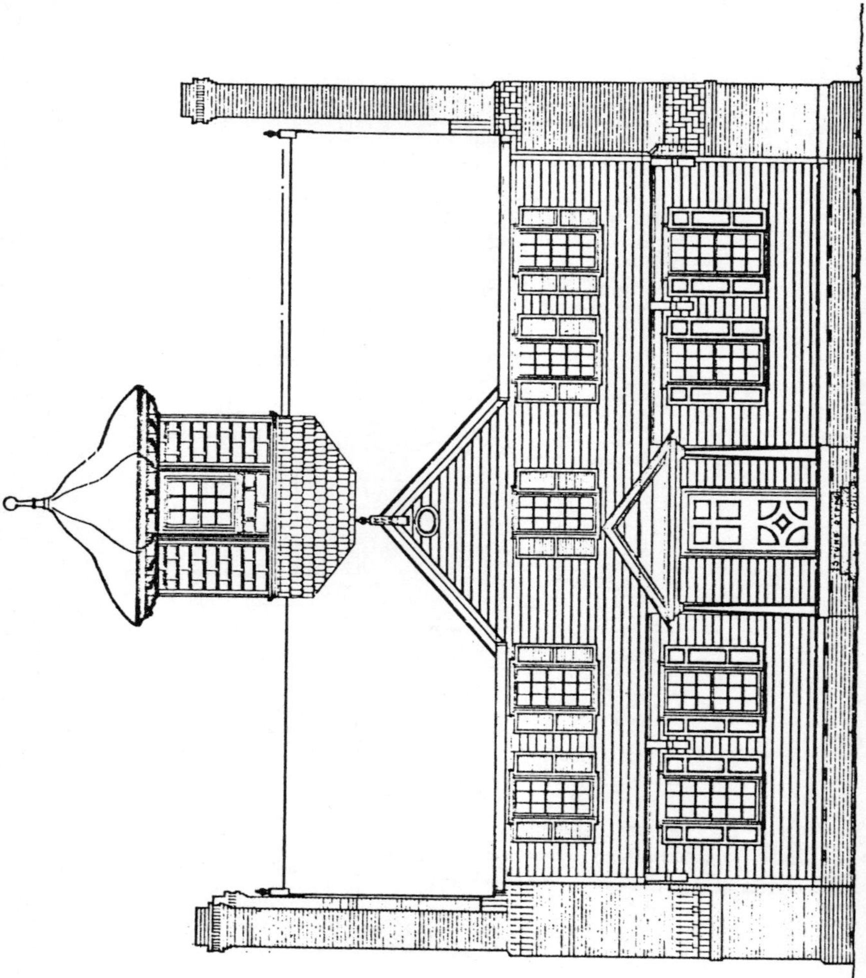

Cupola House

NORTH CAROLINA

AHOSKIE

Ahoskie Downtown HD

1901–1930's - Typical 1 to 3-story brick commercial structures creating a cohesive streetscape. Town originated in simultaneous development in 1880's of large-scale logging and sawmills, and construction of railroad between Tarboro and Norfolk area.

ASHEVILLE

Asheville Downtown HD

Early 20th C. - Excellent examples of Commercial Classical, Neo-Georgian, Romanesque Revival, Art Deco, other styles. Of note: Thomas Wolfe's childhood home (c. 1893, Queen Anne), Plaza Theatre (1922, Mission style), Leader Department Store (c. 1890), Medical Building (c. 1900, Georgian Revival). One of the most complete collections of early 20th C. architecture in the state, with strong period flavor. *Map, Self-Guided Tours*: Chamber of Commerce, Haywood St., POB 1011, Asheville NC 28802, telephone (704)-258-3858. *Annual Homes Tour*: Heritage Week (early May), contact Preservation Society of Asheville and Buncombe County, POB 2806, Asheville NC 28802, telephone (704)-254-2343.

Biltmore Village HD

c. 1898 - An "English Village" designed for George Vanderbilt to complement his Biltmore House mansion complex. Twenty-four of the original structures remain; survivors include 3 designed by Richard Morris Hunt: All Souls Church (1896), Biltmore Railway Station (1896), and Biltmore Estate Office (1896). Despite years of alterations, overall character of the Village has survived. *Map, Self-Guided Tours*:

"Asheville Heritage Tour" brochure for Biltmore Village and other areas is available at Chamber of Commerce, Haywood Street, Asheville NC 28802, telephone (704)-258-3858.

Chestnut Hill HD

Late 19th to early 20th C. - Residential, with over 200 period structures illustrating city's early architectural sophistication. Of note: Beaufort Lodge (1895, Queen Anne), Spears House (1865, Italianate), and Thomas Patton House (1869, Greek Revival). Other styles include Colonial Revival, Shingle. A well-preserved district, with tree-lined streets and substantial segments of surviving brick sidewalks. *Map, Self-Guided Tours*: See **Biltmore Village HD.**

Manor and Cottages HD

1899-1920's - A small district composed of large Manor Inn (1899, Neo-Tudor), and a rambling group of cottages centered around the Inn. Cottages include Milfoil (1914, Shingle style) and Chipmunk (1920, Neo-Tudor). *Map, Self-Guided Tours*: See **Biltmore Village HD.**

Montford HD

1890-1930. Residential, upper middle-class; over 600 well-designed homes built as city's leading residential area, 1890-1930. Of note are 3 homes designed by Richard Sharpe Smith, supervising architect for Biltmore House, all built c. 1900: Rutledge House; Otis Green House; the Clarence Jordan House. Prevalent styles are blends of Queen Anne, Shingle, Bungaloid, half-timbered, and (especially) Colonial Revival. *Map, Self-Guided Tours*: See **Biltmore Village HD.**

Oteen Veterans Administration Hospital HD

1924-1940 - A striking collecton of white-frame Colonial Revival and massive yellow-stucco Georgian Revival structures. Was one of VA's larger treatment centers for tuberculosis and other respiratory diseases. VA still owns many of the older buildings which serve as dormitories, for adjacent hospital built in 1967. *General Information*: Chamber of Commerce, Asheville NC 28802, telephone (704)-258-3858.

BADIN

Badin HD

Early-20th C. - A company town, designed by a French firm for production of aluminum ingots using power from nearby

Narrows Dam. Latter was largest hydro-electric facility in North America when completed in 1917. Notable at the time for the quality of worker housing and a racially integrated work force.

West Badin HD
No further information available at this time.

BATH

Bath HD
18th-19th C. - Small river town contains a number of brick and frame buildings. Of note: St. Thomas Episcopal Church (brick, mid-1700's), Palmer-Marsh House (2-story frame, 1774), and Bonner House (clapboard, 1830's). Bath is state's oldest town, and there have been few modern intrusions. **H A B S** (State Historic site; admission fee). *Map, Self-Guided Tours*: Visitor Center, Box 124, Bath NC 27808, telephone (919)-923-3971. *Special Events*: Living History Weekend (mid-May, early June), Christmas Open House (Sunday in early December); contact Visitor Center.

BEAUFORT

Beaufort HD
18th-20th C. - First settled in 1710, developing into a small maritime village. Has remained small and water-oriented. Contains rows of white frame dwellings with porches, commercial and public buildings, wharves, and Old Burying Ground. A wide variety of styles, including Jacob House (1800-1850's, Federal-Greek Revival) and Gibbs House (1851, Greek Revival). **H A B S**. *Map, Self-Guided Tours*: Historical Association, 138 Turner St., Beaufort NC 28516. *Guided Tours*: See above. *Annual Homes Tour*: Last weekend in June; contact Kathryn Cloud, Beaufort Historical Association, POB 1709, Beaufort NC 28516.

BENSON

Benson HD
1900-1930 - A cohesive grouping of approximately 100 period buildings; commercial, religious, educational, and residential structures. A variety of architectural styles popular in late

19th - early 20th C. Tree-shaded residential streets are setting for an abundance of 1, 1 1/2, and 2-story houses, brick and frame. Many of town's wealthiest citizens lived here, with additional character provided by 6 major church buildings.

BLACK MOUNTAIN (VICINITY)

Black Mountain College HD

1924-1950's - College was a significant experiment in progressive education; supporters included John Dewey, Peggy Guggenheim, and Walter Gropius. Property today is a mix of vernacular wood-shingle cottage style and the smooth International Style associated with Bauhaus movement. Structures include 1920's Grover summer cottages, 1940's buildings in the International Style, and farm buildings from 1940's. Site now is Camp Rockmount for Boys.

Blue Ridge Assembly HD

1912-1930 - An impressive, well-landscaped and beautifully-sited architectural complex of approximately 28 white frame structures derived from Colonial and Neo-Classical Revival styles. Dominant building is Robert E. Lee Hall, an enormous frame structure designed by New York architect Louis Jallade, 1911-1912. Assembly is a YMCA conference center.

BRASSTOWN (VICINITY)

John C. Campbell Folk School HD

1920's-1930's - A campus of 366 acres in rural section of southeastern Cherokee County. A mix of American vernacular structures with buildings of European character; latter are evidence of Danish folk schools on which School is modeled. Campus is a working farm, curriculum chiefly in folk arts. Structures include early 20th C. farm house, variety of workshops and farm buildings, and a mountain farm museum collection of 19th C. log structures.

BURLINGTON

Lakeside Mills HD

1892-1893 - Mill buildings, adjoining mill village, unusually well preserved. Includes mill complex (factory, 3 related buildings), store, and 16 frame houses, 1, 1 1/2, and 2 stories. One of 5 textile mills established in Burlington between 1883-1892. Remains remarkably intact, retaining its original layout and semi-rural character.

West Davis Street - Fountain Place HD
1890-1930 - Residential neighborhood; was home for city's leading businessmen. Still intact, with a collection of fashionable homes; they range from traditional 1-story cottages to some of the finest examples of Queen Anne, Colonial Revival, and Neo-Classical.

BURLINGTON (VICINITY)

Glencoe HD
1880 to early 20th C. - One of North Carolina's best preserved mill villages, offering comprehensive picture of social and commercial organization of a late 19th C. water-powered Southern cotton mill village. Mill complex includes 3-story brick mill in Italianate style; worker tenement housing consists of small frame structures of uniform design. Located on 105-acre site along Haw River.

CAMERON

Cameron HD
c. 1876-1925 - Small linear rural village, with approximately 40 modest frame and brick buildings. Along Carthage St. is a compact community of houses, stores, and churches displaying elements of styles popular between 1875 and 1925. Town's prosperity came from turpentine distilleries, trade, and especially dewberry farming. *Annual Homes Tour*: Candlelight Tour (early December), contact Town of Cameron, POB 108, Cameron NC 28326.

CARRBORO

Carrboro Commercial District
c. 1910-1924 - Sixteen commercial structures, modestly detailed, 1 and 2 stories. District is an extension of adjacent Alberta Mill Complex, composed of mill, turn-of-the-century railroad station, and c. 1883 grist mill.

CATAWBA (VICINITY)

Murray's Mill HD

1913-1940's - Approximately 24 structures set on 150 acres of rolling landscape. Buildings include large 2-story frame mill (1913) and several homes belonging to 3 generations of Murray family, earliest dating from c. 1880. A picturesque district with original mill machinery, typical of water-powered mills once vital to Piedmont's rural economy.

CHAPEL HILL

Chapel Hill HD

18th-20th C. - Includes central campus of University of North Carolina, surrounding residential areas, and adjoining Battle Park area. Of note: East Hall (1795, first university structure), Gothic Revival, Chapel of the Cross (1845-1848), and Playmakers Theatre (1850). Excellent illustration of relationship between a well-planned and successful university, and surrounding community. *Annual Homes Tour*: Candlelight Tour (2nd or 3rd weekend, December), contact Chapel Hill Preservation Society, 610 E. Rosemary St., Chapel Hill NC 27514.

CHARLOTTE

Fourth Ward HD. (L)

No further information is available at this time.

CLEVELAND (VICINITY)

Knox Farm HD

1856 to 1980's - Thirty-three farm-complex buildings and land; location of continuous agricultural practice by the Knox family since John Knox (1708-1758) acquired the core of the farm. Buildings include the family seat, a vernacular Greek Revival house (1854-1856), and buildings of log and frame construction, plus modern factory-made materials. (Private; no public access).

COLERIDGE

Coleridge HD

1882-1930 - Well-preserved North Carolina mill village, with approximately 20 brick or frame structures. Many have Romanesque Revival and Queen Anne elements. Of note: John Caveness house (c. 1900, Queen Anne), and the Enterprise Cotton Mill. Located in North Carolina's oldest industrial area, largely abandoned in 1950's after manufacturing ceased.

CONCORD (HISTORIC CABARUS)

North and South Union Street HD

Mid-19th C. to early 20th C. - (L) North Union contains some 190 residences and religious structures associated with prosperous textile industry (beginning in 1880's). South Union, with about 96 properties, developed during town's industrial boom. Both contain a variety of styles, including vernacular Greek Revival, Italianate, Gothic Revival, and Second Empire. Both retain much of their period appearance. *General Information*: Historic Cabarrus, Inc., POB 966, Concord NC 28025.

Stonewall Jackson Training School HD

1909-1940 - Handsome campus with 50 school and farm buildings, state's first juvenile corrections facility. Most buildings constructed 1909-1930, brick, Colonial Revival, designed by architect Louis H. Asbury. A unified and impressive architectural grouping.

CRAMERTON

Cramerton HD

1906 to 1980's - Approximately 600 structures on 300 acres. Residences predominate, but also includes religious, office, educational, and commercial structures. Most common style is Bungaloid, with examples of Gothic, Romanesque, and Colonial Revival, and late-Victorian era styles. Except for elimination of the original textile mills, this former model mill village looks much as it did in 1920's. An excellent example of early 20th C. industrial planning. **H A E R**

DALLAS

Dallas HD

19th C. - Village of commercial buildings and residences centered around a Greek Revival courthouse. Oldest buildings include county jail, Rhyne Store, Smyre-Pasour House, and Hoffman Hotel (largest, best-preserved mid-19th C. hotel in state).

DANBURY

Danbury HD

Late 19th to early 20th C. - Office buildings, stores, hotels, churches, and homes representing major architectural styles of late-19th and early 20th C. when town was county seat. Imposing Beaux-Arts Neo-Classical Revival courthouse, c. 1900. Nearby mineral springs boasted luxurious resorts. Large shade trees and absence of paved sidewalks contribute to town charm. Little physical change in town's character since 1930.

DOBSON (VICINITY)

Rockford HD

Early 19th C. - Eighteen buildings, mostly frame, representing town's peak of prosperity, 1790-1851; they feature elements of vernacular Federal, Greek Revival, and Gothic Revival styles. Buildings include former courthouse, Masonic lodge, tobacco factory, and inns. *Guided Tours*: On request; contact Evelyn Holyfield, Rockford Preservation Society, Inc., Rt. 2, Box 311 A, Dobson NC 27017, telephone (919)-374-2502.

DURHAM

Bright Leaf HD

19th to early 20th C. - Thirty-five-acre industrial district composed of 24 primary structures, most of them part of the Liggett and Myers Tobacco Company's Durham plant. Of note: 5 warehouses and processing buildings (1890-1910) with elaborate ornamental construction. These structures rank among Durham's most visually exciting architectural landmarks.

Cleveland Street HD

1880-1920 - One of the few surviving portions of the city's most fashionable late 19th C. residential neighborhood, where many business and financial leaders built handsome 1 1/2 and 2 1/2-story homes. Mostly vernacular Queen Anne, interspersed with early Neo-Classical, Colonial Revival. Of note: Holloway-Hutchins House (1880's), and Howerton-Masser House (c. 1890). One of Durham's most significant concentrations of period homes of architectural, historical distinction.

Downtown HD

1900-1940 - A compact and relatively undisturbed commercial area with variety of buildings from city's boom period. They include a castellated fortress-type armory, a Beaux-Arts bank, Art Deco department store, Italianate firehouse, and several Gothic Revival churches. Of note: former headquarters of North Carolina Mutual Life Insurance Co. (**N H L**), largest black-owned business in U.S.

Durham Cotton Mills Village HD

1880's - Fifteen houses from mid-1880's, part of Durham's first mill village. Houses are 1 1/2 stories, 1-room deep, with central chimneys, set in straight rows, all with uniform setbacks. Believed to be unique in the Piedmont region.

Golden Belt HD

1901-c. 1930 - Cigarette-related industrial plants, company-built housing, and a small commercial area. Plants are notable examples of industrial architecture; they are of "slow burn" construction, with classicized treatment of main facades and towers. Also dozens of examples of 2 periods of mill housing: traditional rural house-type from c. 1900, and bungalows, c. 1920's.

Holloway Street HD

1880's-1920's - Residential remnant of what was Durham's most fashionable neighborhood, where many of city's business leaders built handsome houses. Contains noteworthy examples of vernacular Queen Anne and Classical Revival.

Moorehead Hill HD

1870's-1930's - Residential, 14 blocks, approximately 100 buildings of interest. Wide range of types and styles, including outstanding Spanish Colonial Revival and Chateauesque styles. Homes of note: "Greystone", John Sprunt Mill House.

North Durham-Duke Park HD

1880's-1930's - Includes one of Durham's earliest suburbs, an early commercial area, and portions of 1930's residential community. Contains excellent examples of late 19th, early 20th C. styles, including Queen Anne, classical revivals, and Bungalow.

Pearl Mill Village HD

1905-1924 - Twenty-six mill houses, the only intact vestige of one of city's 4 principal late 19th C. textile mills. Twenty-two of the mill houses built as duplexes, c. 1905; 2 stories, 1-room deep, frame, with central brick chimneys. Has retained much of its original appearance

Trinity HD

1890's-c. 1940 - Primarily residential, reflecting city's fashionable architecture. Predominant styles are vernacular Queen Anne, Neo-Colonial, and Colonial Revival. Contains Durham's largest, best-preserved concentration of popular residential architecture of the period.

West Durham HD

1892-1910 - Approximately 90 acres of industrial buildings, company-built housing, and early 20th C. commercial district. Focus is the industrial complex, Erwin Cotton Mills Company's Mill No. 1 and Mill No. 4. Constructed in 1892 and 1910, they exemplify industrial architecture of the time. District also characterized by traditional rural mill house types.

EDENTON

Edenton HD

Early 18th-19th C. - Handsome river community offering a variety of styles, including Federal, Greek and Gothic Revival, Queen Anne, and Bungaloid. Three important Georgian structures are the Cupola House (c. 1725), Chowan County Courthouse (1767), and St. Paul's Church. N H L; H A B S. *Map, Self-Guided Tours*: Historic Edenton, Barker House, (919) 482-2637, POB 474, Edenton NC 27932. *Guided Tours* See above. *Annual Homes Tour*: Edenton Spring Pilgrimage, in odd-numbered years; Christmas Candlelight Tour (mid-December); contact Historic Edenton.

ELIZABETH CITY

Elizabeth City HD

19th C. - Thirty-block area, half residential, half commercial, on the Pasquotank River. A remarkable collection of commercial buildings, including 7 antebellum buildings (Italianate, Greek and Gothic Revival) and a number of well-preserved late Victorians. Other highlights include handsome historic county government buildings and 9 antebellum homes. Oldest is Grice-Fearing House (1789-1808, Georgian). Town is terminus for Dismal Swamp Canal, oldest surviving man-made waterway in U.S.

Downtown HD

(L) No further information available at this time.

West Main St. HD

(L) No further information available at this time.

ELM CITY

Elm City HD

Late 19th to early 20th C. - Primarily residential, approximately 100 structures. Includes modest 1-story frame cottages of 1880's and massive brick Classical Revival residences, c. 1900. Residential streets are broad and lined with mature shade trees. A well-preserved community exhibiting fine examples of architecture; relatively unchanged since 1929.

FAIRFIELD

Fairfield HD

c. 1850-20th C. - Village on north shore of Lake Mattamuskeet, with collection of frame houses, churches, and stores from town's booming canal era. Buildings feature local builders' interpretations of Italianate and Gothic Revival styles. With decline of the Fairfield Canal, this pleasant rural community has survived remarkably intact.

FAYETTEVILLE

Haymount HD

c. 1817-1950 - Residential, 41 significant structures illustrating major architectural trends over 130 years: Federal, Greek Revival, Victorian-era styles, Colonial Revival, Bungalow. Approximately 30 buildings are from 1900-1930. One of city's oldest, most desirable neighborhoods. Of note: Robert Strange Town House (c. 1817, Federal), Smith-Lauder House (c. 1853, Greek Revival), and Dr. Raymond Pittman house c. 1920, Tudor Revival).

Liberty Row HD

Early 1800's-1916 - A total of 14 brick buildings, the oldest being the Liberty Point Store (undated, Federal-period design); other stores date from 1846 to 1916. One of the most cohesive 19th C. commercial rows in North Carolina, with examples of vernacular Federal, Italianate, and Romanesque Revival. A unique area of the city, both historically and architecturally.

Market House Square HD

1884-1926 - Ten commercial buildings surrounding the historic 1830's Market House (N H L), an impressive brick structure modeled after 18th C. English town hall. Other buildings include 2 Italianate store fronts (c. 1884) with cast-iron decoration, a 4-story Second Empire drugstore, and a 5-story Mediterranean Revival office building, c. 1916.

FLAT ROCK

Historic Flat Rock HD

19th C. - Residential area along a winding tree-shaded road, featuring large estates set well back from road and generally not accessible to the public. Wide variety of styles, including Federal, Greek and Gothic Revivals, Second Empire, and Neo-Classical Revival. Of note: Argyle Estate (Federal), St. John-in-the-Wilderness Church (Gothic Revival), and the Saluda Cottages (Second Empire). **H A B S.** *Annual Homes Tour*: First Friday in August,; contact Historic Flat Rock, Inc., POB 295, Flat Rock NC 28731. *General Information*: Historic Flat Rock, Inc., Old Post Office, Greenville Highway, Flat Rock NC 28731.

FRANKLINVILLE

Franklinville HD

19th to early 20th C. - The town was originally 2 antebellum textile-mill villages. Twenty-two pre-1860 structures, including Johnson-Julian House (1819), 9 mill houses (c. 1838), and several others, c. 1850. Also a number of modest 20th C. dwellings with aluminum or asbestos siding. A remarkably intact example of the growth of the textile industry and attendant villages in North Carolina during 19th - early 20th C.

GRAHAM

Graham HD

1880-1940 - Commercial, civic, and residential, centering on courthouse square with handsome 1923 Neo-Classical courthouse. District also includes a few mid-19th C. domestic buildings, several elaborately adorned late 19th C. residences, and an intact late 19th C. neighborhood. Architectural styles in district include Italianate, Second Empire, Queen Anne, Romanesque, Art Deco, and Art Moderne.

GRASSY CREEK

Grassy Creek HD

1812-1950 - Residential-agricultural, including approximately 30 masonry or frame, clapboarded 2 and 2 1/2-story dwellings with numerous dependencies. Of note: Aquilla Greer house (late Federal), the Walter Greer house (with Eastlake porch), and Grassy Creek Methodist Church (Gothic Revival). Has retained its late 19th - early 20th C. agricultural character.

GREENSBORO

Charles B. Aycock HD

1890-1930 - (L) Approximately 250 buildings; major styles are Queen Anne, Neo-Classical Revival, Box, and Bungalow. Of note: Sigmund Steinberger house (1930, Venetian Renaissance Revival), Rucker House (1915, Neo-Classical Revival), and Tar Heel Manor (1920, Colonial Revival). *General Information*: City Planning Dept., One Governmental Plaza, Greensboro NC 27401, telephone (919)-373-2144.

College Hill HD

1880–1920 – (L) Approximately 300 buildings, with Queen Anne, Box, and Bungalow styles prominent. Of note: Bumpass Troy House (1847, Greek Revival), Trogdon House (1900, Queen Anne), and the Wafco Mill, (1893–1913), ornamented brick industrial building. *Map, Self-Guided Tours*: City Planning Dept., One Governmental Plaza, Greensboro NC 27435. *Annual Homes Tour*: College Hill Tour of Homes, POB 5605, Greensboro NC 27435.

Downtown HD

c. 1885–1930 – Primarily commercial; most buildings are simplified Italianate style, oldest dating from 1880's. More ornate structures from 1890's feature cast-iron columns, granite sills, galvanized iron cornices. This modest district typical of urbanization in smaller U.S. cities, from late 19th to early 20th C. *Special Events*: Fun Fourth of July in Old Greensburough, POB 1047, Greensboro NC 27402.

Fisher Park HD

1910–1940 – (L) Approximately 300 buildings; major styles are Neo-Classical, Colonial Revival, and Bungalow. Of note: Latham House (1919, Elizabethan Revival), Julian Price House (1928, Tudor Revival), and First Presbyterian Church (1928, Monumental Early English Gothic Revival). *General Information*: See **Charles Aycock HD**.

HALIFAX

Halifax HD

18th–19th C. – District, near head of the Roanoke River, contains buildings of frame and brick, with 18th–19th C. stylistic elements. Original structures include Constitution House, Owen House (c. 1760), Clerk's Office (c. 1832) and jail (c. 1838). North Carolina State Historic Site. **H A B S**. *Guided Tours*: By arrangement, Halifax Visitor Center, Halifax NC 27839, telephone (919)-583-7191. *Special Events*: Halifax Day (April 13); contact Visitor Center, POB 406, Halifax NC 27839.

HAMILTON

Hamilton HD

19th to early 20th C. – Small riverside town on Roanoke River, with remarkable collection of significant period buildings. Features Greek Revival, Carpenter Gothic, and Queen Anne-style buildings, naively interpreted and boldly executed by a group of local builders. Of note: Edmondson-Purvis House (c. 1810-1820 ?), and the Waldo-Darden Hotel (Greek Revival temple form). Has retained its unique architectural character, and its small-town atmosphere.

HICKORY

Claremont High School HD

1870's-1950's - Intact residential neighborhood contains homes of 3 generations of city's leaders. Buildings provide significant examples of nearly every popular architectural style from 1870's to 1950's. Of special interest: Third Avenue, with Claremont High School (Neo-Classical), 3 fine Queen Anne residences, and 3 imposing early Colonial Revival houses.

Kenworth HD

1913-1920's - Small residential area contains 23 structures, representing 2 periods of town's development: the original 1913 suburb; and the 1920's boom period. Features many diverse examples of the Bungalow, a number of Colonial Revival buildings, and an impressive Neo-Gothic church.

Oakwood HD

Late 19th to early 20th C. - One of the most intact turn-of-the-century neighborhoods in Hickory, with varied collection of frame and brick residences. Includes modest examples of popular styles and a sizeable group of architecturally significant houses representing fashionable house forms, 1880-1940's. Has continued to be an upper-middle class area.

Second Street Place Southwest HD

Early 20th C. - Small district containing the most impressive, relatively intact group of commercial and government structures in town. Includes former Southern Railroad Passenger Station, National Guard Armory (which once contained a livery stable), and former U.S. Post Office.

HICKORY (VICINITY)

Yoder's Mills HD

Late 19th to early 20th C. - Rural milling and farm district, on State Road 1144. Contains farm house with outbuildings and several rural industries (including grist mill, saw mill, brick yard, and sorghum processing plant). A significant undisturbed example of post-frontier development in the Piedmont region.

HILLSBOROUGH

Hillsborough HD

Late 18th - 19th C. Numerous buildings, the majority being Federal and Greek Revival, some with Victorian touches. Of note: Hazel-Nash House (c. 1820, late Georgian), the 18th C. frame Nash-Hooper House (N H L), and the 1823 Eagle Masonic Lodge. H A B S. *Map, Self-Guided Tours*: Orange County Historical Museum, Old Courthouse, Hillsborough NC 27278, 1:30-4:30 p.m., except Mondays. *Annual Homes Tour*: Spring Tour (odd-numbered years), Historical Society, E. Corbin St., Hillsborough NC 27278, telephone (919)-732-8648. *General Information*: Historical Society; also Chamber of Commerce, 228 S. Churton St., Hillsborough NC 27278, telephone (919)-732-8156.

HOPE MILLS

Hope Mills HD

Late 19th to early 20th C. - Site of state's largest antebellum cotton mill as well as 2 post-Civil War cotton factories, one of which reportedly may still be operating. Seventy-four structures of interest, a mix of industrial, residential, commercial, and religious buildings. Oldest structure is Colin MacRae House, c. 1828. Town is typical textile-mill community, with rows of housing, the company store, and bank.

JAMESTOWN

Jamestown HD

18th-19th C. - Quaker settlers from Pennsylvania first held monthly meetings in 1754; town developed into state's leading Quaker community. Features 1-story Jamestown Friends meetinghouse, the 2 1/2-story brick Mendenhall Store, and 1811 Richard Mendenhall Plantation Buildings. **H A B S**

Oakdale Cotton Mill Village HD
1880's - A store and 36 2-story frame houses surrounding a textile factory complex. Factory buildings are 2-story brick, one having a 4-story Italianate tower. Mill belonged to the oldest textile firm in continuous operation in North Carolina. **H A E R**

KENANSVILLE

Kenansville HD
1840-1860 - Rural county seat community with 71 predominantly frame structures, 1 and 2 stories, incorporating elements of Greek Revival. Of note: Dr. David Gillespie house (Greek Revival), and the Neo-Classical Revival Courthouse. Has retained its homogeneous early 19th C. character, with a wealth of Greek Revival architecture.

LAKE LANDING

Lake Landing HD
c. 1800-20th C. - Historic rural landscape on Lake Mattamuskeet, remarkably free of modern intrusions. Contains outstanding examples of antebellum plantation houses, and also typical vernacular examples of domestic, agricultural, and commercial architecture.

LINVILLE

Linville HD
1888-1980's - One of western North Carolina's best preserved and most prestigious resort communities from 19th and early 20th C. Features a collection of rustic cottages covered in chestnut-bark shingles (style initiated by architect Henry Bacon, designer of the Lincoln Memorial), and a later group of rambling Neo-Tudor homes (half-timbered), designed by Harry Stearns. Unblemished atmosphere, free of any commercial intrusions.

LUCAMA

Lucama HD

Late 19th to early 20th C. - Small railroad town with fine examples of commercial, residential, and religious architecture. Approximately 50 period buildings, mostly 1 and 2-story frame residences on tree-lined streets. Of note: c. 1905 train depot, early 20th C. Methodist Church. Has retained much of its turn-of-the-century atmosphere.

MADISON

Academy Street HD

1824-1930 - Residential, featuring finely detailed homes set amidst manicured lawns and lush foliage. Town enjoyed decades of tobacco prosperity and structures reflect 3 periods of development: pre-Civil War, 1865-1900, and 1900-1930. Styles include Federal, Greek Revival, those of the Victorian era, and Colonial Revival. Of note: Twitchell-Gallaway House (1824, Federal-Greek Revival), and Foy-McAnally House (1840-52, Greek Revival).

Decatur - Hunter HD

(L) No further information available at this time.

MILTON

Milton HD

18th-19th C. - Village contains mostly 19th C. 2-story dwellings, some commercial buildings, and several small-scale churches. Styles include Federal, Greek Revival, and Victorian-era. After considerable growth in mid-19th C., town declined for lack of railroad service. **H A B S**. *General Information*: Caswell County Chamber of Commerce, Old Courthouse, Yanceyville NC 27379, telephone (919)-694-6106.

MOORESVILLE

Mooresville HD

c. 1870-1920 - Approximately 80 structures, 3/4's commercial, remainder residential. A broad variety of interesting examples of such styles as late Greek Revival, Italianate, Gothic Revival, Queen Anne, Colonial Revival, and Modernistic. Town growth at turn-of-the-century spurred by Atlantic, Tennessee and Ohio Railroad; depot (replacement built 1914-1925) still marks historical center of town.

MOUNT AIRY

Mount Airy HD

Late 19th to early 20th C. - Two hundred forty-eight commercial and residential buildings within a compact, largely intact 22-block area. Unique in North Carolina due to widespread use of a local light-colored granite. An unusually sophisticated variety of styles including Italianate, Queen Anne, Gothic and Romanesque Revival, Art Deco, Spanish Colonial Revival, and English Cottage. Relatively little modern intrusion.

MOUNT PLEASANT

Mount Pleasant Collegiate Institute HD

1854-1925 - First school on this site founded in 1852 as Western Carolina Male Academy by North Carolina Synod of Evangelical Lutheran Church of America. Frame and brick structures typical of vernacular architecture in North Carolina; they include Main Building (1854-55), and the President's House (1854-55, Greek Revival). Although some alterations, impressive campus has retained the charm and presence of its past.

MURFREESBORO

Murfreesboro HD

18th-19th C. - Central historic area of town contains numerous late 18th and 19th C. dwellings and structures, including William Rea Store (c. 1790), and John Wheeler House (c. 1800). Incorporated in 1787, town was area's principal port by 1792. Has retained its 19th C. appearance. **H A B S.** *Map, Self-Guided Tours*: Murfreesboro Historical Association, 116 E. Main St., Murfreesboro NC 27855, telephone (919)-398-4886. *Guided Tours*: Daily, Monday-Saturday; see above. *Annual Homes Tour*: Christmas Open House (2nd Monday in December); Spring Heritage Weekend (April), even-numbered years. Contact Historical Association.

NAGS HEAD

Nags Head Beach Cottage Row HD

Late 19th to early 20th C. - A densely packed line of starkly handsome wood-shingled frame beach cottages extending nearly 1 mile, overlooking Atlantic. Two major types: pre-1910 cottages and those from 1910-1940. Has retained most of its original character; a resort since pre-Civil War for families of merchants, planters, and professional men of northeastern North Carolina.

NEW BERN

New Bern HD

18th-20th C. - Founded in 1710, town became colonial capitol in 1765; late 18th - early 19th C. commercial growth due to nearby rivers and government support. This impressive and handsome district contains original town center, with government, commercial, religious, and residential structures. Featured styles are primarily Georgian, Federal, and late 19th C. Of note: reconstructed 1765 Governor's Palace and Tryon Palace Complex, Chapman-Taylor House (1790), Coor-Bishop House (1767), and Jones-Jarvis House (1810-1816). **H A B S.** *Map, Self-Guided Tours*: Tryon Palace Visitors Center, Box 1007, New Bern NC 28560, telephone (919)-638-5109; also Chamber of Commerce Visitor Information Center, 211 Broad St., New Bern NC 28560, telephone (919)-637-3111. *Guided Tours*: Casette tape rental, Chamber of Commerce. *Annual Homes Tour*: Christmas Season at Tryon Palace; Spring Historic Homes Tour (April). Contact Chamber of Commerce.

OAK RIDGE

Oak Ridge Military Academy HD

Guided Tours: By arrangement; contact Academy, New Bern NC, telephone (919)-643-4131. *Special Events*: Open House: Mother's Day; 1st Saturday in October; mid-February.

PINEHURST

Pinehurst HD

1895-early 20th C. - Village was designed in 1890's by

Frederick Law Olmstead under patronage of James W. Tufts, Boston inventor, as winter health resort for middle-class northerners. Commercial and residential structures, including Holly Inn, the Casino, general store, boardinghouses, and cottages.

RALEIGH

Blount Street HD

19th C. - (L) Features a fashionable Victorian-era neighborhood, and includes late 19th C. Governor's Mansion on Burke Square. Many former elegant homes now being used as State offices, illustrating adaptive use in historic preservation. *General Information*: Brochure, Historic Districts Commission, Mordecai Historic Park, 1 Mimosa St., Raleigh NC 27604, telephone (919)-832-7238.

Boylan Heights HD

Early 20th C. - A classic early 20th C. residential neighborhood, developed by syndicate of leading realtors, politicians, and local VIPs. Of note: Montfort Hall (1858, Italianate). Considerable restoration after a decline in 1950's-1960's. *General Information*: See **Blount St. HD**.

Cameron Park HD

Early 20th C. - The most exclusive of city's 3 major early 20th C. neighborhoods, launched in 1910 to attract upper middle-class. Features large single-family homes on curving tree-lined streets, and row houses of stucco and half-timber. *General Information*: See **Blount St. HD**; also, contact Cameron Park Association.

Capitol Square HD

19th-early 20th C. - Contains some of city's earliest surviving buildings. Focal point is magnificent granite Capitol (1840, Greek Revival), I. Towne and A. J. Davis, architects,. Of interest: Christ Episcopal Church 1848), First Baptist (1858), First Presbyterian (1900), and First Baptist (1904). *General Information*: See **Blount St. HD**.

Glenwood HD

Early 20th C. - City's first early 20th C. planned residential development. Streetcar lines in 1907 made it possible for growing middle class to move to suburbs. A remarkably intact neighborhood. *General Information*: See **Blount St. HD**.

Moore Square HD

Early 20th C. - Historic commercial neighborhood, featuring a 4-acre wooded park, 1 of 2 surviving downtown parks included in 1792 city plan. Of note: City Market (1914, Spanish Mission style), the historic Tabernacle Baptist Church, and the Montague Building. *General Information*: See **Blount St. HD**.

Oakwood HD

Late 19th C. - Twenty-block residential area; contains brick and frame examples of Greek Revival, Second Empire, and various Victorian-era styles including Queen Anne. Raleigh's only intact 19th C. neighborhood. *Map, Self-Guided Tours*: Capital Area Visitor Center, 301 N. Blount St., Raleigh NC 27601, telephone (919)-833-3005; Convention and Visitor Bureau, Chamber of Commerce, 335 S. Salisbury St., Raleigh NC 27602. *Guided Tours*: Oakwood Publicity, Raleigh NC, telephone (919)-828-3691.

St. Mary's College HD

1842-early 20th C. - Twenty-nine campus buildings, from simple 1830's structures to more decorative Gothic and Neo-Classical buildings, and some contemporary buildings. Of note: Smedes Building, 4-story Greek Revival-Neo-Classical Revival, and the frame Chapel in Carpenter Gothic (attributed to Richard Upjohn). College founded in 1842, has retained its original campus of 23 acres, now heavily shaded with stately oaks.

ROCKFORD

Rockford HD

19th-early 20th C. - A tiny rural town with a handful of buildings, mostly unoccupied. They include the York Tavern (c. 1800, Federal), several c. 1900 frame houses, and the Methodist Church (1912, late Gothic Revival). Other early buildings are the Grant-Burrus Hotel and the Masonic Lodge.

ROCKINGHAM

Rockingham HD

1838-1922 - Over 200 buildings, mostly residential. Oldest structure is the 1838 Steel-Johnson-Cole House. Of note: a number of impressive residences built betwen 1850 and 1870, on main thoroughfare, Fayetteville Road. Much charm, with broad, tree-shaded streets. *General Information*: Public Library (Rockingham Room); also Historic District Commission, 311 E. Franklin St., Rockingham NC 28379; Chamber of Commerce, 220 E. Washington St., Rockingham NC 28379, telephone (919)-895-9058.

ROCKY MOUNT

Central City HD

1890's-early 20th C. - A cohesive collection of commercial and industrial buildings, highlighted by Main Street with railroad tracks down the middle, flanked by blocks of handsome brick commercial buildings. Another impressive streetscape of similar buildings on nearby Washington Street. District defined at south end by an imposing red brick railroad depot, and collection of tobacco warehouses at the north.

ROXBORO

Commercial HD

Late 19th C.-1930 - Seventy commercial and government buildings in 5-block area, with handsome 1930 Neo-Classical Courthouse as focal point. A predominance of early 20th C. vernacular brick commercial structures, but also such styles as Classic Revival and Art Deco. Town's principal growth came after construction of Durham & Lynchburg Railroad in 1890.

SALISBURY

Salisbury HD

18th to early 19th C. - Two hundred forty governmental, residential, and religious structures. Styles include Federal, Richardsonian Romanesque, Spanish Mission, Beaux-Arts, and Neo-Classical Revival. Of note: Greek Revival courthouse, Murdoch-Wiley House (Italianate), and St. Lukes Episcopal Church (late Gothic Revival). Once a major trade and political center for region, district has retained much of its early architectural character. **H A B S**. *Map, Self-Guided Tours*: Chamber of Commerce, 620 W. Innes St., Salisbury NC 28144, telephone (704)-633-4221; also Historic Salisbury Foundation, 100 W. Innes St., Salisbury NC 27144, telephone

(704)-636-0103. *Guided Tours*: Contact Historic Salisbury Foundation. *Annual Homes Tour*: October Tour; contact Foundation, POB 4221, Salisbury NC 28144.

Brooklyn-South Square HD
1840-1930 - Residential neighborhood of approximately 90 structures, with rich variety of late Federal, Greek Revival, Italianate, and late-Victorian period domestic architecture. Among earliest houses: Woodson-Overcash House (c. 1840), and Blackmer-Propst House (c. 1856).

Kesler Manufacturing Co. - Cannon Mills Co. No. 7 HD
1895-1928 - Substantial brick mill complex, warehouses, and an intact surrounding mill village of 1- and 2-story frame houses built in several models. Best preserved mill complex in Salisbury, with attractive village streetscapes.

Livingstone College HD
1882 to early 20th C. - Fine example of a nearly intact black college community of late 19th - early 20th C., with campus and adjoining residential area. College buildings are Victorian eclectic; modest homes provide a pleasing example of a middle-class community from the late Victorian era.

North Long Street - Park Avenue HD
1891-1926 - Residential neighborhood with 46 dwellings, church, and 2 commercial buildings; contains large, elaborate houses of prosperous businessmen, and smaller dwellings of clerks, etc. Area developed over nearly 4 decades, and possesses a rich and varied architectural fabric; provides an interesting record of late Victorian, turn-of-the-century, and Bungalow domestic architecture.

North Main Street HD
c. 1896-1935 - Attractive residential area developed from c. 1900 to 1935, prosperity stimulated by growth of nearby Spencer Shops of Southern Railroad Company. District contains examples of late-Victorian era, Colonial Revival, and Bungalow domestic styles.

SANFORD

Downtown HD
1895-1930 - Commercial, with approximately 100 structures, most of them typical designs of late 19th - early 20th C.,

brick, 1 to 3 stories. Sanford is known as the brick capital of the U.S.; buildings, with their handsome brickwork, terra cotta ornamentation, and brownstone trim, symbolize community's history, especially 1890 - 1930 boom.

SELMA

Selma HD

Late 19th to early 20th C. - Town founded in 1867, prospering because of its location on Atlantic Coast Line Railroad route, and the cotton industry. A number of large hotels and homes reflect boom of the 1880's. Of note: John Parker House (c. 1885), the Selma Cotton Mills (1905), the Dean Oil Co. (c. 1870, late Greek Revival), and the Norwell-Mayerburg-Oliver House (c. 1910, Queen Anne). *Map, Self-Guided Tours*: Chamber of Commerce, 934-9166; Town Offices, 100 N. Raeford St., Selma NC 27576, telephone (919)-965-9841; Thompson Realtors, 211 N. Raeford St., Selma NC 27576, telephpone (919)-965-2366. *Annual Homes Tour*: Railroad Days Festival, 1st weekend, October.

SHELBY

Central Shelby HD

1840's-1930's - An architectural mix characteristic of a North Carolina courthouse town. White frame antebellum houses amidst Gothic Revival cottages, and great columned Colonial Revival homes. Courthouse square dominated by the Courthouse (1907, Classic Revival). Commercial section, early 1900's, features blocks of brick buildings with metal cornices. *General Information*: Economic Development Commission, PO Drawer 207, Shelby NC 28150, telephone (704)-487-6331.

SOUTHPORT

Southport HD

Late 19th C. - Small coastal town which retains its late 19th C. appearance, with meandering streets canopied with large oak trees, no curbs. Modest frame houses, late-19th C., are 1 and 2 stories, and feature repetitive configurations and simple stylistic details. Town's major livelihood was river piloting on Cape Fear River. *Annual Homes Tour*: Spring House and Garden Tour; Southport Candlelight Tour (December). Contact

Southport Historical Society, 501 N. Atlantic Avenue, Southport NC 28461. *General Information*: See Historical Society for purchase of architectural brochure.

SPENCER

Spencer HD

1897–1940 - Town established in 1897 to house management, skilled workers, at Southern Railway's new shops. Residential, with 322 buildings; most houses are conservative examples of Italianate, Queen Anne, Classical Revival, and Bungalow styles. Railroad shops closed in 1960; district has survived with few modern intrusions.

STATESVILLE

Academy Hill HD

1880's–1930 - Neighborhood of approximately 45 residential, educational, and industrial buildings. Most houses are frame, a few of brick. Simplified Queen Anne style very prominent; other influences include Second Empire, Colonial and Classical Revival. Of note: 2 Steele family houses near the old J. S. Steele and Sons brick works; Statesville Male Academy (1874), now a private residence. District has retained much of its late 19th - early 20th C. appearance.

Commercial District

Late 19th to early 20th C. - Oldest commercial area of the town, plus government structures including the old Courthouse with its adjacent statue of a Confederate soldier on marble pedestal. Contains excellent examples of such styles as Late Victorian Commercial, Romanesque Revival, Beaux-Arts, Neo-Classical Revival, and 1920's Eclectic. Most outstanding building: 1892 City Hall, probably finest example of Richardsonian Romanesque in North Carolina.

East Broad Street - Davis Avenue HD

c. 1880–c. 1918 - About 76 residences, mostly single-family. Most buildings well preserved, set amidst large lots and wide, tree-lined streets. One of town's highest concentrations of architecturally significant houses. Displays varying degrees of influence from such styles as Italianate, Gothic Revival, Queen Anne, Colonial and Neo-Classical Revival, and Elizabethan and Tudor Revival.

Mitchell Colleqe HD

Late 19th to early 20th C. - Over 200 buildings, including College and many large frame homes built for middle and upper classes. College is focal point, and includes monumental Main Building (1854-56). Scores of architecturally significant houses exhibiting a wide range of popular period styles. Of note: Friends Meeting House (c. 1875), Congregation Emanual Synagogue (1891).

TARBORO

Tarboro HD.

18th to early 20th C. - Numerous well-preserved homes and buildings, ranging from colonial to antebellum to the Victorian era. Downtown commercial section retains strong turn-of-the-century flavor. Of note: Town Commons (est. 1760, 16 acres), Blount-Bridgers House (c. 1808), the Philips Dependency (c. 1860), and Calvary Episcopal Church (c. 1859). *Map, Self-Guided Tours*: Blount-Bridgers House, 130 Bridgers St., Tarboro NC 27886, telephone (919)-823-4159. *Annual Homes Tour*: Candlelight Tour of Historic Homes (2nd. weekend in October); Blount-Bridgers House, POB 220, Tarboro NC 27886.

Terrell HD

Late 19th to early 20th C. - Small, rural crossroads community, including an 1850's farmhouse of vernacular Greek Revival influence, an outstanding Stick Style house from 1880's, a well-preserved country store and post office typical of late 19th C., early-20th C. grist mill.

TRAPHILL

Traphill HD

1847-1921 - Small rural village community in foothills of Blue Ridge Mountains, with approximately a dozen simple vernacular buildings. They include the Joseph Bryan House (c. 1847), Old Storehouse (1850-79), 2 churches. Town was once an educational center known throughout western North Carolina.

TRENTON

Trenton HD

19th C. - County seat and market center for surrounding agricultural area. A small district with domestic, commercial, and religious structures, mostly frame. Styles include Federal, Gothic Revival, and Eastlake. Of interest: Jacob Huggins House (Federal), and 2 Gothic Revival churches.

WAKE FOREST

Wake Forest HD

(L) No further information available at this time.

WARRENTON

Warrenton HD

1779-20th C. - Over 300 buildings, frame or brick, 1 and 2 stories. Of note is a group of 36 Greek Revival and Greco-Italianate structures built 1840-1860; see the Somerville-Graham House and "Engleside". Town, established as county seat in 1779, developed as a center for the county's plantation society. Has retained much of its antebellum character. *Map, Self-Guided Tours*: Town Hall, Police Station, or County Manager's Office; also Warren County Historical Association, 210 Plummer St., Warrenton NC 27589.

WASHINGTON

Washington HD

Late 18th-19th C. - A river-port town offering an impressive array of residential and commercial structures despite major fires in Civil War and in 1900. Of note: Myers House (1760), Hyatt House (1785), Old Beaufort County Courthouse (c. 1786), Bank of Washington (c. 1852, Greek Revival), Havens house (c. 1820), and the Mallison Building (c. 1870, commercial Victorian). *Map, Self-Guided Tours*: Chamber of Commerce, 138 S. Market St., Washington NC 27889, telephone (919)-946-9168.

WILMINGTON

Wilminqton HD

1720's-20th C. - Urban coastal settlement which has served as major Cape Fear River port, and political-cultural-commercial center. Two hundred-block district includes wide variety of styles ranging from Georgian to 20th C. Neo-Classical Revival, with much Italianate influence. Of note: Burgwin-Wright House (c. 1770, Colonial), Thalian Hall opera house (c. 1858), and Latimer House (1852, Italianate). *Map, Self-Guided Tours*: Public Library, 2nd and Chestnut, Wilmington NC 28402, telephone (919)-763-3303; Thalian Hall, 305 Princess St., Wilmington NC 28402, telephone (919)-763-9328; AAA Motor Club, 17th and Market (Shopping Center), Wilmington NC 28402, telephone (919)-763-8446. *Annual Homes Tour*: Azalea Festival House Tour (April), contact Residents of Old Wilmington, POB 1862, Wilmington, NC 28402; Old Wilmington by Candlelight (December), contact Lower Cape Fear Historical Society, POB 813, Wilmington, NC 28402.

Carolina Heiqhts HD

(L) Primarily residential, 250 structures.

Market Street Mansion HD

1907-1917 - Small residential district of only 4 mansions, brick or frame, 2 and 2 1/2 stories, in Neo-Classical and Georgian Revival styles. Built as part of early-20th C. development of 2 early, progressive examples of suburban planning initiated by Mary Bridgers, wealthy Wilmington heiress.

WILSON

Central Business-Tobacco Warehouses HD

Late 19th to early 20th C. - Includes a number of impressive Renaissance Neo-Classical public buildings, and a large and varied collection of brick vernacular commercial buildings. The 8 massive tobacco warehouses date from 1890 to 1928; the most important such collection in the U.S.

Old Wilson HD

1850's-1920's - Residential, approximately 360 properties among 5 adjacent neighborhoods. Noteworthy examples of all major architectural styles from the 1850's through the 1930's.

Includes a few surviving Italianate and Gothic Revival houses, a fine collection of modest late 19th C. Victorian cottages, a varied group of Queen Anne residences, and a group of early 20th C. Colonial Revival houses. Also, one of finest collections of bungalows in North Carolina, from town's tobacco and cotton boom, 1910's-1920's.

West Nash Street HD

Early 20th C. - A remarkable collection of impressive residences built in the early 20th C. for the city's elites; district stretches for 9 blocks along one of North Carolina's loveliest residential avenues. Includes outstanding examples of Neo-Classical Revival, Colonial and Georgian Revival, and Tudoresque. Most impressive house is the splendid William W. Graves House, Georgian Revival. This district features mature water-oak street trees, shade from a lush canopy of vegetation, and exceptionally deep setbacks for many of the homes.

WINSTON-SALEM

Old Salem HD

18th C. - Museum district is a well-preserved example of an 18th C. colonial community. Includes approximately 22 residential and commercial buildings, mostly of brick, frame, or half-timber construction. Founded in 1766 by Moravians from Bethlehem, Pennsylvania; more than half of the original buildings survive. Of note: Single Brothers House (1768, NHL), and the Salem Tavern (1784). **NHL; HABS.** *General Information*: See Museum Reception Office for admission charges, brochure, and such Special Events as "Christmas in Old Salem".

Reynolda HD

1913-1917 - Covers 178 acres and includes Reynolda House (a gracious Colonial Revival mansion), Gardens, Village, and Presbyterian Church. Once part of a larger self-sufficient country estate developed by founder of R. J. Reynolds Tobacco Co. Gardens designed by Thomas W. Sears, mansion by Charles Barton Keen, Philadelphia architect.

WINSTON-SALEM (VICINITY)

Bethabara HD

18th to early 19th C. - Encompasses the Moravians' original settlement, established in 1753 and used as base while Salem was being constructed, 1766-1772. Of note: 1788 Church (in regular use until 1953), the 1782 Potter's House, and the 1803 Brewer's Residence (museum). Now a facility of Winston-Salem Dept. of Recreation. Handsome restorations amidst outdoor setting, evoking atmosphere of the past. *Map, Self-Guided Tours*: Museum-Reception Center, Historic Bethabara, Winston-Salem NC, telephone (919)-924-8191; 727-2063.

Bethania HD

1759 to early 1800's - Approximately 20 structures, predominantly of log, brick-nogged, or wood frame construction. Of note: brick Bethania Moravian Church (1806), and God's Acre, the original graveyard laid out in 1759. This district, the second Moravian settlement in North Carolina, is a well-preserved example of Moravian town planning; it retains the intimate scale and character of early 19th C.

YANCEYVILLE

Yanceyville HD

18th-19th C. - Contains numerous domestic and commercial structures as well as Courthouse Square; predominant style is Greek Revival. Has retained its mid-19th C. character, with residences such as Dongola and the Johnston House reflecting the antebellum prosperity from expanding tobacco industry. **H A B S**. *Special Events*: Bright Leaf Hoedown (September); Caswell County Chamber of Commerce, POB 29, Yanceyville, NC 27379, telephone (919)-694-6106. *General Information*: Caswell Historical Museum, Old Courthouse on the Square; also Chamber of Commerce.

Bennett's Rice Mill

SOUTH CAROLINA

ABBEVILLE

Abbeville HD

18th–20th C. - Commercial, centered around old town green; contains many original 19th C. buildings, some brick-paved streets, mounting blocks and watering troughs. Majority of dwellings are frame, in variety of styles from Greek Revival to those of Victorian era. Town, founded in 1785, was site of Confederate Government's last council of war, 2 May 1865. *Map, Self-Guided Tours*: Chamber of Commerce, 104 Pickens St., Abbeville SC 29620, Monday–Friday, 9–5, telephone (805)-459-4600. *Guided Tours*: By appointment; contact Chamber. *Annual Homes Tour*: Abbeville Spring Festival (2nd weekend in May); contact Abbeville County Development Board, POB 533, Abbeville SC 29620, telephone (803)-459-2181.

AIKEN

Aiken Winter Colony HD's I, II, and III

c. 1882–c. 1948 - Known as the "Winter Polo Capital of America" in its heyday, Aiken has been a winter resort for affluent Northerners since the 1870's. Three districts contain 177 properties, many of them large estates along tree-lined roads (unpaved for comfort of the many horses). Styles include Second Empire, Queen Anne, Shingle, and Georgian Revival. Of note: the Sandhurst property (c. 1900), Joye Cottage (c. 1897), and the Idylwood property (c. 1923).

ANDERSON

Anderson HD

19th-20th C. - Residential; numerous 19th - early 20th C. structures in a wide variety of styles including Greek Revival, High Victorian Italianate, and Georgian Revival. Town, created in 1826, flourished around cotton milling after Civil War.

Downtown HD

Late 19th to early 20th C. - Commercial and civic, with approximately 100 commercial structures, County Courthouse, City Hall, Victorian fountain, and 2 historic monuments. Commercial structures are mostly of brick, 2 and 3 stories. Well-maintained collection of buildings with courthouse and square as focal point; very few modern intrusions, and has retained a strong "Victorian" appearance.

AUGUSTA (NORTH AUGUSTA)

Georgia Avenue-Butler Avenue HD

c. 1859-c. 1930 - Sixteen properties illustrate growth of the area from the time it was part of an antebellum plantation through its development first as winter resort and then as year-round residential community (c. 1900) for Augusta-area professionals. Most buildings constructed between 1900 and 1930, and offer a range of vernacular designs. Of note: Star of Edgefield, a red brick plantation home, c. 1859.

BEAUFORT

Beaufort HD

18th-20th C. - Approximately 170 public and private buildings, in tree-shaded community on Beaufort River. Primarily early 18th to mid-19th C.; a good number of plantation-style houses fronting the river. Of note: John Mark Verdier House (c. 1790), Barnwell-Gough House (1789), and Marshlands (c. 1814, NHL). **N H L; H A B S.** *Map, Self-Guided Tours*: Historic Beaufort Foundation, 801 Bay St., Beaufort SC 29902, Wednesday-Saturday, 11-3; also Chamber of Commerce, 1006 Bay St., Beaufort SC 29902, telephone (803)-524-3163, weekdays. *Annual Homes Tour*: Spring Tours of Beaufort (April); contact POB 11, Beaufort SC 29902.

BENNETTSVILLE

Bennettsville HD

Late 19th to early 20th C. - Commercial section with courthouse as focal point, surrounded by residential sections. Most structures date from late 19th to early 20th C. Of note: Marlboro County Courthouse (c. 1885, altered c. 1951), the McColl Block (c. 1889, elaborate cast-iron facade), "Magnolia" Home (c. 1853), and the D. D. McColl House (c. 1882, Queen Anne).

BENNETTSVILLE (VICINITY)

Welsh Neck-Long Bluff-Society Hill HD

18th-19th C. - Contains the rural community of Society Hill and sites of 18th C. communities, Welsh Neck and Long Bluff. Includes numerous frame dwellings, 2 and 2 1/2 stories, all with ful-width front porches.

CAMDEN

Camden HD

18th-20th C. - A village laid out along wide streets, plus 178 acres of parkland. Includes numerous structures dating largely after 1813 fire; many Greek Revival residences and public buildings, including several designed by Robert Mills. Of note: Bethesda Presbyterian Church (1820), and courthouse (remodeled 1826). *Map, Self-Guided Tours*: Chamber of Commerce, 700 W. DeKalb St., Camden SC 29020, telephone (803)-432-2525; Camden Archives, 1314 Broad St., Camden SC 29020, telephone (803)-432-2342; Historic Camden, POB 710, Camden SC 29020, telephone (803)-432-9841. *Annual Homes Tour*: Candlelight Homes Tour (early December), Spring Tour of Homes (mid-April); contact Chamber of Commerce.

Kendall Mill HD

1899-1923 - Focal point is the Wateree Plant of Kendall Mills (1899, Romanesque Revival). Mill faces landscaped 10-acre Kendall Park. On park's eastern border are the mill supervisors' houses, 1900 - c. 1925. Mill operatives' housing consists of frame houses, 1900-1923. Most buildings have retained original architectural features, are in good repair.

CHARLESTON

Charleston HD

18th–19th C. - Over 1,000 residential, commercial, civic, and religious structures. Founded in 1670, city became the largest and wealthiest 18th C. city south of Philadelphia; with prosperity based on rice and indigo trade, it was the leading seaport and cultural center of antebellum South. Includes many notable residences and retains much of its 18th–19th C. appearance. **N H L; H A B S.** *Map, Self-Guided Tours*: Chamber of Commerce Visitor Information Center, 85 Calhoun St., Charleston SC 29403, telephone (803)-722-8338; Preservation Society Information Center, corner King/Queen Sts. *Guided Tours*: See Chamber of Commerce (including cassette tape tours). *Annual Homes Tour*: Annual Festival of Houses (3 weeks in late March, first half of April), sponsored by Historic Charleston Foundation. Contact Festival of Homes, 51 Meeting St., Charleston SC 29401, telephone (803)-722-3405. *Special Events*: Contact Chamber of Commerce for such events as Christmas in Charleston, Candlelight Tours of Homes and Gardens, and House and Garden Tours.

CHERAW

Cheraw HD

Late 18th to early 20th C. - More than 30 commercial, residential, and public buildings of frame or brick. Many Greek Revival structures, and some good examples of late-19th C. styles. Offers a sense of unity with its many frame houses on tree-shaded streets, and its overall well-preserved character.

CHESTER

Chester HD

19th–20th C. - Commercial area, with central public square and numerous 19th C. residential and commercial structures. Predominant structures are Italianate commercial blocks and Greek Revival dwellings. Settled in 1750's, was important rail center during Civil War.

CHESTERFIELD

East Main Street HD

c. 1798-1937 - Twenty-two properties, mainly residential but also includes the old Courthouse (c. 1885), the handsome Bank of Chesterfield, and a church. Of note: John Craig House (c. 1798, Federal), and Minor James Hough and Dr. Lewis Trotti Houses, both early 20th C.

West Main Street HD

19th C.-1930 - Core of an intact residential neighborhood; a large number of fashionable and substantial buildings from early 20th C. (town's era of greatest prosperity), and 5 structures from 19th C. Of note: Austin-Craig House (pre-Civil War, Gothic Revival), the John T. Hurst House, and Dr. Teal House.

CLINTON

Clinton Commercial HD

1875-1930's - A large section of the city's central business district with approximately 40 significant properties. Store buildings predominant, but also includes two bank buildings, former city hall, and a Masonic temple. A variety of architectural features, including ornamental Victorian-era brickwork, pressed-metal cornices of the early 20th C., and geometric designs of the Art Moderne style. Of note: the Bee Hive Department Store (c. 1910, with cast-iron facade), the former City Hall/Fire Station (c. 1906), and the Masonic Temple (c. 1921).

CLIO

Clio HD

Late 19th to early 20th C. - Unusually intact collection of period vernacular architectural design. Approximately 138 structures, both residential and commercial. Of note: Sternberger-Welsh-Hammer House (1901, late Queen Anne), J. C. Covington House (c. 1905, Colonial Revival), and the Bennett-Sistare House (c. 1912, Classical Revival). Majority of buildings continuously in use since construction, and in good repair.

COKESBURY (VICINITY)

Old Cokesbury HD

1824 - Small, rural district; developed by Methodists, as one of South Carolina's earliest planned communities. Organized around a school, and contains modest domestic and commercial structures, the majority reflecting Greek Revival influence. Of note: Masonic Female College (1854, Greek Revival temple form). *Map, Self-Guided Tours*: Masonic Female College, or nearby custodian's home.

COLUMBIA

Allen University HD

1891-1941 - School founded in 1881 by the African Methodist Episcopal Church (A.M.E.); one of several universities established by A.M.E. Church in the South, post-Civil War. District contains 4 major university buildings of red brick with white columns, surrounding campus green. Oldest building is Arnett Hall, c. 1896.

Arsenal Hill (Historic District I)

19th C. - Predominantly residential, mostly frame construction. Of note: Governor's Mansion (1855), the Lace House (1854, ornate ironwork), and the Caldwell-Hampton-Boylston House (1820-1830). Latter, one of city's finest examples of Greek Revival architecture, has outstanding gardens with ironwork.

Historic District II

18th-19th C. - Residential, mostly brick and frame structures, various styles. Antebellum prestigious neighborhood, which suffered much Civil War destruction. Extensive rebuilding did not occur until 1880's. Of note: Hale-Elmore Siebels House (c. 1790), one of Columbia's oldest houses; Ainsley Hall House (1823, NHL), designed by Robert Mills. *Map, Self-Guided Tours*: Historic Columbia Foundation, 1616 Blanding St., Columbia SC 29201, telephone (803)-252-7742. *Guided Tours*: By reservation for groups of 10 or more (bus or walking tours); contact above. *Annual Homes Tour*: Christmas Candlelight Tours (first full week in December); contact above.

Old Campus HD

19th C. - Original campus section of South Carolina College

chartered in 1801; rechartered in 1865 as University of South Carolina. District, surrounded by brick wall, contains numerous academic buildings. Of note: Rutledge College (1805) and the Maxey Monument (1827), both built by Robert Mills; South Carolinian Library (c. 1840); and the gymnasium (1855), designed by Jacob Graves as a chapel.

DARLINGTON

St. John's HD

1880–1925 - Approximately 20 residential properties of architectural or historical significance, in a 5-block area of oak-tree lined streets. Focal point is the St. John's School complex and the Academy Green (campus). Of note: Trinity Methodist Episcopal Church (c. 1834, now a residence), Haynesworth House (c. 1895, Colonial Revival), and the Old Gibson House (c. 1884, Downing cottage style). Thirty-six other buildings contribute to district's character. *General Information*: Darlington County Historical Commission, 104 Hewitt St., Darlington SC 29532.

DAUFUSKIE ISLAND

Daufuskie Island HD

1890–1930 - Accessible only by boat; roads, unpaved and unnamed, are lined with moss-draped pines and oaks. Approximately 24 properties, mostly folk housing built from 1890 to 1930 but reflecting a much earlier building technology. Also on island are 2 lighthouses, architectural ruins, and 5 antebellum slave cemeteries. *Guided Tours*: Vagabond Tours, Hilton Head, daily by boat, March 1 - November 1. *Annual Homes Tour*: Daufuskie Day (June), with boats from Hilton Head, SC, and Savannah, GA; contact Mrs. Billie Burn, historian, Daufuskie Island SC 29915.

DUE WEST

Erskine College HD

c. 1840–c. 1941 - Eighty-one properties centered around college campus (c. 1842), plus adjacent residential and commercial areas. Buildings portray architectural evolution from town's early settlement to early 20th C. Of note: Philomathean Society Hall (1859, Italian Renaissance

Revival), the Nickles House (c. 1886, Victorian farmhouse), and the Erskine Building (1892).

EDGEFIELD

Edgefield HD

18th-20th C. - Small town laid out around courthouse square, originally the village green. Approximately 40 structures from 19th C.; majority of dwellings are frame with center entrances and fanlights. First settled in 1760's, town was home of many prominent political figures including 10 former state governors. *Map, Self-Guided Tours*: Courtesty Center/Archives, Courthouse Square, POB 468, Edgefield SC 29824. *Guided Tours*: Cassette-tape walking tour may be available; see above.

FROGMORE (VICINITY)

Penn Center HD (Penn School)

Mid 19th-20th C. - The first school for free blacks in the South; approximately 18 buildings, mostly brick and frame. The oldest is Brick Church (1855, Greek Revival elements). School also served the community as health clinic, farm bureau, and repository for preservation of the Gullah heritage and history unique to St. Helena Island. School closed in 1948, but with continued use for community services and cultural preservation. **N H L**

GEORGETOWN

Georgetown HD

18th-19th C. - South Carolina's third oldest city, on north side of Sampit River. District contains numerous residential, religious, and public structures; 29 from the 18th C., and 18 pre-Civil War 19th C. Includes both simple frame dwellings from colonial period, and later elaborate antebellum homes. By the 1850's, city was world's largest exporter of rice. *Map, Self-Guided Tours*: Chamber of Commerce, 600 Front St., POB 1776, Georgetown SC 29442, telephone (803)-546-8436. *Guided Tours*: Contact above. *Annual Homes Tour*: Plantation and Town House Tour (March); contact above, or Prince George Winyah Episcopal Church, Broad & Haymarket, Georgetown SC 29440.

GLENN SPRINGS

Glenn Springs HD

19th to early 20th C. - Historic nucleus of small rural community that developed around a popular 19th - early 20th C. resort hotel. Nineteen significant properties including several residences, 2 boarding houses, 2 churches, store, and post office. Several buildings represent various vernacular and high-style period modes. Of note: John Zimmerman House (c. 1854), Charlie Zimmerman House (c. 1890), and Calvary Protestant Episcopal Church (1897, Carpenter Gothic). Tree-shaded, very few modern intrusions.

GRANITEVILLE

Graniteville HD

1845-1867 - Consists of the Graniteville Canal (1846), the original Graniteville Mill (1849, 2 1/2 stories), 26 original workers' houses in early Gothic Revival (exteriors virtually unaltered), 9 other units of mill housing, the 1847 Academy, and St. John's Methodist Church (1849, early Gothic Revival). This first typical Southern cotton-mill village was created by pioneer industrialist William Gregg. **N H L**

GREENVILLE

Hampton-Pickney HD

Late 19th to early 20th C. - Tree-shaded residential neighborhoods, one of oldest in Greenville. Approximately 47 structures, ranging from Greek Revival through Italianate and Queen Anne, to Prairie Style and Neo-Classical. Of note: W. P. McBee House (c. 1835, Greek Revival), J. M. Geer House (c. 1894, Queen Anne), and the Matoon Presbyterian Church (1887), city's oldest black church building. *Map, Self-Guided Tours*: Tours Around Greenville, Arts Council, 615 S. Main St., Greenville SC 29601. *Guided Tours*: See above. *Annual Homes Tour*: Showhouse (October), Box 9178, Greenville SC 29604; Holiday Showhouse (November), Symphony of Homes Tour (October), contact Metropolitan Arts Council, 615 S. Main St., Greenville SC 29601.

JOHNSTON

Johnston HD

1880–1920 - A 3-block commercial area surrounded by residential neighborhoods; approximately 145 properties, displaying a variety of styles and with relatively little alteration. There are 17 buildings of special architectural or historical significance, including John Payne House (c. 1883), and the Carwile-Huiet House (c. 1874).

KINGSTREE

Kingstree HD

1900–1920 - Forty-eight properties, including courthouse, public library, railroad station, and numerous commercial buildings. Town prospered as a retail and tobacco marketing center, between 1900 and 1920. A fine collection of 19th C. vernacular architecture.

LANCASTER

Downtown HD

c. 1880–c. 1935 - Contains 12 significant buildings and is the most intact section of town's early commercial area. Key buildings are the Springs Block (c. 1905), Bank of Lancaster/Opera House (c. 1907), Farmers Bank and Trust Co. (c. 1920), and Post Office (c. 1927). Several fine examples of commercial architecture. *Map, Self-Guided Tours*: Chamber of Commerce, 604 Main St., Lancaster SC 29720, telephone (803)-283-4106; or Main Street Program, c/o City Hall, 201 W. Gay St., Lancaster SC 29720.

LATTA

Latta HD's No. 1, 2

c. 1890–1930 - Town contains 2 Historic Districts, Number 1 with 55 properties, Number 2 with 12. Various trends in Victorian-era vernacular architecture, including Queen Anne, Neo-Classical, and Georgian Revival. Most buildings are frame residences, set on streets lined with large oaks. Has retained much of its early 20th C. character.

LAURENS

Laurens HD

19th to early 20th C. - Focal point is 4-acre Courthouse Square. Era of textile-industry prosperity reflected in many of the buildings. Of note: Courthouse (c. 1840, 1911), Episcopal Church (1846), Governor Simpson House (1839), Octagon House (c. 1859), and the Franks House (1859, Italian Villa). *Map, Self-Guided Tours*: Chamber of Commerce, 409 W. Main St., POB 248, Laurens SC 29360, telephone (803)-984-0322. *Annal Homes Tour*: Pride of the Piedmont Jubilee, Laurens County (mid-May); contact POB 519, Laurens SC 29360.

MARION

Marion HD

19th C. - Established in 1798, was important as county seat and a railroad town. Early frame structures, antebellum homes with Greek Revival porticos, vernacular raised cottages, and homes from Victorian era.

MAYESVILLE

Mavesville HD

Mid-19th C. to early 20th C. - Eighty significant structures include examples of commercial, residential, and religious buildings. A broad range of vernacular architectural design of the period, and representative of the development of a small 19th C. South Carolina community. Of note: Baptist Church (1878), J. M. Cooper House (c. 1880), Railroad Depot (1905), and P. M. Teller House (1907). *Map, Self-Guided Tours*: Mayesville Historical Society, or Ethel Cooper Turner, Box 149, Mayesville SC 29104.

MCCLELLANVILLE

McClellanville HD

c. 1860-1935 - Approximately 105 properties, including residential, commercial, religious, and educational buildings; they illustrate evolution of a pinelands resort village into a small but stable year-round fishing village. Styles include Carpenter Gothic, Queen Anne, and vernacular center-hall farmhouses. Of note: William P. Beckman House (c. 1868), the New Wappetaw Presbyterian Church (c. 1877), and the L. P. McClellan summer house (c. 1891).

MCCONNELLSVILLE (VICINITY)

Brattonsville HD

18th-19th C. - Tiny district of 3 distinctive houses owned by the Bratton family, built between 1776 and 1855: the 1776 Revolutionary House (1 1/2 story, logs); the c. 1830 Greek Revival Homestead; and a 1855 Jeffersonian Classical brick house.

MOUNT CARMEL

Mount Carmel HD

Late 19th C. - Approximately 40 properties in heart of small town which developed in 1880's thanks to Savannah Valley Railroad. Includes residential, commercial, institutional, and industrial buildings offering a range of turn-of-the-century architecture. Of note: Baker's Store (c. 1890), John Cade House (c. 1890), and the John Morrah House (1896) with numerous original outbuildings.

MOUNT PLEASANT

Mount Pleasant HD

18th-20th C. - Residential community; contains numerous 1-story cottages and more elaborate 19th C. dwellings. Predominant styles are Greek, Gothic Revival. Town, first settled c. 1776, was county's oldest summer resort, developing rapidly as a summer retreat for planters.

MURRELLS INLET

Murrells Inlet HD

Mid-19th to early 20th C. - A significant concentration of 19 residential structures reflecting area's transition from 2 rice plantation estates to a 20th C. resort community. Of note: 2 antebellum homes, both local interpretations of Greek Revival - Sunnyside, c. 1850, and The Hermitage, c. 1848. Vernacular 20th C. resort homes of wood construction with large screened porches. Houses, most overlooking saltwater creek and marsh, are surrounded by moss-draped live oaks and cedars.

NEWBERRY

Boundary Street - Newberry Cotton Mill HD

A collection of classical and vernacular upper and middle-class houses, 1857-1898, and a relatively intact mill village surrounding 1884 mill (still operative as late as 1979).

Caldwell Street HD

Eight residences, dating from 1885 to 1915; styles range from upcountry plantation through decorated Victorian to Neo-Classical. Of note: Zaccheus Wright Mansion, Neo-Classical.

College Street HD

Nineteen residences built between c. 1880 and c. 1930. Styles range from Victorian vernacular to California Bungalow. A faculty residential area for Newberry College since 1880's.

Harrington Street HD

Two blocks of important residences reflecting city's most prosperous era, from 1870 to c. 1930; includes Victorian raised cottages, Neo-Classical mansions.

Main Street HD

A relatively unchanged upper-class neighborhood reflecting a century of development. Styles include Greek and Gothic Revival, Eastlake, and Neo-Classical. Many large 2-story homes of asmymetrical form typical of the Victorian period.

Newberry HD

The town's central square contains 2 and 3-story brick and stone buildings, governmental and cultural, and many 2-story commercial buildings. A variety of late-19th C. styles. Of note: Old Courthouse (c. 1850, Greek Revival), and Newberry Opera House (1882, Romanesque Revival).

Newberry College HD

Contains nucleus of college campus, including 4 brick buildings from late 19th and early 20th C. Of note: Smeltzer Hall (1877) and Keller Hall (1895), both incorporating Italianate elements. College established 1856 by Lutheran Synod of SC.

Vincent Street HD
A small and compact collection of late 19th and early 20th C. residences, and 1 Greek Revival home.

West Boundary Street HD
Four residences, each representing a different predominant architectural style, 1840-1935.

NEWRY

Newry HD
1893-1910 - Rural textile-mill village of 118 properties. Includes mill complex, office, company store, church (late Gothic Revival details), and approximately 80 period workers' houses. Outstanding example of a textile-mill village, little changed since early 20th C.

ORANGEBURG

Amelia Street HD
c. 1890-1929 - Residential district of 15 homes, most of them large, 2-story frame structures with decorative woodwork. Of note: the Judge Moss House (c. 1890), the Ilderton Bowman House (c. 1890) and the James Albergotti House (c. 1915). Many houses were owned by prominent local citizens, built on a grand scale, and have considerable architectural distinction. District offers a streetscape of historical character.

Claflin College HD
Five brick educational buildings in historic core of the college campus. Of note: Lee Library (1898), and Tingley Memorial Hall (1908, Georgian Revival) by black architect William Wilson Cooke. An intact collection of early-20th C. educational structures in a college noted for important contributions to black education in South Carolina in early 20th C.

Downtown HD
c. 1850-c. 1935 - Forty-four buildings (mostly brick) in city's core, including stores, a textile mill, livery stable, 2 churches, 2 lodge halls. Reflects city's boom period, 1883-1925. Of interest: St. Paul's Methodist Church (c. 1896, Romanesque Revival), Blythewood Building (1915), and Orange Cotton Mill (c. 1880-1950).

East Russell Street Area HD

c. 1850–c. 1930 - A basically intact residential neighborhood, with wide range of architectural types reflecting original mix of affluent whites and servant-class blacks. Approximately 55 significant structures, including substantial brick and frame homes and modest frame houses.

Ellis Avenue HD

1900–1931 - A significant concentration of 7 substantial frame turn-of-century residences, basically unaltered. Also 2-story brick Ellis Avenue School (1931), an important example of collegiate design of James B. Urquhart, prominent South Carolina architect.

Treadwell Street Area HD

c. 1890–c.1930 - Contains the intact sections of an early 20th C. black neighborhood; was regarded as one of the most well-to-do black residential sections of the city. Approximately 40 buildings, 39 of them originally residences. Most are 1-story, weatherboarded frame with simple design and detailing, set on small lots with mature shrubs, trees.

Whitman Street Area HD

c. 1880–c. 1925 - Residential, with approximately 12 period buildings. Was a high-income area, with large homes displaying fashionable architectural modes of the times. A small but relatively intact portion of a once much larger neighborhood.

PAWLEY'S ISLAND

Pawley's Island HD

18th–20th C. - One of state's earliest summer beach communities, settled in late 1700's by affluent rice planters. Numerous 1 1/2-story frame dwellings, each with wide porch for ventilation, and a high brick foundation providing protection against gale tides. *Annual Homes Tour*: Annual Pawley's Island Tour of Homes (mid-May); contact The Episcopal Churchwomen, All Saints' Episcopal Church, Waccamaw, Pawley's Island SC 29585.

PENDLETON

Pendleton HD

18th–19th C. – Approximately 50 period structures around the town green; architecture reflects building practices and preferences popular in Charleston area and Mid-Atlantic colonies. Of note: Old Stone Church (1802), Elam Sharpe House (1802), and Farmers Society Hall (1828, Greek Revival temple form). *Map, Self-Guided Tours*: Pendleton Historical and Recreational Commission, 125 E. Queen St., POB 565, Pendleton SC 29670, telephone (803)-646-3782. *Guided Tours*: See above for cassette-tape tours in English, French. *Annual Homes Tour*: Historic Pendleton Spring Jubilee (early April); contact above.

PINOPOLIS

Historic District North

c. 1834–c. 1883 – Small district of 7 properties, 4 of which are 19th C. planters'-retreat houses which characterized this pineland village. All are frame, weatherboarded, with large porches and absence of styling pretensions. Strong ambience from very heavy foliage, no paved roads, and absence of contemporary buildings.

Historic District South

19th C. – Thirteen properties comprising historic core of this planters'-retreat community. Includes Dr. Morton Waring House (1 of first 2 buildings in town), other pre-Civil War buildings, and numerous others from late 19th C. District set in heavy pine forest.

RIDGEWAY

Ridgeway HD

1860–c. 1925 – Thirty-three properties of significance, both residential and commercial. Styles include Queen Anne, Neo-Classical, and Georgian Revival. Approximately 70 percent of the buildings constructed between 1890 and 1915. Commercial block unified by a predominance of 2-story brick buildings with ornamental cast-iron and brick work. Most residences are of frame and weatherboard construction.

ROCKVILLE

Rockville HD

19th-20th C. - Summer resort village on north bank of Bohicket Creek; contains numerous simple frame dwellings featuring raised foundations, large porches, and central-hall plans. One of nation's oldest surviving summer resorts; first established as summer retreat for island planters. One of main landings for the Edisto Island Ferry.

SENECA

Seneca HD

19th-20th C. - Numerous residential structures in wide variety of period styles, plus 3 churches, 1 museum. *Map, Self-Guided Tours*: Chamber of Commerce, Main St., Seneca SC 29678, telephone (803)-882-2097; also, *History of Seneca* for sale, c/o F. Holleman, POB 143, Seneca SC 29679.

SPARTANBURG

Converse College HD

1891-1915 - Includes 9 brick structures, 2 to 4 stories. Styles include Gothic Revival, Richardsonian Romanesque, Neo-Classical Revival, and vernacular. Oldest building is Pell Hall, 1891. Founded as women's liberal-arts college.

Wofford College HD

Mid-19th C. - The original section of Wofford College; contains 8 Italianate structures flanking Old Main, a Greek Revival and Italianate building dominating the complex. All buildings are c. 1854, when college was founded.

SULLIVANS ISLAND

U.S. Coast Guard Station HD

1891 - Coastal lifesaving station contains 5 structures, including the 1891 boathouse (frame), administration building, and carriage house (now a garage), plus the 1962 lighthouse. Oldest surviving lifesaving installation in South Carolina. A Federal facility, U.S. Coast Guard.

SUMMERVILLE

Summerville HD

1809-1880's - Residential, commercial, and civic, with approximately 700 structures; primarily frame construction, 1 1/2 and 2 stories, many with standing-seam metal roofs. Styles include Federal, Greek Revival, Queen Anne, and Colonial Revival. Has retained much of its 19th C. character. *Map, Self-Guided Tours*: Chamber of Commerce, 104 Civic Center, POB 670, Summerville SC 29483, telephone (803)-873-2931. *Special Events*: Christmas Parade (early December), Flowertown Festival (late March); contact Chamber of Commerce or Family YMCA, 900 Crosscreek Dr., Summerville SC 29483, telephone (803)-871-9622.

SUMTER

Sumter HD

c. 1828-20th C. - Commercial, approximately 84 structures of brick or stone, 1 to 4 stories. Most were built from 1880 to 1930, incorporating elements of a variety of styles, late 19th - early 20th C. Of note: Town Hall and Opera House (1893, Richardsonian Romanesque). Contains city's original business district; reflects turn-of-the-century development as county seat, commercial center.

SUMTER (VICINITY)

Stateburg HD

18th-19th C. - Residential neighborhood; contains mostly domestic frame and *pise de terre* structures in wide variety of styles, including Greek, Gothic Revival. Of note: the Borough House (c. 1756). An important antebellum residential area, until seriously damaged in the Civil War.

UNION

South Street HD

1850-1915 - Residential, 43 homes, primarily of frame construction, 1 to 2 1/2 stories, large and well-developed yards and gardens. Most houses exhibit characteristics of Queen Anne style. A typical upper-income residential sector of a small town of the era; little alteration since 1915.

WALTERBORO

Walterboro HD

1800-1945 - Residential, approximately 175 buildings; includes large portion of the town's historical residential areas. Majority of buildings date from early 19th C. to pre-World War II, representing variety of styles and periods. Of note: Lucas House (early 1800's, Federal raised cottage), Little Library (c. 1820, Federal woodwork), and St. Judes Episcopal Church (1855, 1879, Carpenter Gothic).

Hickory Valley HD

1821-1929 - Residential district of 19 properties, representing the major styles of 19th and 20th C. Styles include Federal, Greek Revival, Neo-Classical, and Federal Revival. Includes a group of early homes from town's heyday as pinelands resort village for low-country planters. Of note: Elmore-Henderson House (c. 1821), the Edward B. Fishburne House (c. 1829), and the Paul House (c. 1847). Well-preserved residences, set amidst mature trees of landscaped yards.

WINNSBORO

Winnsboro HD

18th-20th C. - Primarily residential section of a typical upcountry town in South Carolina; a number of early, simple frame houses by Scotch-Irish builders, and more sophisticated Greek Revival dwellings built by later prosperous planters. Of note: Ketchin Building (c. 1830, Federal), Robertson House (1852, Greek Revival), and the c. 1833 town clock (reputedly oldest continuously running clock in the United States). *Map, Self-Guided Tours*: Chamber of Commerce, Town Clock Building, Congress St., Winnsboro SC 29180; also Fairfield County Museum, S. Congress St., Winnsboro SC 29180, telephone (803)-635-4242. *Guided Tours*: Contact Chamber of Commerce. *Annual Homes Tour*: Contact Chamber of Commerce, POB 297, Winnsboro SC 29180.

WINNSBORO (VICINITY)

Liberty Church - Feasterville Academy HD

1830-1945 - Small rural district of 4 buildings comprising a significant collection of period religious and educational structures. School complex (c. 1842) is an unusually intact grouping from an antebellum academy; church (c. 1832) is state's only known remaining 19th C. Universalist church.

Rockton and Rion Railroad HD

c. 1883-c. 1945 - Industrial district of 45 properties along 12-mile stretch of Rockton and Rion Railroad, in south central Fairfield County. Includes Rion and Anderson granite quarries, granite residences for quarry managers, and 2 steam locomotives (1903, 1920). Local granite enjoyed a national reputation and was used in such construction as New York Flatiron Building.

White Oak HD

Late 19th to early 20th C. - Rural trading community consists of 9 properties constructed between c. 1876 and c. 1925. Includes 3 residences, church and manse, 2 store buildings, and a cotton warehouse. Of interest: F. G. Patrick Store (c. 1876), McDowell's Store (c. 1885), and the T. G. Patrick House (c. 1903). A relatively intact example of a prosperous turn-of-the-century village.

YORK

York HD

Early 1800's-1906 - Ten-block residential district, with approximately 50 significant structures, most of them dwellings from first half of 19th C. Of note: Robert Latta House (1825, Federal), Joiner-Grist House (c. 1850, Greek Revival), and McElwee House (1899, Queen Anne). *Map, Self-Guided Tours*: Chamber of Commerce, 3 Roosevelt St., POB 97, York SC 29745, telephone (803)-684-2590; Historical Society, 8 Cottage Ave., POB 1122, York SC 29745; City Hall Information Center. *Annual Homes Tour*: Historic Awareness Day (Spring), Christmas Parlor Tour (early December); contact President, Yorkville Historical Society, 8 Cottage Ave., York SC 29745.

TENNESSEE

ARLINGTON

Arlington HD

1880–1920 - Primarily residential, with 29 turn-of-the-century vernacular homes. Also eight commercial buildings, three churches. Tree-lined streets, a strong sense of neighborhood.

BEERSHEBA SPRINGS

Beersheba Springs HD

19th C. - Located in Grundy County along Tennessee Route 56. Approximately 55 log and frame structures with white columns, balustrades, and verandahs. Primarily a resort area. Of interest: Beersheba Hotel Complex (1856–1858), Old Northcutt Store (1856–1860), Armfield Cottage (1833–1839).

BELL BUCKLE

Bell Buckle HD

1850–1940 - Residential, commercial, religious, and educational structures; styles include Greek and Gothic Revival, Italianate, Eastlake, and Commercial. Founded in mid-19th C., prospered with coming of railroad in 1852.

BERLIN

Berlin HD

1856–1920 - An intact collection of primitive and simple buildings, many of log and frame construction, 7 miles north of Lewisburg (Marshall County). Includes the Finley Farmstead (1856), the Lunn House (1840's), and the 1857

Methodist Church. The heart of a much declined but historically important village.

BLOUNTVILLE

Blountville HD

18th-20th C. - Small town features simple 2-story frame residences; includes some late 18th C. examples of log construction, and commercial and governmental structures in brick and frame. Of note: Old Deery Inn (c. 1794, Federal elements), and Anderson Hall (1780's-1790's, Georgian). County seat since 1795, active commercial center for most of 19th C.; has retained much original atmosphere.

BOLIVAR

Bills-McNeal HD

1830's-c. 1900 - Nine significant buildings in proximity to the court square. Most are residential, ranging from 1830's Federal-style examples to Gothic Revival, Greek Revival, and Italianate. Also two church buildings, 1869-1870 Gothic Revival.

Bolivar Court Square HD

Late 19th C. - Forty buildings, 28 of which are of significance; includes commercial, religious, government, and residential buildings. Of interest: Rexall Drugs (1878), Western Auto Store (c. 1890), Ragon Building (1878).

North Main Street HD

1849-1925 - Residential, 25 buildings; styles include Greek Revival, Carpenter Gothic, Victorian Vernacular, and Bungaloid.

BROWNSVILLE

College Hill HD

19th to early 20th C. - Seventy-seven residences and four commercial buildings. Of interest: Harbert-Hooper House (1859, Greek Revival), Anderson-Austin-Moss House (c. 1867, Gothic Revival), Bond House ("Whitehall", 1868, Greek Revival). Also Haywood County High School, 2-story brick built in 1852 as Brownsville Baptist Female College.

CHARLOTTE

Courthouse Square HD

1804-c. 1920 - Twenty-two buildings of interest, a mix of public, residential, and commercial. Of note: Dickson County Courthouse (1833), Old Masonic Lodge (1830), Voorhie-James House (1806). A once thriving trade center, town now has population under 1,000. Has retained much of the appearance of a typical 19th C. rural Tennessee town. *Special Events*: Fall Festival (Charlotte Lions Club), Candlelight Tour (Historical Society). *General Information*: Historical Society, Courthouse Square, Dickson TN 37036; Chamber of Commerce, 100 Clement Place, Dickson TN 37036, telephone (615)-446-2349.

CHATTANOOGA

Chattanooga

Group Tours: Convention and Visitors Bureau, 1001 Market Street, Chattanooga TN 37411. *General Information*: Historical Society, POB 8755, Chattanooga TN 37411.

Ferger Place HD

1915-1930 - A cohesive residential area of 59 buildings and a 2-acre neighborhood park. Popular styles include Colonial and Tudor Revival, Bungalow, plus simple vernacular.

Fort Wood HD

1880-1920 - Residential downtown area adjacent to campus of University of Tennessee. Approximately 120 buildings in 12 square blocks. Predominant style is Queen Anne but also includes Eastlake, Italianate, Romanesque, Tudor, and Classical Revival.

Market Street Warehouse HD

1904-1929 - Eight row warehouse structures in city's downtown. The only surviving examples in Chattanooga, they form a highly cohesive and monumental unit. Have retained their architectural integrity.

Martin Luther King Blvd. HD

1890's-c. 1917 - This district contains 36 commercial buildings, mostly brick. The thoroughfare (formerly East Ninth

Street) has been a principal center of city's black life since the mid-1800's. Some alterations, and many of the structures in poor condition.

St. Elmo HD

Late 19th C. - A planned streetcar suburb with some 620 buildings, primarily residential. Built for the middle-income working class, predominantly frame, 1 and 2 stories. Styles include Gothic Revival, Tudor, Queen Anne, Bungalow, Shingle, Classical Revival, and such vernacular styles as the shotgun.

CLARKSVILLE

Clarksville Architectural District

1840's-1880's - Commercial, approximately 40 significant masonry structures, two and three stories. Styles include Italianate, Greek Revival, and Second Empire. Of note: Poston Block (Federal style), eclectic City Hall, and the fanciful City Department of Electricity with its Chateauesque elements. Retains some of its 19th C. character. *Map, Self-Guided Tours*: Tourist Commission, 312 Madison St., POB 513, Clarksville TN37041, telephone (615)-647-2331.

Clarksville Industrial District

1859 - Five significant structures, primarily brick, 1 1/2 to 3 stories, vernacular utilitarian design. Includes a tobacco warehouse, railroad freight station, a Pratt-truss swinging bridge, and remnants of the city gasworks.

Dog Hill HD

1890's - Primarily residential, with typical late 19th C. cottages, mostly frame. Of note: Goodlett, Peay, and Hurt Building (c. 1874). Community reputedly so named because neighborhood canines howled at whistles of nearby steamboats, trains.

COLUMBIA

Columbia

Columbia offers a number of significant antebellum homes, including "Rattle and Snap" (1845, Greek Revival, NHL), the Athenaeum (1835, Gothic Revival), and Vine Hill (1836 plantation mansion). *Annual Homes Tour*: Columbia's Fall Spectacular, POB 942, Columbia TN 38401, telephone (615)-388-5113; Columbia Academy Associates Fall Tour, 1101 W. 7th Street, Columbia TN 38402, telephone (615)-388-5363. *General Information*: Chamber of Commerce, 308 W. 7th Street, Columbia TN 38402.

Columbia Commercial District

1820's-1940 - Predominantly commercial, with 91 buildings arranged around the Maury County Courthouse. Styles include Federal, those of the Victorian era, and Beaux-Arts. Majority are of brick, 1 to 4 stories. Encompasses "Mink Slide" area, a black commercial district.

West Sixth Street - Mayes Place HD

1870's-1930 - A neighborhood of 55 buildings and sites, developed by upper-income residents; contains many well preserved examples of vernacular architecture dating from 1820.

DANDRIDGE

Dandridge HD

Late 18th to early 20th C. - Town center of small antebellum community; approximately 26 interesting buildings from 19th C. including 3 early 19th C. taverns, 2-story County Courthouse (1845) and a number of brick and frame residences. Of note: Swann House (1855-1860), with hipped roof. Town named after Martha Dandridge Washington; developed as a river and stage stop but declined in prosperity after Civil War. *Map, Self-Guided Tours*: Historical Society, Old Vance Building, POB 329, Dandridge TN 37725; Dandridge City Hall. *Special Events*: Founding Festival, second weekend in June.

DIXON SPRINGS

Dixon Springs HD

1830-1910 - Rural residential area, approximately 30 frame and log dwellings, 1 and 2 stories, from late 19th C. Developed as trading center for neighboring farms. Of note: William Martin Young house (1870, Greek Revival), the Phillips Merchandise Co. (1900), and Dixon Springs Bank (1910). Has retained much of its 19th - early 20th C. integrity.

DUCKTOWN

Burra Burra Mine HD

Early 20th C. - Thirteen surviving structures and entrance to the Burra Burra mine, illustrating almost all aspects of deep copper mining, early 20th C. Set amidst bare hills, denuded of vegetation by sulfur dioxide fumes and fuel cutting. Approximately 40 miles west of Chattanooga, on edge of Cherokee National Forest.

ELIZABETHTOWN

Elizabethtown HD

18th-20th C. - Frame residences, soldier's monument on courthouse circle, the courthouse, and a covered bridge. The numerous structures reflect town's 19th C. development. **H A E R**

FAYETTEVILLE

Mulberry - Washington - Lincoln HD

General Information: Chamber of Commerce, 104 N. Main St., POB 515, Fayetteville TN 37334, telephone (615)-433-1234.

FRANKLIN

Franklin HD

19th-20th C. - Center of city, with residential, commercial, religious, and government structures. Features 1 1/2 to 3-story brick and frame structures in Federal, Greek Revival, late 19th C. styles. Franklin grew from a frontier town to the center of law practice by many political figures, including John Marshall and Thomas Hart Benton. Includes many fine examples of period architecture. Of note: Eaton House (1805, Federal), Williamson County Courthouse (1858, Greek Revival elements), and the Akers House (late 19th C. Victorian eclectic). *Map, Self-Guided Tours*: Tourism Committee, County Courthouse; Chamber of Commerce, City Hall, (615)-794-1225. *Guided Tours*: Heritage Foundation, (615)-790-0378. *Group Tours*: Downtown Franklin Association, POB 807, Franklin TN 37065, telephone (615)-790-7094. *Annual Homes Tour*: Carter House Neighborhood Candlelight Tour (1st weekend in December), Town and Country Tour (last weekend in April); contact Chamber of Commerce, POB 156, Franklin TN 37064, telephone (615)-794-1225.

Hincheyville HD

c. 1828-1930's - Primarily residential, with 92 buildings, mostly single-family homes. Architectural influences represented include Federal, Greek Revival, Italianate, Queen Anne, Eastlake, Four-Square, and Bungalow. Porches with gingerbread trim, large trees, and iron fences all add to the strong sense of neighborhood.

GATLINBURG (VICINITY)

Roaring Fork HD

1800 to late 19th C. - Mountain settlement contains six frame or log 1-story gabled structures. Includes the Ephraim Bales cabin (c. 1800) and barn, and Alfred Reagan House (1886-1894) and tub mill (c. 1900). Well-preserved examples of vernacular structures reflecting settlers' difficult living and farming conditions. (Federal; National Park Service) **H A B S**

GREENEVILLE

Greeneville HD

18th-20th C. - Business section flanked by residential areas with numerous structures. Of note: Valentine Sevier House (Federal), the 1850 home of President Andrew Johnson, and First Presbyterian Church (Greek Revival). Settled by Scotch-Irish after 1783 and developed commercially due to its position on an early trade, stage route. **H A B S**

HENDERSONVILLE (VICINITY)

Shackle Island HD

19th C. - A small rural community consisting of a few scattered commercial buildings, plus 5 period homes and 1 church. Of interest: 1804 farm home, "Old Brick".

JACKSON

East Main Street HD

General Information: Convention and Visitors Bureau, 400 S.

Highland, Jackson TN 38301, telephone (901)-423-2341; Chamber of Commerce, POB 1904, Jackson TN 38302, telephone (901)-423-2200.

JONESBORO (JONESBOROUGH)

Jonesboro HD

18th-19th C. - Oldest town in Tennessee; established in 1779, was site of early legislative sessions of proposed state of Franklin. Approximately 150 structures (religious, public, commercial, residential); major styles are Federal, Greek and Gothic Revival, and Italianate. Of note: Robert May House (Federal-Italianate), and Irwin House (Gothic Revival). *Map, Self-Guided Tours*: Visitors Center, (615) 753-5961; also, Jonesborough Civic Trust, POB 451, Jonesboro TN 37659, telephone (615)-753-5281. *Guided Tours*: May-October; contact Civic Trust. *Annual Homes Tour*: Christmas in Olde Jonesborough, December; Christmas Progressive Dinner and Homes Tour (by reservation only). Contact Civic Trust.

KINGSPORT

Boatyard HD

18th-19th C. - Located near the Holston River; includes residential areas of Christianville, Rossville, and Rotherwood, various fort and battle sites, and 18th C. Cherokee campground sites. Town was early center for road and river traffic, later active in boat building. *Map, Self-Guided Tours*: Chamber of Commerce, 408 Clay Street, Kingsport TN 37660, telephone (615)-246-2010. *Special Events*: August Fun Fest, Annual Christmas Party; contact Netherland Inn Museum, POB 293, Kingsport TN 37662, telephone (615)-247-3211.

Church Circle HD

1915-1930's - Consists of two small city parks with surrounding buildings, on edge of downtown business district. Includes commercial, religious, and public brick buildings in Georgian Revival style, and 2 1/2 story brick and stucco dwellings in Jacobethan Revival style. Focal point is a circular park with four churches in semi-circle. *Map, Self-Guided Tours*: See **Boatyard HD.**

KNOXVILLE

Fort Sanders HD

1880-1910 - Residential neighborhood with approximately 350 structures at least 50 years old. Developed during a boom period in Knoxville, area contains such styles as Shingle, Queen Anne, Eastlake, and Bungalow. Of note: G. W. Pickle House (c. 1889), the Ross Home (1894, Queen Anne-Romanesque), and the Carson House (1903). Many homes and buildings have been restored. *Map, Self-Guided Tours*: Knoxville Heritage Inc., 807 S. Gay Street, POB 1242, Knoxville TN 37901, telephone (615)-523-8008; Visitor Information Center, 500 Henley Street, Knoxville TN 37902, telephone (615)-523-2316.

Fourth and Gill Street HD

c. 1880-c. 1930 - Primarily residential, with nearly 300 homes in such styles as Queen Anne, Stick, and Shingle. Also a substantial collection of Colonial Revival, American Four-Square, and Tudor styles. Larger and more impressive residences are of classic Queen Anne architecture.

Jackson Avenue Warehouse District

Late 19th to early 20th C. - A relatively unaltered area of warehouses which once played an important role in city's commerce. Buildings mostly 3 to 5-story brick, with stone, brick, or terra cotta trim; also large brick or metal cornices, and cast-iron storefronts on the ground floors. **H A B S.** *Map, Self-Guided Tours*: "Downtown Knoxville", from Knoxville Heritage (see **Ft. Sanders HD**).

Knoxville College HD

1886-1929 - Campus district contains original core of this school founded as black college in 1875 by the United Presbyterian Church. Structures include President's Residence (1886-1905), Wallace Hall (1890), McKee Hall (1895), and Elnathan Hall (1898). *Map, Self-Guided Tours*: Visitor Information Center, 500 Henley St., Knoxville TN, telephone (615)-523-2316.

Market Square Commercial District

Late 19th C. - Historic central business district contains 20 buildings retaining varying degrees of their historical appearance. Buildings around the square offer Italianate and Neo-Classical detailing; most are of brick.

Mechanicsville HD

Late 19th to early 20th C. - Residential, in two areas, developed in late 1800's. The Middleton and Weatherford Addition (c. 1895-1910) area contains large number of almost identical shotgun houses. Larger area contains Italianate and Queen Anne houses built for factory owners, businessmen. Historically many black residents, and population continues to be integrated. Neighborhood, with tree-shaded streets and a number of ornamental iron fences, has retained much of its original ambience. *Map, Self-Guided Tours*: See **Ft. Sanders HD**.

LAGRANGE

LaGrange HD

1825-1840's - Southern antebellum community of approximately 75 buildings (most of brick or frame), with range of period styles. Town, laid out in 1825 in grid imitating plan of Philadelphia, PA., developed as thriving commercial-cultural center. Of note: Hillcrest House (1840), Immanuel Episcopal Church (c. 1843), and Hancock Hall (1857). A well-preserved example of its type.

LAKEWOOD

Lakewood HD

1926-1930 - Five commercial structures of frame or brick, the only remaining grouping of early 20th C. commercial architecture in the communities of Rayon City, Lakewood and Old Hickory (See also **Old Hickory HD**).

LOUISVILLE

Louisville HD

19th-20th C. - Predominantly residential, with approximately 30 structures, including Federal and Victorian-era-style dwellings, a commercial building, and Masonic Lodge. First developed as important 19th. C. Tennessee River port, commercial center.

MARYVILLE

Maryville College HD

1869-1922 - An 18-acre campus with 9 buildings representative of architectural trends, 1869-1922. Oldest building is Anderson Hall, 1869.

MEMPHIS

Annesdale Park HD

Early 20th C. - An important and almost undisturbed collection of early 20th C. architecture reflecting the transitional period between ornate Victorian-style houses and bungalows. Built for upper-middle class, and known as "the First Subdivision of the South."

Annesdale-Snowden HD

Early 20th C. - Residential, with a number of 1-story cottages and bungalows.

Beale Street HD

Early 20th C. - A 2-block section of Beale Street, considered the birthplace of the "blues". Area originally was a notorious gambling and entertainment section. Buildings of note include the Palace and Daisy Theaters, the Hole-in-the-Wall Saloon, and Peewee's Saloon; latter was headquarters for W. C. Handy who wrote "St. Louis Blues", etc. **N H L**. *Map, Self-Guided Tours*: Visitors Information Center, 207 Beale Street, Memphis TN 38103, telephone (901)-526-4880. *Guided Tours*: Memphis Heritage, Inc., POB 3143, Memphis TN 38173, telephone (901)-327-3086.

Central Gardens HD

C. 1900 - A large residential district of approximately 1,540 structures, mostly single family residences. Significant for its architecture, community planning, and for prominent citizens who have lived in the area.

Cotton Row HD

1848-1928 - By 1887, Memphis boasted the world's largest inland spot cotton market, and cotton factors (brokers) had become city's social elite. Most of the cotton offices still standing were built between 1848 and 1928. *General Information*: See **Beale Street HD.**

Court Square HD

1860–1965 - Thirty-nine commercial buildings, from 1 to 20 stories; a few vernacular structures, and good examples of the eclectic use of Romanesque, Byzantine, and Renaissance elements. Also two landscaped parks, Court Square (1819), and Confederate Park (1908).

Evergreen HD

1890's–1930's - Primarily residential, with 1,366 buildings; majority are Bungalows and Four-Squares, but there are excellent examples of Colonial Revival, Beaux-Arts, Mediterranean, Spanish Colonial Revival, and Tudor Revival. Encompasses **Stonewall Place HD**.

Gayoso–Peabody HD

1880–1927 - Commercial, originally including hardware, dry goods, and grocery stores which serviced cotton industry during its heyday. District named for its once-elegant hotels, the Gayoso (opened in 1842), and the Peabody (opened in 1869). Of note: Lemmon-Gale Building (Romanesque), the Cast Iron Twins (c. 1891), and the Majestic Theatre (c. 1913). *General Information*: See **Beale Street HD**.

Greenlaw Addition HD

1890–1910 - City's first suburb, laid out in 1856; approximately 30 blocks. Majority of dwellings are from 1890-1910, in Victorian-era styles; many feature irregular roof lines, shingles on the eaves, porches, and gingerbread trim. Of interest: the Mill House, Love House, and the Sambucetti House. *General Information*: See **Beale Street HD**.

Madison - Monroe HD

1860–1935 - Thirty-nine commercial buildings, 1 to 18 stories, of brick, terra cotta, and stone. Good local examples of Romanesque, Beaux Arts, Neo-Classical, and Art Deco styles plus simple vernacular structures.

Overton Park HD

c. 1900 - Some 342 acres of open meadow and dense forest, in mid-town Memphis. Exemplifies enlightened principles of late 19th C. landscape architecture; also contains a number of significant buildings and statues.

Pinch–N. Main Commercial District

Late 1800's to early 1900's - Thirty-eight significant buildings (historically or architecturally), nearly all of brick, many with cast-iron columns on facades of the first floor. Heights vary from 1 to 4 stories.

South Main Street HD

1900-1930 - Primarily commercial, with 105 buildings of brick, terra cotta, and cast stone. Facades employ a wide range of early 20th C. architectural details showing strong influences of Beaux Arts, Georgian Revival, and Chicago Commercial style. Relatively few alterations.

Stonewall Place HD

Early 20th C. - A 4-block residential area with 84 architecturally significant residences. Primary architectural style is the American Four-Square; a cohesive neighborhood, with park-like street landscaping.

Vance-Poncotoc HD

1858-1918 - Residential area, containing Queen Anne and other Victorian-era style frame houses and a large collection of outstanding Italianate townhouses. Most of the homes (many in disrepair) built between 1858 and 1918. Of note: Robert Bowles and Patrick S. Hayley Houses. *General Information*: See **Beale Street HD.**

Victorian Village HD

19th-20th C. - Downtown residential area features 1 and 2-story frame and brick dwellings constructed from 1840's to 1890's. Architecture reflects city's economic boom as a center of steamboat and railroad transportation. Of note: Bartholomew House (1840's, Federal and Greek Revival elements), the Kirtland-Mallory House (1852, Italianate Villa), and the Taylor House (1886-1890, Queen Anne). *Guided Tours*: Memphis Heritage, Inc. POB 3143, Memphis TN 38173, telephone (901)-327-3086. *General Information*: Victorian Village, 680 Adams Ave., Memphis TN 38105, telephone (901)-526-1469.

MOCASSIN BEND

Stringer Ridge HD

No further information available at this time.

MONTEAGLE

Monteagle Sunday School Assembly HD

1882-1930 - Founded in 1882 as the "Chatauqua of the South"; encompasses 96 acres with 162 cottages, mostly frame, and 23 other structures. Predominant architectural influence is Victorian, with Queen Anne and Carpenter Gothic most common.

MORRISTOWN

Morristown Colleqe HD

1892-1968 - Thirty acres with 13 brick and frame buildings; styles represented are Queen Anne, Georgian Revival, Eclectic, vernacular. College founded in 1881.

MURFREESBORO

East Main St. HD

Late 19th to early 20th C. - A significant concentration of residential structures built by city's most historically prominent families. Approximately 100 buildings, with styles including Federal, Greek Revival, and (especially) Colonial Revival.

North Maney Ave. HD

1870-1920 - A major collection of 129 buildings, mostly residential, presenting a diversity of architectural styles and materials from 1835 to 1935. Most are vernacular clapboard, with Classical, Colonial Revival, or Queen Anne ornamentation. Has retained much of its historic ambience, with heavy shade, brick sidewalks, and few exterior alterations.

NASHVILLE

Belmont-Hillsboro HD

c. 1900-1930 - A 20-block residential district with approximately 600 buildings, most middle-class, single-family dwellings of modest scale. Major types include 1 1/2-story houses with Neo-Classical or late Victorian-era decorative treatment, the boxy "four-square", and the bungalow. Over 300 examples of the bungalow type, displayed in astounding variety of designs. *General Information*: Belmont-Hillsboro

Neighbors, c/o Sam House, 2009 Cedar Lane, Nashville TN 37212.

Broadway HD

Late 19th to early 20th C. - Primarily commercial; begins one block from Cumberland River, encompassing some of city's oldest blocks. Has strong historical associations with the furniture trade (see H. Brown Building, 1902, and Harley-Holt Building, 1906), and particularly strong associations with the Grand Ole Opry (here until 1974). Despite decay and modifications, district retains some of the original detail from its heyday. *General Information*: Metropolitan Historical Commission, 701 Broadway (Customs House), Nashville TN 37203, telephone (615)-259-5027.

Buena Vista HD

Late 19th to early 20th C. - Primarily residential, with approximately 200 structures in 10 square blocks. A wide variety of styles, including Gothic Revival, Queen Anne, Eastlake, shotgun, and simple Victorian cottage. Also several fine examples of Second Empire storefronts, and a number of important churches. Wide, tree-lined streets and brick sidewalks contribute to period atmosphere. *General Information*: See **Broadway HD.**

East Nashville HD

Late 19th to early 20th C. - Middle-class residential area, approximately 400 buildings. Mostly single-family houses, in such styles as late-Victorian-era, Neo-Classical, and Bungalow. Largely intact, although in a larger area of urban decline. *General Information*: East End Association, c/o Roger Elliot, 1211 Woodland Street, Nashville TN 37206; Lockeland Springs Neighbors, c/o Sylvia Byrn, 1604 Forrest Avenue, Nashville TN 37206.

Edgefield HD

Late 19th C.-1920's - Contains only sizeable concentration of Victorian-era residential architecture left in Nashville. Approximately 200 buildings, with excellent examples of late 19th C. architecture; includes churches, luxurious residences of the wealthy, and modest middle-class clapboard cottages. A unique neighborhood in Nashville, with its mix of architecture, tree-lined streets, and sections of original brick sidewalks. *Annual Homes Tour*: May; contact Historic Edgefield, Inc., c/o Lucy Gibson, 816 Russell Street, Nashville TN 37206.

Fifth Avenue HD.

Late 19th C. - Downtown business section, with approximately 25 significant structures; from 2 to 6 stories, masonry construction, the majority reflecting Italianate, Chicago, commercial, and Art Deco styles. While changes to some storefronts, majority have retained their original architectural characteristics. *General Information*: See **Broadway HD.**

Fisk University HD

1860's-1970's - Approximately 70 structures of various styles. University founded in 1866, regarded as "Harvard" of historic black college system. Of note: Jubilee Hall (1876, Stephen D. Hatch, arch.), Academic Building (1908, Moses McKisack III, arch.), and the former Gym (1888, White and Means, architects). Campus has retained strong turn-of-the-century atmosphere. *General Information*: See **Broadway HD.**

Germantown HD

1850's-1920 - Eight blocks, primarily residential, approximately 124 buildings of historical or architectural significance. Area associated with German immigrants of 19th C.; contains wide cross-section of styles, types of residences, as well as several significant commercial and industrial structures. Includes shotguns, workers' cottages, grand 2-story townhouses, and refined turn-of-the-century residences. *Special Events*: Oktoberfest, 2nd Saturday in October; contact Germantown Neighborhood Association, c/o Ginger Pennic, 1239 Sixth Avenue North, Nashville TN 37208.

Printers Alley HD

Late 19th to early 20th C. - Fifteen downtown buildings form an excellent collection of rich architectural styles, illustrating Nashville transition from Victorian to modern architecture (and the technological advances that made it possible). Late-Victorian buildings are very elegant, with others showing early influence of the Chicago School. Has historical connections with printing, entertainment industries. *General Information*: See **Broadway HD.**

Richland-West End HD

c. 1910-1920's - Residential 12-block neighborhood, about 300 buildings. One of the largest, best-preserved collections of bungalow architecture in Nashville. Retains atmosphere of early 20th C. *General Information*: See **Broadway HD.**

Rutledge Hill HD

Late 19th to early 20th C. - Developed as fashionable residential neighborhood of elegant 19th C. townhouses and educational institutions (Vanderbilt University, George Peabody College, and Montgomery Bell Academy). A wide variety of styles, dating from city's earliest years to 20th C. bungalows; contains last remaining cluster of 19th C. buildings in the area. *General Information*: See **Broadway HD.**

Scarritt College HD

1925-1982 - Includes 12 buildings, five of which are original campus. Designed in late Gothic Revival style, presenting unified whole. Six modern buildings from 1940-1960's are visually compatible with the original complex. *General Information*: See **Broadway HD.**

Second Avenue Commercial District

1870's-1880's - One of the most outstanding collections of cast-iron and masonry storefronts in the U.S., covers three blocks. Brick Italianate, 3 and 4 stories, built as shops and stores; they are a full block in depth, and overlook the Cumberland River. Exteriors relatively unaltered, with nice brick work, heavy stone cornices with brackets. **H A B S.** *Special Events*: Market Street Festival (late September); contact Director, Historic Nashville, Inc., 100 Second Avenue North, Nashville TN 37201.

Warner Park HD

1927-1941 - Park district of 2,664 rolling acres was developed between 1927 and 1930, with extensive Works Progress Administration (WPA) construction, 1935-1941. Man-made features have been built with great sensitivity to the natural environment; they include entrance gates, retaining walls, bridges, stables, and even a steeplechase course. Latter is only racetrack built by the Federal Government; designed in late 1930's by William I. du Pont, Jr., of Wilmington, Delaware. *General Information*: See **Broadway HD.**

Waverly Place HD

1880-1935 - Small suburban subdivision with 222 relatively intact late 19th and early 20th C. buildings, most of them houses. Developed as "streetcar suburb" in the 1880's, quickly popular with middle and upper-middle class families. Designed by English engineer James A. Jowett, district's curving streets are lined with late-Victorian styles, "four-squares", and bungalows. Design reflects popularity of the "romantic suburb" pioneered by Frederick Law Olmstead and Horace W. S. Cleveland. *General Information*: See **Broadway HD.**

Whites Creek HD

1870's to early 20th C. - Rural agricultural community with wide variety of styles: 19th C. Tennessee Vernacular, Italianate, vernacular Victorian, Eastlake, Colonial Revival, and English Cottage. Best remaining example of a rural community in Davidson County, which has undergone extensive suburban development.

Woodland In Waverly HD

1893-1930 - An urban residential neighborhood with approximately 80 residences. Houses, 1 to 2 stories, are frame, with brick, stone, and weatherboard veneers; they range from large Queen Anne and Colonial Revival residences to vernacular cottages. Relatively unaltered since 1930, has retained much of its original character. *General Information*: Ridley-Benton Neighborhood, c/o Allen Ramsaur, 744 Benton Avenue, Nashville TN 37204.

NORRIS

Norris HD

1934-1937 - Planned community, covering 4,000 acres, includes approximately 400 structures, mostly residential. The last project totally planned and built by T.V.A. Structures featured use of innovative building techniques, e.g., cinderblock construction, large-scale electric heating. Was based on Ebenezer Howard's "Garden City" town planning ideas.

OLD HICKORY

Old Hickory HD

1917-1918 - A company town established for the DuPont Powder Plant in World War I. Contains 276 period residences in 10 different types reflecting Colonial Revival, Bungalow, and Vernacular styles. Has retained much of its original architectural character (see also **Lakewood HD, LAKEWOOD**).

PALL MALL

Sergeant York HD

19th-20th C. - Sparsely settled rural area contains simple private and commercial structures; includes log-and-frame houses, stone Bible School, chapel, mill, and natural landmarks. Home of Alvin C. York, World War I hero and winner of Congressional Medal of Honor.

PRIMM SPRINGS

Primm Springs (also White Sulphur Springs) HD

A somewhat deteriorated collection of 16 vernacular frame structures comprising what was a spa resort, 20 miles east of Centerville (Hickman County). Includes a large hotel, dance hall, a boarding house, and 6 summer cottages.

PULASKI

Pulaski Courthouse Square HD

1860's-1930's - Primarily commercial, with 92 buildings in 9-block area around the 1909 Giles County Courthouse. Facades exhibit a variety of architectural influences in their detailing, from Italianate to Art Deco. First-story storefronts of many buildings have had extensive alterations.

ROGERSVILLE

Rogersville HD

Late 18th to early 20th C. - Town district features tree-lined streets, central square, cemetery, and approximately 30 public and private buildings, many built 1800-1850. Hale Springs Hotel, built in 1824 as a stage-route tavern, was in use as late as 1970's. Styles include Federal and Greek Revival, and buildings with Victorian detailing. A relatively undisturbed area of a 19th C. town laid out in 1787.

RUGBY (VICINITY)

Rugby Colony HD

1880's - Rural museum district includes 17 buildings remaining in a community established in 1880 by British reformer-author Thomas Hughes. Community emphasized the value of manual labor, a cooperative economic system, and education. Most buildings are frame, with Gothic Revival and Italianate elements. *Guided Tours*: Daily tours, March 1 - December 15.

SAVANNAH

Savannah HD

1869-c. 1930 - Small residential area of 16 period buildings, many in Queen Anne and Colonial Revival styles. Most are largely unaltered.

SHELBYVILLE

Shelbyville Courthouse Square HD

1870-1980's - Fifty-nine buildings in a 9-block area surrounding the Bedford County Courthouse. Most are 2-story brick Victorian commercial row buildings.

SOMERVILLE

Somerville HD

1835-1925 - One hundred residential, commercial, and church structures; majority are from the Victorian Period, with much use of Gothic and Italianate styles. Also some Greek Revival. Of note: "Frogmore" House, c. 1829.

SPRINGFIELD

Springfield Town Square HD

1890-1925 - Thirty-four commercial and governmental buildings in a 4-block area surrounding the Robertson County Courthouse. Of interest: Beasley Building (c. 1899), Robertson State Bank Building (c. 1899). A cohesive unit majestically situated atop a hill overlooking entire town.

TOWNSEND (VICINITY)

Cades Cove HD (in Great Smoky Mountains Nat'l Pk)

1826-1895 - Small rural district encompasses 11 miles of scenic park roads and a number of vernacular structures, most of latter reflecting the frontier period, 1826–1850. Of note: John Oliver cabin (c. 1826), the Missionary Baptist Church (1894), the Gregg-Cable House (1879), and restorations at the Cable Mill Complex. *Map, Self-Guided Tours*: By automobile from Cades Cove Visitor Center, National Park Service. *Guided Tours*: Walking tours, Cable Mill Complex, daily, mid-April through October.

TRENTON

Trenton HD

1830's to early 20th C. - Primarily residential, with 97 significant buildings. Styles include Greek Revival, Queen Anne, Neo-Classical, and Bungalow. Relatively few intrusions or major alterations.

TUSCULUM

Tusculum College HD

Map, Self-Guided Tours: Tusculum College Development Office, McCormick Hall, POB 5040, Greeneville TN 37743, telephone (615)-638-1111, ext. 204.

WASHINGTON COLLEGE (VICINITY)

Broylesville HD

Late 18th to early 20th C. - Eight significant but scattered rural properties. (residential, commercial) the remains of the once thriving community of Broylesville, approximately 10 miles southeast of Jonesborough. Includes Broylesville Inn (c. 1797), the Telford House (c. 1815, Federal).

Reed's Row

VIRGINIA

ABINGDON

Abingdon HD

18th-19th C. - Primarily residential, extending along both sides of Main Street. Many fine examples of Federal design and of 19th C. revival designs; structures of brick, frame, and stucco. A typical 19th C. rural Virginia town. *Map, Self-Guided Tours*: Chamber of Commerce, 304 Depot Square, Abingdon VA 24210, telephone (703)-628-8141. *Annual Homes Tour*: House Tour, second weekend of Virginia Highlands Festival; Candlelight Tour, second weekend, December. Contact Chamber of Commerce, 304 Depot Square, Abingdon VA 24210.

ACCOMAC

Accomac HD

Early to mid-19th C. - Many examples of early to mid-19th C. regional building types, several important mid-19th C. builder and architect-designed houses, and a distinctive late-Victorian county courthouse complex. *Map, Self-Guided Tours*: Chamber of Commerce, No. 1 Courthouse Ave., POB 147, Accomac VA 23301, telephone (804)-787-2460. *Annual Homes Tour*: Historic Homes and Gardens (last Friday-Saturday in April); contact Mrs. C. A. Turner, Kendall Grove, Eastville VA 23347, telephone (804)-678-5325 or (804)-442-5768.

ALDIE

Aldie (Mill) HD

Early 19th C. - mill complex includes mill, miller's house,

and the manor house. Three-part brick mill is one of best preserved and equipped in Virginia.

ALEXANDRIA

Alexandria HD

Late 18th to early 19th C. - Riverside district, contains probably Virginia's largest concentration of late 18th and early 19th C. urban architecture. Some structures from Colonial and Victorian periods, but most are Federal style, brick or frame. Of note: Christ Church (1767, **N H L**), Gadsby's Tavern (18th C., **N H L**), and Carlyle House (1752, Georgian). Was Virginia's principal upstate seaport and commercial center until Civil War. District, with several surviving sections of cobblestone streets and widespread preservation-restoration, has retained its picturesque quality. **N H L; H A B S.** *Map, Self-Guided Tours*: Ramsay House Visitors Center, 221 King St., Alexandria VA 22314, telephone (703)-549-0205. *Annual Homes Tour*: Old Homes/Gardens Tour (late September), contact Alexandria Hospital Auxiliary Board (703) 751-3391. *Special Events*: Annual Scottish Christmas Walk (early December), contact Alexandria Community Y, (703)-549-0111; Old Town Christmas Candlelight Tour (mid-December), contact Ramsay House Visitors Center.

ARLINGTON

Fort Meyer HD

1863-20th C. - Military post (U.S. Army), featuring 6-building headquarters, and Generals' Row, a series of officers' large residences. Also includes numerous brick and frame structures, stables, etc. Originally built as defensive fortification of Washington, D.C.; was site of aviation demonstration by Orville Wright in 1909. **N H L**

ASHLAND

Ashland HD

Late 19th to early 20th C. - Predominantly residential, with a commercial core. Focal point is Center Street, with full range of Victorian styles from Italianate and Second Empire to Eastlake and Queen Anne. Large collection of late-Victorian and Edwardian frame dwellings and a brick commercial section, set among hundreds of trees; has preserved much of its turn-of-the-century character. *Map, Self-Guided Tours*: Municipal Building, Thompson Street, at Hanover Avenue, Ashland VA 23005, telephone (804)-798-9219.

BEDFORD

Bedford HD

1884-1930's - Includes residential, commercial, and industrial areas, with 240 structures; architectural styles range from Greek Revival, Italianate, Carpenter Gothic, and Romanesque Revival, to Bungalow and Spanish Colonial Revival. City prospered throughout most of the 19th C. as a major tobacco manufacturing center; many of the commercial and residential structures were constructed after a disastrous fire in 1884.

BLUEMONT

Bluemont HD

c. 1900 - Village (originally Snickers Gap, then Snickersville) that arose along a primary trade route 18th and 19th C. Town's post-Civil War decline was reversed by arrival of railroad in 1900 and promotion of the area as a small mountain resort. Has retained much of its turn-of-the-century quality and charm.

BREMO BLUFF (VICINITY)

Bremo Bluff HD

1820-1844 - Rural district in Fluvanna County; 3 plantation house groupings and their outbuildings and dependencies, all built on Bremo Plantation, 1803-1845. Principal residence, Upper Bremo, is Palladian style, 1820; Thomas Jefferson's advice was sought during its construction and it has been described as the most nearly perfect "of all the houses in the Jeffersonian tradition." The entire grouping forms one of the most remarkable collections of early 19th C. structures in the United States. Outstanding architectural interest, and remarkably well-preserved. **N H L** (private)

BRIDGEWATER

Bridgewater HD

Mid-19th C. to early 20th C. - One of the largest and finest collections of vernacular architecture in Rockingham County. Focal point is Main Street with its rows of closely packed mid-19th C. dwellings; also includes a number of fine antebellum brick residences and the original pre-1910 portion of the Bridgewater College campus.

BROWNSBURG

Brownsburg HD

19th-20th C. - Typical early village of the region. Residential and commercial structures in various styles popular in early 19th C. and between 1870-1910. Many are 2-story brick, in local interpretation of the Federal style. Has maintained its 19th C. character.

BUCKINGHAM

Buckingham Courthouse (Village) HD

19th C. - A complex of court buildings; includes 2-story Greek Revival courthouse, several taverns, and number of brick and frame dwellings in Federal, Greek Revival, and Italian Villa styles. Typical of a 19th C. village which developed around a courthouse establishment. *General Information*: Mr. Gordon Baldwin, Pres., Historic Buckingham, Inc., POB 53, Buckingham VA 23921.

BURKE'S GARDEN

Burke's Garden Rural HD

Early 19th C. to early 20th C. - Scattered farmsteads over 40 rural acres plus two churches, and a former store; homes range from sole surviving example of German Lutheran settlers' stone buildings (Peter Gose House, (early 19th C.) to substantial brick and frame residences of the late 19th and early 20th C. A significant rural landscape with few modern intrusions.

CHARLOTTESVILLE

Albemarle County Courthouse HD

Early to mid-19th C. - The original heart of town; includes Federal and Greek Revival public buildings and town houses flanking 2 sides of town green. Of note: courthouse with pedimented tetrastyle Ionic portico, and Levy Opera House. Has retained its 19th C. character. *Map, Self-Guided Tours*: Chamber of Commerce, 5th and E. Market St., POB 1564, Charlottesville VA 22902, telephone (804)-295-3141. *Annual Homes Tour*: Dogwood Festival (2nd - 4th weeks of April), Charlottesville-Albemarle Jaycees, c/o Towe Insurance Service, 416 E. Main St., Charlottesville VA 22901, telephone (804)-295-5191.

Rugby Road - University Corner HD

1890-1930 - Twenty city blocks; contains the majority of surviving nonacademic buildings (commercial, residential, institutional) associated with the University of Virginia, 1890 - 1930. Of interest: the President's House on Carr's Hill, the Bayley Museum, and approximately 30 fraternity/sorority houses. An outstanding and well-preserved example of a period university neighborhood, featuring distinguished architecture, large, well-planted yards, and expansive open spaces.

University of Virginia HD

19th-20th C. - University, chartered in 1819, had Thomas Jefferson as its first planner and architect. Original campus reflects Jefferson's ambition to create a community of scholars living and studying in an architecturally unified complex. Includes Jefferson's 1819 Rotunda at the North end, Sanford White's Cabell Hall at South end. **N H L; H A B S**

Wertland Street HD

c. 1900 - The most cohesive collection of Victorian vernacular design houses remaining in the city; has remained relatively unchanged since turn-of-the-century. Well-preserved, and with historic associations with both city and the University. *General Information*: Chamber of Commerce, 5th and E. Market Street.

CLIFTON

Clifton HD

Mid to late 19th C. - Small rural village of some 56 buildings of interest, majority of frame construction. Town grew because of railroad and such industries as lumbering, sawmilling, farming, and talc mining. Retains much of the appearance of a 19th C. community.

DANVILLE

Danville HD

19th C. - Residential, contains a number of 2 and 2 1/2-story brick, frame, and stucco dwellings. Includes fine examples of buildings with elements of various Victorian styles. Of note: the Public Library (1857, Italian Villa), where Confederate President Jefferson Davis signed his last official proclamation (April 4, 1865). Has retained its turn-of-the-century character. *Map, Self-Guided Tours*: Visitor Center, 614 Lynn Street, POB 1538, Danville VA 24543, telephone (804)-797-9437 or (804)-799-5149.

Tobacco Warehouse and Residential HD

19th-early 20th C. - Three hundred fifty-acre district, with approximately 600 structures representing all the elements of a period tobacco manufacturing town. Well-preserved industrial and residential architecture.

DAYTON

Dayton HD

Mid-19th C.-20th C. - A commercial center for a large Old-Order Mennonite population. Town was established in 1833. Streets are lined with rows of vernacular structures, recalling town's former prosperity.

EASTVILLE

Northhampton County Courthouse HD.

18th - 19th C. Government and commercial structures around the court square. Of note: 1731 brick courthouse (much altered), late 18th C. frame Eastville Inn (altered), and the 1899 brick courthouse (Georgian Revival). Considered one of Virginia's most complete county seat complexes. **H A B S**

FALLS CHURCH

Falls Church HD

1770–1910 – (L) A mix of residential, public, and commercial; approximately 125 buildings built pre-1910. Predominant styles are from late Victorian period, when city grew as a prosperous commuter suburb of Washington, D.C. Of note: Falls Church (1769, Georgian), Cherry Hill farmhouse (1840's–1870's, Greek Revival vernacular). *General Information*: Friends of Cherry Hill Foundation, 408 Lincoln Avenue, Falls Church VA 22046; also Historical Commission, 120 N. Virginia Avenue, Falls Church VA 22046.

FALMOUTH

Falmouth HD

18th–19th C. – Riverport town, with frame, brick, and stone dwellings and brick commercial structures. Predominant style is Federal, with buildings varying from low riverside rows of houses to larger homes overlooking the town. Town, laid out in 1727, was leading mercantile center until mid-19th C. **H A B S**. *Special Events*: Historic Falmouth Autumn Walking Tour, c/o Historic Falmouth Towne, POB 5250, Falmouth VA 22403.

FINCASTLE

Fincastle HD

18th–19th C. – Small agricultural county-seat community. Wide variety of styles, including Greek and Gothic Revival, and those of the Victorian period. Numerous buildings, unified by scale and use of local materials. **H A B S**

FRANKLIN

Franklin HD

Late 19th to early 20th C. – Commercial and residential, with majority of buildings dating from town's boom in late 19th C. after the Union Camp Corp. established its headquarters here. Large residential neighborhood west of the downtown features picturesque streetscapes of high-style and vernacular dwellings. Commercial architecture on Main Street includes many fine examples of Italianate and Colonial Revival styles. District has maintained an exceptional level of architectural integrity.

FREDERICKSBURG

Fredericksburg HD

18th-20th C. - Government, religious, and residential structures in city's original downtown area. Numerous brick and frame dwellings from the 18th and 19th C., 1 and 2 1/2-stories. Of note: Courthouse by architect James Renwick, Kenmore (mid-18th C., Georgian, N H L), the 1758 law office of James Monroe (N H L), and the 1760 Rising Sun Tavern (NHL). **H A B S**. *Map, Self-Guided Tours*: Visitor Center, 706 Caroline St., Fredericksburg VA 22401, telephone (703)-373-1776. *Guided Tours*: By advance reservation only; contact above. *Annual Homes Tour*: Fredericksburg Day (late April, part of Historic Garden Week in Virginia); Christmas Candlelight Tour (1st Sunday in December). Contact Tourism Dept., Visitor Center.

GLOUCESTER

Gloucester County Courthouse Square HD.

18th-20th C. - Numerous buildings on the Square and its borders. A wide variety of civic, commercial, and religious structures, representing styles from the mid-18th C. to the 20th C. Of note: Long Bridge Ordinary (mid-18th C., clapboarded), and the 2-story Botetourt Hotel, restored in 1968 for office use. **H A B S**. *Annual Homes Tour*: Garden Club Tour of Historical Homes (last weekend, April); contact Chamber of Commerce. *General Information*: Chamber of Commerce, POB 296, Gloucester VA 23061, telephone (804)-693-2425; Information Center, "Debtors Prison", weekdays, 8:30 a.m. - 4:30 p.m.

GOOCHLAND

Goochland County Court Square HD

19th C. - A county-seat complex arranged around brick, 2-story 1826 courthouse (with Tuscan portico). The square, enclosed by original brick wall, includes 2-story stone jail

(1848), a 1-story clerk's office (of brick), and a Confederate monument. **H A B S**

GORDONSVILLE

Gordonsville HD

19th to early 20th C. - A rich assemblage of residential, commercial, and institutional buildings; many of the 19th C. residences are set on a tree-shaded section of Main Street. Town's growth reached its zenith in 2 decades following the Civil War.

GRAVEL HILL (VICINITY)

Buckingham Female Collegiate Institute HD

Mid-19th C. - Rural structures and sites associated with one of the earliest efforts to provide higher education for state's young women during the 19th C. Complex includes the President's House (c. 1853), Institute Store and Tavern, and hostelry. *General Information*: Mrs. John Francis West, Rte. 1, Box 184, Gravel Hill - Dilwyn VA 23936.

GREAT FALLS

Patowmack Canal HD

Late 18th to early 19th C. - Surviving principal elements of the canal system (in varying degrees of preservation) include large Wing Dam, Upper, Lower Guard Gates, and series of 5 locks. Canal company was organized in 1785, George Washington serving as first president; one of the earliest canals in U.S. with locks. **N H L; H A E R**. *General Information*: Visitors Center, Great Falls Park, Fairfax County.

HALIFAX

Mountain Road HD

19th to early 20th C. - Residential district in courthouse town of Halifax, highly regarded for distinguished architecture and beautiful landscapes. A fine collection of 19th and early 20th C. residences in styles ranging from late Federal to Bungalow. Of note: Masonic Hall (1828), St. Mark's Church

(1831), and St. John's Church (1846). A strong 19th C. ambience.

HAMPDEN-SYDNEY

Hampden-Sydney College HD

19th C. - College, one of Virginia's oldest, opened in 1776. Most buildings are 19th C. in their original settings, combined with 20th-C. Georgian Revival structures. Of note: the Alamo (1817), and Cushing Hall (1822).

HAMPTON

Hampton Institute HD

19th C. - Founded for training freedmen after the Civil War, opening in 1868; Booker T. Washington is a famous alumnus. Contains over 100 structures on 200 acres. Of note: Virginia Hall, Academic Hall (Richard Morris Hunt, architect), and the Memorial Church (J. C. Cady, architect). **N H L**

Victoria Boulevard HD

1890's-1920's - An excellent example of a turn-of-the-century streetcar suburb, originally laid out in 1888. Dwellings offer a variety of popular architectural styles from c. 1895 to 1920's while cohesiveness comes through similarity of scale and common building materials.

HANOVER

Hanover County Courthouse HD

18th-20th C. - Historic core of the original village. Includes Courthouse (c. 1735, Georgian, NHL), Hanover Tavern (18th C.), and 1835 jail and clerk's office. **H A B S**. *Guided Tours*: Barksdale Theatre, PO Box 7, Hanover VA 23069, telephone (804)-798-6547. *Annual Homes Tour*: Hanover Garden Tour, 1st Saturday of 1st full week in April; contact Historical Society. *General Information*: Hanover County Historical Society, POB 91, Hanover VA 23069.

HILLSBORO

Hillsboro HD

19th C. - Contains many 2-story, gable-roof stone residences, illustrating influence of Pennsylvania vernacular building types on Northern Virginia. Many homes feature Victorian porch and bay window additions. Scenic location; town grew along a trade route in early 19th C. *Annual Homes Tour*: First week in December; contact Hillsboro Community Association, Hillsboro VA 22132.

HOPEWELL

City Point HD

Late 18th to early 20th C. - This site, at confluence of Appomattox and James Rivers, is one of oldest continuously occupied settlements in America. An important late-Colonial-era port; neighborhood contains buildings dating from late 18th through early 20th C.

LANCASTER

County Courthouse HD

c. 1800 to early 20th C. - A tiny village district, with late antebellum courthouse as focal point. Structures include a c. 1800 tavern, mid-19th C. post office, a Carpenter Gothic church, and numerous detached 19th and early 20th-C. dwellings. Virtually free of modern intrusions, with much of its original atmosphere. *General Information*: Mary Ball Washington Museum and Library, POB 97, Lancaster VA 22503, telephone 462-7280; Tuesday-Friday, 10 a.m. - 4 p.m.

LANGLEY (VICINITY)

Langley Fork HD

Mid-19th C. - An interesting assemblage of local vernacular buildings. Six major structures are: Langley Ordinary (c. 1850), Langley Toll House (mid-19th C.), Friends' Meeting House (1853), the Mackall House (now the site of Happy Hill Country Day School), Gunnell's Chapel (post-1865), and Hickory Hill (residence of late Senator Robert F. Kennedy). Has retained its historic identity and appearance despite intense regional development in the vicinity of Washington, D.C.

LEESBURG

Leesburg HD

18th-19th C. - Residential community, with a large number of late 18th and early 19th-C. houses, plus commercial, public buildings. Of note: Greek Revival courthouse, and county office building (c. 1844). Town established in 1758, and became a prosperous center before Civil War. **H A B S**. *Map, Self-Guided Tours*: Visitors Center, 16 W. Loudon St., Leesburg VA 22075, telephone (707)-777-0519.

LEESBURG (VICINITY)

Oatlands HD

19th C. - District retains what was once plantation acreage; also contains Oatlands mansion, the 1-room Mountain Gap Schoolhouse (c. 1827), Church of Our Savior (c. 1875), and ruins of a mill complex. Oatlands, an elegant brick, stuccoed Federal home with Adamesque detailing, was designed and built in 1800 by George Carter. *Special Events*: Christmas at Oatlands Mansion (November - early December); (703)-777-3174.

LEXINGTON

Lexington HD

18th-20th C. - District encompasses the campuses of Washington and Lee University and the Virginia Military Institute (V.M.I.), and contains many commercial, residential, and religious structures. Features a variety of 19th C. styles, including Washington Hall (1823, Jeffersonian Classical), the Gothic Revival buildings by A. J. Davis at V.M.I., and various small brick and frame cottages. Has retained its late 19th C. character. **H A B S**. *Map, Self-Guided Tours*: Historic Lexington Foundation Visitor Center, 107 E. Washington St., Lexington VA 24450, telephone (703)-463-3777. *Guided Tours*: Motorcoach groups only; contact above. *Annual Homes Tour*: Blue Ridge Garden Club Homes Tour (late April), Christmas Holiday in Lexington (weekend in early December); for both, contact Historic Lexington Foundation above.

Virginia Military Institute Barracks HD

19th C. - A military educational complex containing 2 connecting quadrangles along the parade ground, with barracks as focal point. V.M.I., founded in 1839, was patterned after West Point. Burned in 1864, it now contains 40 major buildings. Famous graduates include "Stonewall" Jackson and George C. Marshall. **N H L** *General Information*: See **Lexington HD.**

Washington and Lee University HD

19th C. - University, founded in 1749, is 6th oldest in United States. The "Front Campus" presents an impressive view of columned and pilastered buildings covering 150 years of the school's history. Antebellum buildings are the highlights of a complex that has maintained its architectural integrity. Of note: Washington Hall (1823), Lee-Jackson House (1865-68), and the Robert E. Lee Memorial Episcopal Church (1883). **N H L** *General Information*: See **Lexington HD.**

LINCOLN (AND VICINITY)

Goose Creek HD

18th-20th C. - A cohesive rural area, with unusually high degree of unspoiled pastoral beauty. District, centered on town of Lincoln, contains a rich collection of 18th, 19th and 20th C. rural vernacular and town architecture; of note is the superb stone masonry craftsmanship. Area once held largest concentration of Quaker settlers in Virginia, beginning in 1730's.

LUNENBURG

Lunenburg Courthouse HD

19th C. - Small village contains 19th C. buildings, outbuildings. Highlight is the courthouse square dominated by the Jeffersonian Classical courthouse (1827); also of interest are an early 19th C. tavern and the Hotel Gary. Has retained its picturesque character.

LYNCHBURG

Daniel's Hill HD

Early 19th to early 20th C. - Residential, with a rich variety of styles and types. Focal point is Point of Honor Mansion, famous Federal residence built by Dr. George Cabell. Concentrated building activity began in 1840's, following subdivision of the plantation established in the late 18th C. by Cabell. The only thoroughfare, Cabell Street, is lined with an impressive progression of mid- and late 19th C. mansions. By contrast, district also contains a large quantity of c. 1900 vernacular factory workers' houses.

Diamond Hill HD

c. 1900 - Was one of city's most fashionable residential neighborhoods. Numerous residences, ranging from speculative rental units to stately architect-designed houses, were built c. 1900. A number have survived, many of the larger houses in Georgian or Colonial Revival styles.

Federal Hill HD

Early 19th to early 20th C. - Residential, approximately 12 blocks; a notable assemblage of free-standing dwellings in styles ranging from early 19th C. through Edwardian styles of early 20th C. Of note: an important collection of early Federal-style townhouses, which includes some of city's oldest, finest homes. Residential area for merchants, civic leaders.

Garland Hill HD

19th-20th C. - Small residential district with numerous early 19th C. and late 19th C. - early 20th C. houses. Styles include early Greek Revival, Queen Anne, and eclectic Victorian. Of note: Watkins House (1898), Burroughs House (1899). A prosperous late-Victorian neighborhood, developed by leaders in local tobacco, shoe industries. *Map, Self-Guided Tours*: Chamber of Commerce, 2015 Memorial Ave., POB 2027 Lynchburg VA 24501, telephone (804)-845-5966; also City of Lynchburg, 900 Church St., Lynchburg VA 24504. *Guided Tours*: City-Scape Tours, Ltd., POB 3424, Lynchburg VA 24503, telephone (804)-384-8699, (804)-384-1794. *Annual Homes Tour*: Garden Clubs of Lynchburg (April); contact Chamber of Commerce.

MADISON

Madison County Courthouse HD

1830's to late 19th C. - County seat and commercial hub since its formation in 1793; focal point is the 1830 Roman Revival courthouse. Contains a number of noteworthy structures from the early to mid-19th C., a late 19th C. commercial core, and a number of fashionable Victorian residences. Has retained much of its historic courthouse village character.

MANASSAS

Old Town HD, Liberia HD

19th C. - (L) This rail-junction city was devastated during Civil War. Old Town, however, contains number of late-Victorian structures. Of interest: "Liberia" (1825, Federal), County Courthouse (1892, Romanesque), Old City Hall - Firehouse (1914, Edwardian). *Map, Self-Guided Tours*: Manassas City Museum, 9406 Main St., Manassas VA 22110, telephone (703)-368-1873.

MIDDLEBROOK

Middlebrook HD

1880's - One of the oldest rural villages in Augusta County; an excellent grouping of 19th C. vernacular architecture, sited on the original town plat. Rows of closely spaced dwellings and stores lining main road retain the 1880's character of the village.

MIDDLEBURG

Middleburg HD

Late 18th to early 20th C. - Village in Virginia's hunt country, founded in 1787. By 1850's it had become an important commercial and institutional center, declining in wealth, power after Civil War. Beginning in 1920's, developed into a social and sporting capital of international reputation. An impressive and diverse collection of styles, from late 18th to early 20th C. Has retained picturesque qualities of its formative years, with tree-lined streets, brick sidewalks, and harmonious scale of structures.

NEW CASTLE

New Castle HD

19th C. - Contains 5 county and commercial buildings, including impressive Greek Revival courthouse, the sheriff's house, and a hotel. The area's most complete antebellum county seat. **H A B S**

NEW MARKET

New Market HD

18th–19th C. - Contains commercial and religious structures, and dwellings (primarily 2-story frame and brick). Most constructed from early to mid-19th C. Of note: limestone Henkel house (c. 1800, with Federal elements), and Emmanuel Lutheran Church (Romanesque Revival). Town laid out in 1785, becoming active mercantile center in early 19th C. Among German inhabitants was Ambrose Henkel, founder of the oldest Lutheran Press (1806) in America, **H A B S**. *Map, Self-Guided Tours*: Tourist Information Center, I-81, exit 67, New Market VA 22844; Chamber of Commerce, POB 57, New Market VA 22844, telephone (703)-740-3212. *Annual Homes Tour*: Heritage Days (2nd weekend in May); contact Chamber of Commerce.

NEWPORT NEWS

Hilton Village HD

20th C. - One of the first planned communities built with Federal funds; constructed to relieve local housing shortage during World War I. Contains groups of frame houses with stucco or clapboard exteriors and steeply pitched slate roofs. Includes play areas, row houses, 1- and 2-family dwellings, stores, schools, parks, churches, and city square. Francis Y. Joannes, architect. *Guided Tours*: By arrangement, with Newport News Historical Committee.

North End HD

1900–1935 - Residential neighborhood encompassing 22 blocks. In 1900–1910 period, middle managers from Newport News Shipbuilding and Dry Dock Company (founded in 1886) and skilled workmen resided here. Large numbers of dwellings were erected between 1910 and 1920, due to area's growth from World War I. Homes include residences of former Shipyard presidents and prominent politicians.

NEWTOWN

Newtown HD

19th C. - Began in the late colonial period as crossroads settlement; prospered in the antebellum period and was locale of a long succession of private schools and academies. Survives today in a predominantly rural setting, with 19th C. atmosphere.

NORFOLK

Ghent HD

1890-1905 - Norfolk's first suburb to offer such modern amenities as sewer, water, and gas lines. Fronts on Smith's Creek, with banks landscaped by John Graham, Philadelphia engineer, who laid out the community. Suburb quickly attracted middle-to-upper-middle class residents who built numerous stately homes between 1890 and 1905. A rich collection of domestic architecture set off by plan and landscaping.

West Freemason St. Area HD

18th-20th C. - Predominantly residential, at edge of city center; contains 2 and 3-story detached or semi-detached brick dwellings set close to the street on deep, narrow lots. Of note: Whittle House (1791, Federal), Weston House (1890's, Second Empire), and Roper House (1893, Georgian Revival). Variety of styles provides excellent illustration of city's architectural development. **H A B S**

OCCOQUAN

Occoquan HD

Late 19th to early 20th C. - Interesting riverside collection of vernacular residential and commercial structures, preserving a port-village image of the period. Of note: Rockledge (c. 1760, Georgian), Mill House (late 18th C), and the Hammil Hotel (c. 1830). Town predates 1759, was once a prosperous flour milling center. *Map, Self-Guided Tours*: At local merchants; also Historic Occoquan, Inc., Mill House Museum, POB 65, Occoquan VA 22125; (Museum open daily, July-October; Sundays, 1-5 p.m., April-October).

PALMYRA

Fluvanna County Courthouse HD

Mid-19th C. - A county seat complex containing an 1829 stone jail, the 1831 Greek Revival temple-form courthouse (locally attributed to General John Hartwell Cocke), and an early lawyer's office. Has retained its original appearance in an undeveloped setting.

PETERSBURG

Centre Hill HD

Early 19th to early 20th C. - An architecturally interesting enclave of period residential buildings surrounded by more recent commercial and industrial development. Focal point is 1823 mansion, Centre Hill; styles represented include Federal, Greek Revival, Italianate, Queen Anne, and early 20th C. eclectics.

Folly Castle HD

18th-19th C. - A 1-block residential district containing 14 houses from late 18th and 19th C., plus 19th C. church. Formerly one of town's leading residential neighborhoods. Of note: Folly Castle (1763), Georgian), the Rambout-Dounan House, and the Johnathan Smith residence.

Old Town HD

Early to late 19th C. - Approximately 250 buildings on 190 acres, in downtown Petersburg, one of Virginia's oldest cities (1733). Significant for its diversity of residential, commercial, and industrial architecture. Of interest: a rich collection of fine early to late 19th C. houses lining High Street, a group of early worker cottages, and industrial structures along Appomattox River. Has preserved one of Virginia's most notable assemblages of building types.

Poplar Lawn HD

Mid to late 19th C. - Small district composed primarily of single-family residences grouped around a 2-block public green. The green, sometimes called "Central Park", was focal point for early military exercises and social gatherings.

POCAHONTAS

Pocahontas HD

Late 19th–20th C. – Mining town, containing residential areas with religious and commercial structures. Features primarily 2-story duplex frame dwellings with weatherboarding or board-and-batten siding (many with Italianate elements, a few with pressed metal facades). Of note: Italianate city hall (1895) and nearby brick bank building with Richardsonian Romanesque elements. Established c. 1881 by a mining concern which constructed housing, support facilities; mining continued until 1955.

PORT REPUBLIC

Port Republic HD

19th C. – A once booming river port, founded in 1802. Small town laid out on grid plan, with its growth and eventual decline reflected through the collection of surviving buildings. *Map, Self-Guided Tours*: Society of Port Republic Preservationists, POB 47, Port Republic VA 24471. *Annual Homes Tour*: Festival Day (3rd Saturday in September); contact above.

PORT ROYAL

Port Royal HD

18th–19th C. – Predominantly residential, with notable architecture from 18th, early 19th-C. Town, founded in 1744, quickly developed into major tobacco shipping port. Declined with advent of railroad. Has had few modern intrusions to mar its charm. **H A B S**

PORTSMOUTH

Park View HD

c. 1894–1914 – Portsmouth's first streetcar suburb, reflecting eclectic architectural styles and tastes during a boom period in city's economic growth. Some 300 structures, including outstanding examples of such styles as Queen Anne, Colonial Revival, American Four-square, and Bungalow.

Portsmouth (Old Towne) HD

18th-20th C. - Encompasses the entire area of Olde Towne, containing 2- and 3-story Federal and Greek Revival townhouses, primarily brick and wood. Also some post-Civil War and early 20th-C. structures. Bounded on one side by Elizabeth River; district has distinctive architectural quality due to frequent use of the high English basement.

Craddock HD

1918 - One of nation's first planned 20th-C. communities; built by Federal Government to house World War I influx of workers at Norfolk Naval Station. Approximately 700 dwellings, predominantly frame, in range of eclectic styles including modified English Cottage, Bungaloid, and Colonial Revival. Also a town square, small commercial center.

Port Norfolk HD

c. 1900-1920's - Turn-of-the-century residential neighborhood, a planned suburb of Portsmouth. Styles range from elaborate and well-preserved Queen Anne examples to the popular Bungalow. Few modern intrusions, and outstanding examples of middle, upper-middle class housing typical of the period.

Truxtun HD

c. 1917-1918 - Forty-two-acre neighborhood built by Federal Government in World War I to house a part of growing work force in Norfolk Naval Shipyard, Portsmouth. Was the first wartime U.S. housing project constructed exclusively for blacks. Residential portion is characterized by close-knit, 5-room structures with jerkinhead roofs. Has retained much of its original character despite some moderate alterations since 1920's.

POWHATAN

Powhatan Courthouse HD

19th C. - Features a relatively unaltered group of 19th C. structures around and adjacent to the town green. Included are the 1-story Courthouse (1848-49, Greek Revival), an 18th C. clerk's office, and a 1-story Italianate frame office building.

PULASKI

Pulaski Historic Commercial District
Late 19th C. - Town's historic commercial-industrial center, with 100 buildings including commercial structures, industrial buildings, multi-family dwellings, two railroad depots, church, county courthouse, the former high school, and town park. Retains the context and fabric of a turn-of-the-century boom town.

REEDVILLE

Reedville HD
1870's to early 20th C. - Picturesque and charming maritime village developed after the Civil War; its growth was based on introduction of the menhaden fish-oil industry from New England by Elijah Reed. Features an unusually fine and well preserved collection of late Victorian and early 20th C. residences built for sea captains, wealthy industrialists, and merchants. Also has preserved a number of modest 1870's frame dwellings built by Reed family for factory workmen and families.

RICHMOND

Richmond
Map, Self-Guided Tours: Metro Richmond Convention and Visitors Bureau, 300 E. Main Street, Richmond VA 23219, telephone (804)-782-2777; Visitors Information Center, 1700 Robin Hood Road, Richmond VA 23220, telephone (804)-358-5511; Historic Richmond Foundation, 2407 E. Grace Street, Richmond VA 23223, telephone (804)-643-7407. *Guided Tours*: Grayline Tours (seasonally); Metro Richmond, all year. *Annual Homes Tour*: Historic Garden Week tours (last full week in April), Garden Clubs of Virginia, 12 E. Franklin Street, Richmond VA 23219 (804) 644-7776; Historic Church Hill Candlelight Christmas Tour, week before Christmas; Fan District Christmas Tour (804)-730-2364.

Boulevard HD
Early 20th C. - A combinaton of public buildings, apartment houses, town houses, and the Boulevard with its handsome trees, landscaping and street lamps. A fashionable address during the early 20th C., the 13-block Boulevard district offers

a display of popular architectural styles of the period including Colonial and Tudor Revival, and Spanish Eclectic. Of note: Battle Abbey (home of the Virginia Historical Society), the Tuscan Villas, and the Henry E. Baskerville House.

Commonwealth Club HD

Late 19th C. - A well-preserved cluster of turn-of-the-century upper-class townhouses around 400 Block, W. Franklin Street. Focal point is the architecturally luxuriant Commonwealth Club, designed in 1890's by Carrere and Hastings, New York. Era's stylistic diversity is well illustrated, with houses in Italianate, Romanesque, Colonial Revival, and Classical styles.

East Franklin Street HD (100 Block)

Mid to late 19th C. - Small urban neighborhood, 1 1/2 blocks in area, contains interesting, varied collection of brick townhouses, two and three stories. Of interest: the prodigious Kent-Valentine House. Neighborhood is a good example of preservation of the historic fabric of a busy downtown area.

Fan Area HD

Late 19th to early 20th C. - Large residential neighborhood encompassing 85 blocks of good urban design. Reflects demand for better housing by a new, white, urban middle class, especially from 1885 to 1915. Attractive streetscapes, with a strong sense of neighborhood unity.

Ginter Park HD

Late 19th to early 20th C. - A 21-block residential area containing 352 buildings. Planned by noted Richmond philanthropist Lewis Ginter at end of the 19th C.; key elements in his plan were relocation of Union Theological Seminary from Farmville, Virginia and new streetcar service. This architecturally rich neighborhood offers such styles as Tudor and Colonial Revival, Bungalow, American Four-square, Queen Anne, and Shingle. *General Information*: Ginter Park Residents Association.

Grove Avenue HD (2900 Block)

19th-20th C. - Tiny residential district containing four stone and brick 2 1/2-story dwellings; three were built in the late 1890's, and feature Queen Anne turrets and porches. Fourth is square residence, built 1912. Behind the houses are carriage houses (frame), featuring cupolas and scrollwork. Developed in 1886, this block has retained its quiet residential atmosphere.

Jackson Ward HD

1800–1900 - Residential, approximately 600 dwellings, two and three stories, primarily of brick. Styles include Georgian, Federal, Greek and Gothic Revival, Italianate, and late 19th C. Was the city's 19th C. center of black business and community life. Has retained much of its 19th C. character. **N H L; H A B S**

Monroe Park HD

Late 19th to early 20th C. - An exceptional demonstration of eclectic architectural tastes. Of note: the monumental Grace and Holy Trinity Church (1895, Gothic), Cathedral of the Sacred Heart (1906, Italian Renaissance), and the Auditorium (1927, Moorish Mosque). These buildings, plus several late 19th C. townhouses and two impressive apartment houses from the 1920's, form an architectural ensemble unique in Virginia.

Monument Avenue HD

19th–20th C. - Predominantly residential, along an unusually wide avenue with numerous monuments honoring heroes of the Confederacy. The area, virtually unaltered, contains Georgian Revival and Second Renaissance Revival townhouses and terrace rows. Also several Greek Revival churches.

Shockoe Slip HD

18th–19th C. - Five-block commercial area, featuring two to four-story brick buildings constructed primarily in the 19th C. Some are stuccoed, many have Italianate elements, and a number of storefronts incorporating iron columns and pilasters. **H A B S**

Shockoe Valley and Tobacco Row HD

19th C. - Approximately 530 buildings encompassing the area of city's earliest residential, commercial and manufacturing activity. Of note is the imposing "Tobacco Row" warehouses row. District is architecturally significant for the stylistic diversity of its varied buildings.

St. John's Church HD

18th–19th C. - Predominantly residential, styles ranging from Federal and Greek Revival to Victorian. Majority of structures are brick and frame townhouses. City's oldest row houses, Carrington Row (1818), are Federal style, with stuccoed brick. Focal point is the frame 1-story St. John's Church, site of the Virginia Convention of 1775. **H A B S**

West Franklin Street HD
19th-20th C. - Fashionable post-Civil War urban residential, with attached and detached townhouses, apartment buildings, and religious structures. Features primarily 2 1/2-story residences of brick and stone in a variety of late 19th and early 20th C styles. Of note: Millhiser House (late 19th C., Jacobethan Revival elements), Second Renaissance Revival residence at 810 W. Franklin (c. 1900). The 200 block (technically a separate HD) contains eight significant townhouses; included in the complex are the Cole-Diggs House (Federal), the Palmer House (Greek Revival), and the Schoolcraft House (Second Empire).

RICHMOND (VICINITY)

James River and Kanawha Canal HD
1840 - Extends from Ship Locks to Bosher's Dam, also in city of Richmond. Includes a canal section with earthen excavations, stone locks, bridges, culverts, basins, and towpaths. Completed in 1840 but its importance waned with growth of railroads and impact of the Civil War. **H A E R**

ROANOKE

City Market HD
Late 19th to early 20th C. - Over 60 structures, displaying full range of late 19th to early 20th C. commercial styles. Centerpiece is the City Market Building on Market Street, built in 1922. District is notable for its harmony of materials and appealing human scale. Has been a major target of city's centennial revitalization efforts.

Southwest HD
1882-1930 - Approximately 1,700 structures in large urban residential neighborhood; most architecturally cohesive residential area of the inner city. Three distinct neighborhoods: Old Southwest; Mountain View; and, Hurt Park. A remarkable collection of turn-of-the-century and early 20th C. residences, ranging from modest bungalows to large mansions.

Warehouse HD

1889-1902 - Consists of five brick warehouses, "Wholesale Row", erected 1889-1902 for transit storage of wholesale foods. Buildings exemplify the functional tradition of early industrial warehouse design. Characterized by gabled ends, rows of segmental arched deep-set windows, and cast-iron window, door moldings.

SCOTTSVILLE

Scottsville HD

1700-1900 - Small town, with a variety of residential, commercial, and industrial structures representing styles popular in Virginia before and after the Civil War. Established in 1732, was county seat 1741-1762. Town declined following extensive Civil War destruction in 1865. Has retained much of the character of a 19th C. Virginia river town. **H A B S**

SINGERS GLENN

Singers Glenn HD

1880-1900 - Originally a Mennonite village, later site of considerable publishing activity. Contains some structures erected during early and mid-19th C. but most buildings are from 1880-1900. Latter include a number of elaborate albeit provincial versions of popular architectural.styles. Other buildings include T. Funk and Sons Store and the Swank Carriage Factory.

SMITHFIELD

Smithfield HD

18th-20th C. - One of best-preserved and most picturesque of state's colonial seaport towns. Predominantly 19th C. residential, but with styles from 1750 to present. Also a small commercial district, with several modern structures. Town is world famous for the production of a special type of ham. **H A B S** *Map, Self-Guided Tours*: Chamber of Commerce, Old Courthouse, Main Street, POB 38, Smithfield VA 23430, telephone (804)-357-7131. *Annual Homes Tour*: In odd years; contact Chamber.

SNOWVILLE

Snowville HD

19th C. - Small village on the Little River which by 1850's was a manufacturing center using such local raw materials as iron ore, lumber, and wool. Surviving buildings along S.R. 693 are dominated by the Snowville Christian Church. Has few modern intrusions and retains a sense of 19th C. isolation typical of many pre-railroad villages.

SOUTH BOSTON

South Boston HD

Mid-19th to early 20th C. - Encompasses much of the city, featuring a variety of industrial, commercial, and residential buildings dating from mid-19th C. Includes a large number of brick tobacco warehouses, a railroad depot, and an impressive collection of commercial buildings along Main Street. Résidential neighborhoods feature architectural styles ranging from modest vernacular housing to large and stylish Queen Anne-style houses. *General Information*: South Boston Downtown Revitalization Committee; Chamber of Commerce, 505 Main St., POB 399, South Boston VA 24592, telephone (804)572-3085.

SPERRYVILLE

Sperryville HD

19th C. - A crossroads town virtually unchanged from the 1920's. Prosperity following tannery established in 1867 resulted in construction of simple wooden residences which give town its charm, architectural identity. Intermingled are postbellum houses influenced by the 19th C. Romantic Revivals. Also of interest: a scattering of late 19th C. workers' houses, an early brick and frame tavern.

SPOTSYLVANIA

Spotsylvania Courthouse HD

1800-1840 - Site of one of Civil War's bloodiest battles. Chief landmark is the Roman Revival courthouse (1840), largely rebuilt after the War. Four other buildings standing from the battle: a c. 1800 tavern, two antebellum churches, and a c. 1840 farmhouse. *Map, Self-Guided Tours*: Spotsylvania Historical Association, POB 64, Spotsylvania VA 22553, telephone (703)-582-5672; weekdays, 10 a.m. - 3 p.m., at Old Berea Christian Church (County Museum).

STAUNTON

Beverly (Downtown) HD

19th to early 20th C. - One hundred fifty buildings in 11 blocks of the central business district. Compact, well-preserved district presents an image of a classic Victorian main street. Of note: Augusta County Courthouse, the old YMCA, and the Masonic Building. *Map, Self-Guided Tours*: Historic Staunton Foundation, 120 S. Augusta Street, Staunton VA 24401, telephone (703)-885-7676. *Annual Homes Tour*: Christmas House Tour (1st Sunday in December); contact above.

Gospel Hill HD

Late 19th C. - Residential area contains a great number of sophisticated, elaborate late 19th C. residences. Includes birthplace of Woodrow Wilson. Many of the distinctive residences designed by Staunton architectural firm, T. J. Collins. *Map, Self-Guided Tours*: See **Beverly HD**.

Newtown HD

18th to early 20th C. - Staunton's oldest continuously occupied residential area, with many fine buildings representative of domestic architectural styles of the 19th - early 20th C.; also significant individual examples of late 18th C. architecture. *Map, Self-Guided Tours*: See **Beverly HD**.

Stuart Addition ("North End") HD

19th to early 20th C. - A diverse older neighborhood adjoining the campus of Mary Baldwin College and the former Staunton Military Academy; contains a number of buildings on the National Register of Historic Places. Of note: 18th C. clapboarded log house at 215 N. Augusta, the Waddell home (c. 1875, Italianate), and St. Francis of Assisi Church (1895, Gothic Revival). *Map, Self-Guided Tours*: See **Beverly HD**.

Wharf Area HD

19th-20 C. - Warehouse and commercial district contains numerous 2- and 3-story brick buildings with Italianate elements. Of special interest: eclectic C & O railroad passenger station, and the cast-iron facade at 119-123 S. Augusta Street. District reflects town's growth and prosperity in the late 19th C.

STRASBURG

Strasburg HD

Late 1700's-1890's - Founded in 1749, Strasburg by the early 19th C. was prosperous flour milling center; in the antebellum period, town was associated with manufacture of high grade pottery. By 1890 was an important industrial center. Exhibits a rare continuum of architectural styles, periods, and building types covering two centuries.

SUSSEX

Sussex County Courthouse HD

19th-20th C. - Primarily county government buildings, including the clerk's office, jail, treasurer's office, and county office building. Focal point is the Jeffersonian Classical courthouse. The town, with its brick Greek Revival public buildings and white frame residences, has retained its 19th C. character.

TAPPAHANNOCK

Tappahannock HD

18th-20th C. - Commercial, residential, governmental, and religious structures in a wide variety of styles, reflecting town's maritime and political history. Of note: Anderson House (c. 1750); Scot's Arms Tavern, early 19th C. **H A B S**

TAYLORSTOWN

Taylorstown HD

18th-19th C. - This picturesque location, with its steady supply of water power, attracted millers of the 18th C. Milling industry flourished in this small hamlet for over 200 years; its history symbolized by Thomas Taylor fieldstone mill, now a private residence.

UPPERVILLE

Upperville HD

18th-20th C. - Stretching one mile along VA. 50, this linear district contains primarily residential and religious structures, plus some commercial buildings at one end. Features 2-story brick, frame, and stone dwellings, with end chimneys, gabled roofs, and Federal elements. District has many associations with equestrian sports; has retained its rural quality. **H A B S**

WARRENTON

Warrenton HD

Late 18th to early 20th C. - Prosperous courthouse town, offering an exceptional collection of governmental, residential, and commercial architecture reflecting a wide range of 19th C. styles. The locale of numerous fine private academies and seminaries, and has preserved a remarkable number of structures associated with Civil War era. *Map, Self-Guided Tours*: Fauquier National Bank, Warrenton VA 22186, telephone (703)-347-2700; Fauquier Historical Society, POB 675, Warrenton VA 22186.

WASHINGTON

Washington HD

19th C. - Approximately 70 structures in town center, predominantly frame or brick, 1 to 2 1/2 stories, incorporating elements of a variety of 19th C. styles. Of note: courthouse (1833, Jeffersonian Classical) by architect James Leake Powers. Town built on grid plan laid out in 1749 by George Washington for a group of private proprietors; named for him in 1796 when town was organized. A well-preserved example of a 19th C. Virginia county seat.

WATERFORD

Waterford HD

18th-19th C. - Relatively unaltered mill town of the 18th-19th C., predominantly residential. Approximately 90 historic structures in stone, brick, frame, and log; 25 date from 18th C., 40 from 1801-1835, 15 from 1836 to 1853, and 10 from

1854 to 1882. Town first settled by Quakers in 1733; has maintained its country character. **N H L; H A B S.** *Annual Homes Tour*: Waterford Homes Tour-Crafts Exhibit (3 days, starting 1st. Friday in October); contact Waterford Foundation, Inc., Waterford VA 22190, telephone (703)-8882-3018. *General Information*: See above.

WHITE POST

White Post HD

Late 19th C. - Crossroads village with approximately 21 residences, two churches, old post office, and several abandoned commercial structures. Architecture is representative of a building period in the region at the end of 19th C. Of note: Bishop Meade Memorial Church (1875), an unusually ornate and finely crafted example of rural Gothic Revival. District is a visually cohesive grouping.

WILLIAMSBURG

Williamsburg HD

17th-18th C. - This world-famous 130-acre museum district contains approximately 500 brick and frame structures restored or reconstructed to their 18th C. appearance. Settled in 1663, capital of Virginia, 1699-1779; a center of leadership and influence throughout the period preceding the Revolution. Of note: Wren Building, College of William and Mary (1702, NHL), Bruton Parish Church (1712-1715, NHL), Randolph Peyton House (c. 1715, Georgian, NHL), and the Wythe House (c. 1755, Georgian, NHL). **N H L; H A B S.** *General Information*: Contact Visitors Center for information on admission fee, tours, special events, map, etc.

WINCHESTER

Winchester HD

1870's-1920's - Approximately 45 city blocks of commercial and residential properties. Styles representative of all periods of the city's growth, dating from late 18th C., and also of the varied backgrounds of settlers. Has become center of Virginia apple industry during 20th C. *Annual Homes Tour*: Christmas Time (mid-December); contact Preservation of Historic Winchester, 8 E. Cork Street, Winchester VA 22601, telephone

(703)-667-3577. *General Information*: Chamber of Commerce, 2 N. Cameron St., Winchester VA 22601, telephone (703)-662-4118; Historical Society, POB 97, Winchester VA 22601, telephone (703)-662-6550.

YORKTOWN

Yorktown HD

18th C. - Small riverside neighborhood, with about 12 significant 18th C. structures scattered over some 8 blocks. Considerable modern intrusion. Many historical associations with Revolutionary War and siege of 1781. Famous Yorktown Battlefield nearby. *Map, Self-guided tours*: Visitors' Center, National Park Service, Yorktown Battlefield, Yorktown VA.

ZION CROSSROADS (VICINITY)

Green Springs HD

18th-20th C. - Agricultural district set among broad fields and forested areas; features fine examples of a variety of 19th C. buildings and styles. Of note: Westend (1849, Greek Revival), Hackwood (1854 Italian Villa by Alexander Jackson Davis), and St. John's Chapel (1888, Gothic Revival). First settled c. 1720; became nationally-important wheat producer in mid-19th C. N H L